TAMSIN JOHNSON

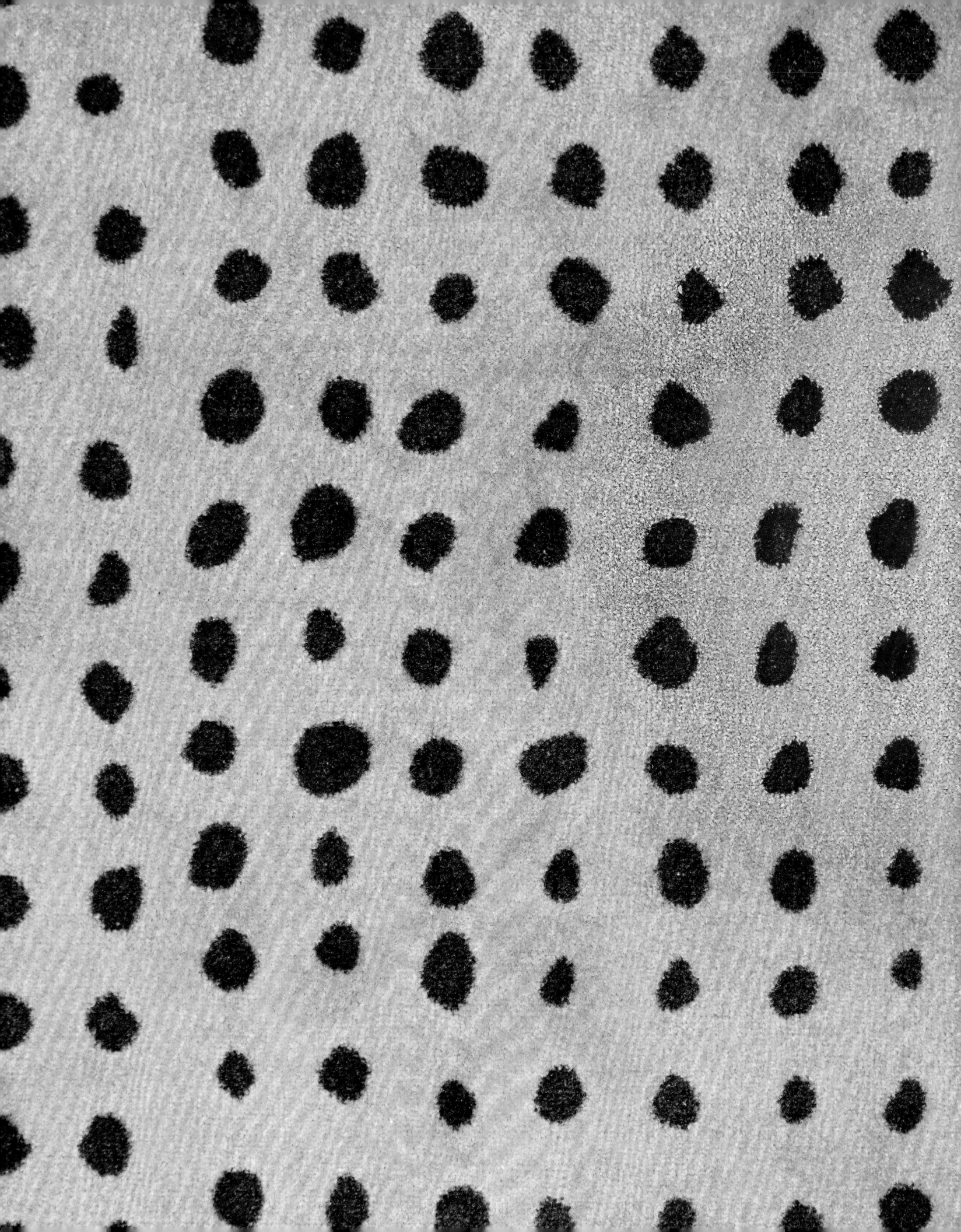

TAMSIN JOHNSON

Spaces for Living

Foreword by Edward Clark

Written by Tamsin Johnson and Fiona Daniels

Rizzoli
NEW YORK

New York · Paris · London · Milan

What is style? It's a good question, and one of the hardest to answer. Maybe the best answer is, we really don't know — but we know it when we see it. When I first saw Tamsin's work, it was clear that she had it.

—

Alex Eagle

If you are lucky enough to enter any space that Tamsin has designed, bets are on that you will never want to leave.

—

Lucy Folk

Contents   *Foreword*   14   *Introduction*   18

SANDCASTLE
Ashley Street, Tamarama, Sydney — 25

HIDEAWAY
Barrenjoey Road, Palm Beach, Sydney — 42

ATELIER
Thomas Street, Windsor, Melbourne — 67

BUNGALOW
Hastings Parade, North Bondi, Sydney — 79

VILLA
Avondale Road, Armadale, Melbourne — 95

TREEHOUSE
Domain Road, South Yarra, Melbourne — 110

SANCTUARY
Tivoli Road, South Yarra, Melbourne — 129

PIED-À-TERRE

Rue des Tournelles, Le Marais, Paris — 147

CAPSULE

Irving Place, Gramercy Park, New York — 165

TOWNHOUSE

Edgecliff Road, Woollahra, Sydney — 178

VAULT

Huntingtower Road, Armadale, Melbourne — 197

GREENHOUSE

Wallaroy Road, Woollahra, Sydney — 216

RETREAT

Raes on Wategos, Marine Parade, Byron Bay — 235

Acknowledgments — 256

Foreword by Edward Clark

The eye has to travel

— Diana Vreeland

Tamsin has never stayed long in one place. Perhaps it was the gypsy caravan existence she enjoyed as a child. Sometimes we lived in the city, above my antiques shops—there were at least nine of them operating during her childhood, in locations ranging from the Melbourne suburb of Armadale, to the small Victorian town of Mount Macedon, to the busy high streets of Sydney and London. Sometimes we lived by the seaside, once in an historic house with seven acres of gardens.

Once we lived in Lorne, a quaint beach town in Victoria, where we converted a tumbledown cottage of no particular design into a charming weekender using French doors and leaded windows found in the south of France. Just these few architectural features transformed that tired little bungalow on a large block of land overlooking the sea into a weekend paradise for the family. As a dealer often thinks, "I wish I'd never sold it."

Tamsin spent her childhood surrounded by antiques, paintings, and an ever-changing mural of architectural elements, lighting, and garden features. She observed her parents restoring buildings, shops, stables, an enormous bakery and a century-old ceiling rose factory. And, just as the family settled in to each new place, the inevitable furniture vans would arrive to move us all on to another opportunity, another adventure or folly. Throughout all these escapades, Tamsin was forever asking questions, forever curious, and would often inquire, "How much did you pay for that?" I'd tell her the price and she would say, "You'll never sell that!" or "Oh Dad, you've still got the last one you bought, and you haven't been able to sell that." "Yes, but now we've got a pair! Twice as easy to sell," I'd reply. As we hauled her around the Paris flea markets, the London salerooms, to endless galleries and decorators in Los Angeles and New York, and to countless exhibitions, I watched her absorbing all she saw, with both insight and foresight. She developed a taste for Italian glass of the 1950s; she admired the work of Galle, Daum, and Lalique, and became interested in art deco furniture and the wrought iron of Edgar Brandt, Prouvé, and Jansen.

Opposite - My parents loved converting buildings to incorporate both a residence and a business—Dad called them "shop and dwellings"—and among these was the former site of the Golden Crust Bakery in Armadale, Victoria. The exterior (top) still shows the old bakery façade, while they added a courtyard at the rear (below).

At the fairs, she'd remark on cane and rattan furniture, art deco buffets, and crazy '50s colorful glass hanging lights, while I'd urge her to keep walking, continuing my search for early Spanish tables, etc. Now, at the Drouot and on the Left Bank of Paris, I see that early '40s and '50s decorative pieces have made a resurgence, and are now highly regarded.

When Tamsin moved to London after university, it was clear that she'd caught the family bug. While studying interior design, she began accompanying her mother and me on our regular antiques-buying forays in Europe. From a tiny flat on Portobello Road, we now had a handy agent covering the sales—and bringing to light some exciting discoveries. One discovery caused her to ring me (in Australia) in the middle of the night. "Dad, are you still buying silver-mounted emu eggs?" "Yes, of course I am. Why, have you found one?" "Will you be here next Saturday? I've got something for you in Portobello Road, and the dealer will hold it for you." As Tam explained, an elderly London dealer had retired, but was still making the pilgrimage to his stall on Portobello Road. Not only was he keeping aside an emu egg desk set, but he had several other pieces of colonial silver. On arrival, I went directly to the market, where I met the aged dealer, who was smiling from ear to ear while he said, "Hello, the man from Melbourne, are you interested in kangaroos too?" He started to open packages wrapped in newspaper. The desk set he produced was a museum-quality piece, by Wendt of Adelaide, circa 1880. It was a masterpiece! Oh, and the kangaroos he mentioned? A pair of sterling silver bookends by Drummond of Melbourne, circa 1900, beautifully engraved and presented to a vicar returned to England. I think there were about seven pieces in all; all wonderful, and I bought the lot.

On her return to Australia, Tamsin embarked on her own peripatetic lifestyle, moving with her husband, tailor Patrick Johnson, between countries and cities, establishing their respective work spaces in a number of different contemporary and historic buildings. With each new venture, Tamsin continued to demonstrate her fine eye for detail, her subtle use of color, her flair for designing with decorative lighting and antique furniture. Tamsin has the unique ability to rework the old with the new in a way that's modern, clean, and relevant today, in a style she has made her own.

Today, she is the one making regular buying trips, and juggling these with her own busy family life and her thriving business. Current projects include the restoration of a historic apartment in Paris, the interiors of two hotels in Dubai, the refit of a luxury super yacht moored in Sydney Harbour, and ongoing projects in Australia—from a seaside home in Palm Beach, New South Wales, to a cliffside mansion in Sorrento, Victoria. For now, Tamsin's office sits at the top of a tiny Victorian building in the Sydney suburb of Paddington, just off the high street, in a building that is both shop and dwelling. It seems history has a way of repeating itself.

Opposite - I wanted to create a gallery-like space for my store, with a clean backdrop to allow for the ever-changing display of pieces inside. The sculptural plaster detail on the walls, the custom-made steel bookshelves, and the mirrored ceilings to let in more light are the only decorative features.

Introduction by Tamsin Johnson

I'd been accompanying my parents on buying trips since the age of four, so in that respect this one was no different. The same brutal 5 a.m. start, heading off in the dark to a local antiques fair in a European city. The same thrill on arrival, with the earliness of the hour soon forgotten amid the cornucopia of sights, sounds, and smells. Once I was there, I never wanted to leave. On this particular trip, we were in Rome for the weekend, on our way to visiting an antiques fair in Bologna. I was twenty-one years old and living in London while interning at renowned fashion house Stella McCartney. The worlds of fashion and interiors had always enchanted me, but having studied the former for three years at Victoria's RMIT University, it was my chosen path at that time. My internship was an incredible experience, during which I met inspiring and talented people from around the globe and learned valuable lessons about design and life. But while my head was turned towards fashion, my heart lay somewhere else.

I'd quite literally grown up under the nineteenth-century Spanish tables and among the many Louis chairs in my father's antiques stores around Melbourne. In my teens, he'd pay my sister and me to help out on Saturdays, when we'd rush around measuring items and looking up details in his files so we could appear knowledgeable when customers inquired about a piece. This latest buying trip was nothing new, except that by now I had developed a very real knowledge of—and a deep appreciation for—what I was looking at. Yet something had changed. Perhaps it was the fact that I'd recently bought my first painting back in London, a French still-life I found at a vendor on Portobello Road, which would mark the start of my lifelong passion for collecting art. Perhaps it was having the chance to look at my path through a different lens, being far from my childhood home and on a break from my adopted one. All I know is that sitting in a hotel in Rome that weekend, I listened to my heart, and it was speaking to me of interiors.

How do you explain the whisperings of instinct? How do you account for that sense of contentment and peace when you know something just "feels right?" For me, the sense came with the realization that my voice sounded strongest and at its most authentic in this arena, and every decision I made from that point felt natural. Instinct led me to spend another year in London studying interior design at Inchbald School of Design. Instinct brought me home again to start work with an Australian firm, Meacham Nockles McQualter, and to start a new life in Sydney with my now-husband, Patrick, who was also returning from London as part of his next career move. And five enriching years later, instinct dictated that it was time to branch out on my own. It is that same instinct—a most precious resource—that shapes my design choices.

There's a certain balance I seek, where a space looks appealingly layered but not "decorated," where a design appears effortless rather than forced. I am by no means a minimalist, but my instinct guides me in the process of removing the unnecessary to ensure a space doesn't feel cluttered. I add, and edit, and remove, and assess, until the space feels right. For me, that occurs when the pieces appear as if they have always been there, regardless of the era when they were created.

This sense of timelessness is something I strive for in my designs. When I buy a piece of furniture, I always ask: will it still be good in fifty or even a hundred years' time? Beauty does not date, and "good design" may enjoy many lives and many homes. The way pre-loved objects can defy the decades and evolve through different life cycles is one of the things I love about them. Another is that it is of course near impossible to come across the same piece twice. Antiques enable me to bring something unique to each space, wrapped in a slight air of mystery that interweaves with the familiar and the contemporary.

Custom designs also allow me to introduce one-off pieces, and it is that mix of the old and the new that I believe gives a home its spirit. Aesthetics is a beguiling realm, with its own language of context, subtext, concord, and (necessary) discord. The straight and the uneven line, the refined and the organic texture—they all have a place in an interior design as long as there is purpose and beauty in each element. I like to think of the result as a "tactful disharmony," where unexpected pieces and finishes merge, surprising you with the character they bring to a space, yet not dominated by any single object. To me, that quote by fashion icon Diana Vreeland—"The eye has to travel"—resonates here, with an interior design being a journey of discovery through a changing realm.

Opposite - The store, in the Sydney suburb of Paddington, used to be a former fashion boutique and dwelling—clearly I inherited the family preference for these combined spaces. I bought the building in 2019 from the designer who created my wedding dress.

But as much as I enjoy collision, complexity, and drama, I welcome rest, calmness, and comfort, and just as important as the dynamic mix are the moments of repose. I want to create spaces for living: rooms that are beautiful without being fussy; functional designs that allow for every corner to be used and enjoyed by all. Spaces that are full of life, where the layers of furniture, lighting, soft furnishings, and art reflect the lifestyle, personality, and passions of their owners. With two children of my own, who accompany Patrick and me everywhere and who will no doubt join us on future buying trips, I know that the exceptional and the livable can go hand in hand.

As a keen collector of interior design books, I find it a humbling and inspiring experience to enter the world of other people's homes, to explore a space through someone else's eyes, to be gifted with a glimpse of someone else's vision so that by the time I reach the final page I feel as if I know them. The projects in this book reveal a little of my vision, inspirations, and design aesthetic. They range from a grand family house to a seaside escape, from a city apartment in Paris to a beach bungalow in Bondi. They also include a couple of the homes Patrick and I have lived in, and you'll see some pieces there that have gone on to enjoy another incarnation elsewhere in the book. I hope you enjoy your travels through these spaces. Spaces for living, but also spaces for sharing.

x x

Tamsin Johnson

Opposite - I designed the custom carpet on the stairs, which lead from the store to office space on the first floor and a sample library above that.

SAND CASTLE

*Ashley Street,
Tamarama, Sydney*

It's no secret that my house is something of a second showroom, with its own revolving door. During the four years we have lived in this beachside cottage, the place has seen six different coffee tables and three dining settings. Several armchairs have spent quality time with us, each bringing its unique beauty of line and texture before moving on to residences new. Like international guests, some of the pieces I've discovered on buying trips will arrive, stay for a while to the enjoyment of all, then head off on a new adventure with a client. Sometimes, too, when my clients' style or space requirements change, they'll return a piece to me and I will welcome it back like an old friend. Since I would never buy anything for a client that I wouldn't love in my own home, this works out just fine.

When Patrick and I bought and renovated this four-bedroom house for our growing family, we wanted to create a relatively subtle backdrop, partly to complement frequent changes of furnishings and partly in response to the commanding view outside. The 1940s residence looks out over Sydney's Tamarama beach, also known as "Glamarama" for its style-savvy regulars. The electric blue water, an intricately curved coastline, and the little surf club below—all these are iconic sights of the area that we were keen to soak up. When we discovered the house, its main floor featured only a few small windows facing the ocean, so one of our first moves was to completely open up the space to the view and add steel-framed bifold doors that allow for optimal ocean gazing. Removing internal walls and opening up spaces was pretty much our focus here, given that the place hadn't been touched in fifty-odd years and was a series of dark rooms. One happy discovery during this process was a concealed high pitched ceiling, which we restored, retaining the beams and adding lining boards painted in a gorgeous glossy white enamel. Simple white tones with a little texture to them form the basic canvas of the house, with Venetian plaster featuring on the bathroom walls and in the kitchen. This finish is not a traditional choice for a kitchen counter top, but dedicated weeks of hand-layering have given it a smooth and divinely tactile effect that I adore. Paired with the whites are warmer sandy hues under foot, created by larch floorboards with a white stain, and Belgian sisal in the bedrooms.

Previous pages - The neutral backdrop of white walls and white-stained larch floors allows the focus to remain on the view of Tamarama beach outside and the shifting canvas of furnishings within.

Opposite - Two Audoux Minet rope chairs bring a strong textural element to this coastal space. While they have since moved to another beachside residence, other pieces will always stay with us, such as the Rietveld-inspired chair I made in woodwork and the Gaetano Pesce "his" and "hers" side tables ("his" is pictured here, while "hers" is on the previous page).

Starting with this calm, natural palette and the ocean view as anchor, we worked our way back through the rooms, introducing color, energy, and surprise with furniture and art. Some pieces came from our previous apartments, such as a white cotton sofa and cloud-like wool Fritz Neth chairs, which continue the lightness of touch established by the walls, ceilings, and floors. Among our favorites is a pair of concrete side tables by Gaetano Pesce with a cheeky "his" and "hers" design. From here, we built up a collection to suit this new home, adding discoveries from trips and late-night internet trawls.

I wanted the house to feel international in its aesthetic but also possess that very Australian sense of coastal comfort, where indoors and outdoors merge, and a relaxed, beachy vibe prevails — where nothing appears too contrived or unapproachable. I believe that houses and the pieces that fill them should be durable, comfortable, and functional as well as beautiful. It was also important to me that we utilized every available space. At the entrance, I transformed a large cupboard into a little nook with banquette seating, which increases the size of the hallway and establishes a mood of elegant repose. I always prefer a piece of furniture to built-in storage, and so sideboards and consoles feature prominently in the house, perfect for displaying art as well as showcasing the artistry of their own design. In the living area, a glossy black USM cabinet reinforces the monochromatic impact of a series of photographs that we've added to over time. In the master bedroom, a 1940s Belgian oak cabinet with verdigris copper inlays brings extra punch to a pair of vibrant green, bamboo-shaped lamp bases. The rugged rattan lampshades and the sun-kissed look of the cabinet have a textural, calming quality that balances the strong hit of color.

At the time of writing, our collection of furniture is undergoing another evolution. The well-traveled Fritz Neth chairs, having wended their way here from Denmark via New York and Paris, have moved to a house in Sydney's eastern suburbs, while a pair of Audoux Minet rope armchairs now reside in another beach house in neighboring Bondi. But some pieces are stayers: the black and gray kitchen bar stools, which were custom made to fit under the counter; a chair in the corner of the living room, which I made during weekly woodwork classes, inspired by the work of Gerrit Rietveld; and a nineteenth-century French carved timber trunk from my parents' collection, which my sister and I used to fight over to sit on during phone calls back in the days when we had landlines. And then there are our artworks, which we'd never sell but happily shuffle between home and showrooms. Patrick and I have been collecting art for many years, often looking to our generation of emerging local artists as we enjoy watching their styles develop. In the living area, the monochromes of an abstract painting by Kirsty Budge sit above the fireplace, near the rich terracottas of an Australian landscape painted by Luke Sciberras and, between them, a strip of sky-blue metal riddled with bullet holes by Saskia Folk. I think this trio sets the tone for the house — cool and coastal with elements of surprise and a robust, enduring beauty.

Opposite - Among the many artworks in our place, the series of black-and-white photographs that sits above a USM cabinet is a constantly evolving scene. Those incredibly soft Fritz Neth chairs have also left us for another home now.

Above - Layers of Venetian plaster give the most beautiful finish to the kitchen countertops. The painting of the rooster by Lucy Culliton is one of our oldest artworks — I love its thick brushstrokes and sandy tones.
Opposite - A magnolia branch in a Murano vase provides a vivid burst of color in the room. I think fresh flowers are an essential part of a room's design. Lighting choices such as the pendant and the triangular wall sconce are sculpturally appealing but don't dominate the space, keeping the focus on the view outside.

Opposite - A collection of ceramics makes an arresting display under a bullet-ridden artwork by Saskia Folk.
Above - I transformed this unused entrance space into a welcoming nook with a custom white linen French-buttoned banquette cushion. A spiky Murano glass wall sconce, Josef Hoffmann brass hooks, and a Jacques Adnet umbrella stand lend their intriguing shapes to the rich colors of velvet cushions and an artwork by Pino Manos.

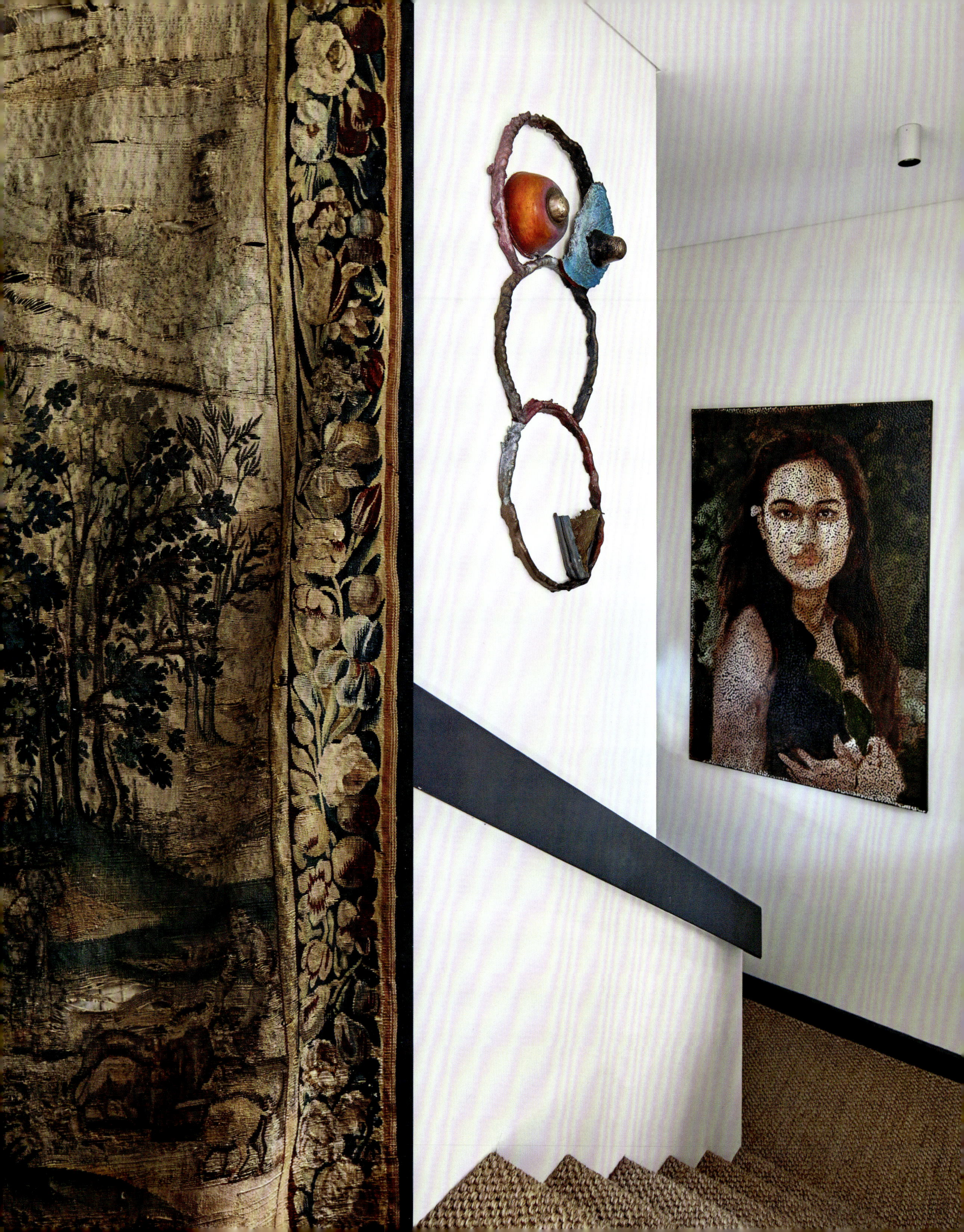

ED VAN DER ELSKEN
CAMERA IN LOVE
PRESTEL
JEAN-LOUIS DENIOT INTERIORS
SIMPLICITY
NANCY BRAITHWAITE
The Houses of VERANDA
LISA NEWSOM
ROTHKO SUGIMOTO
PACE LONDON
HAPPY TIMES / LEE RADZIWILL
ASSOULINE
BRANCUSI
DE KOONING
Florida Modern
HOTEL IL PELLICANO
PETER BEARD
TASCHEN

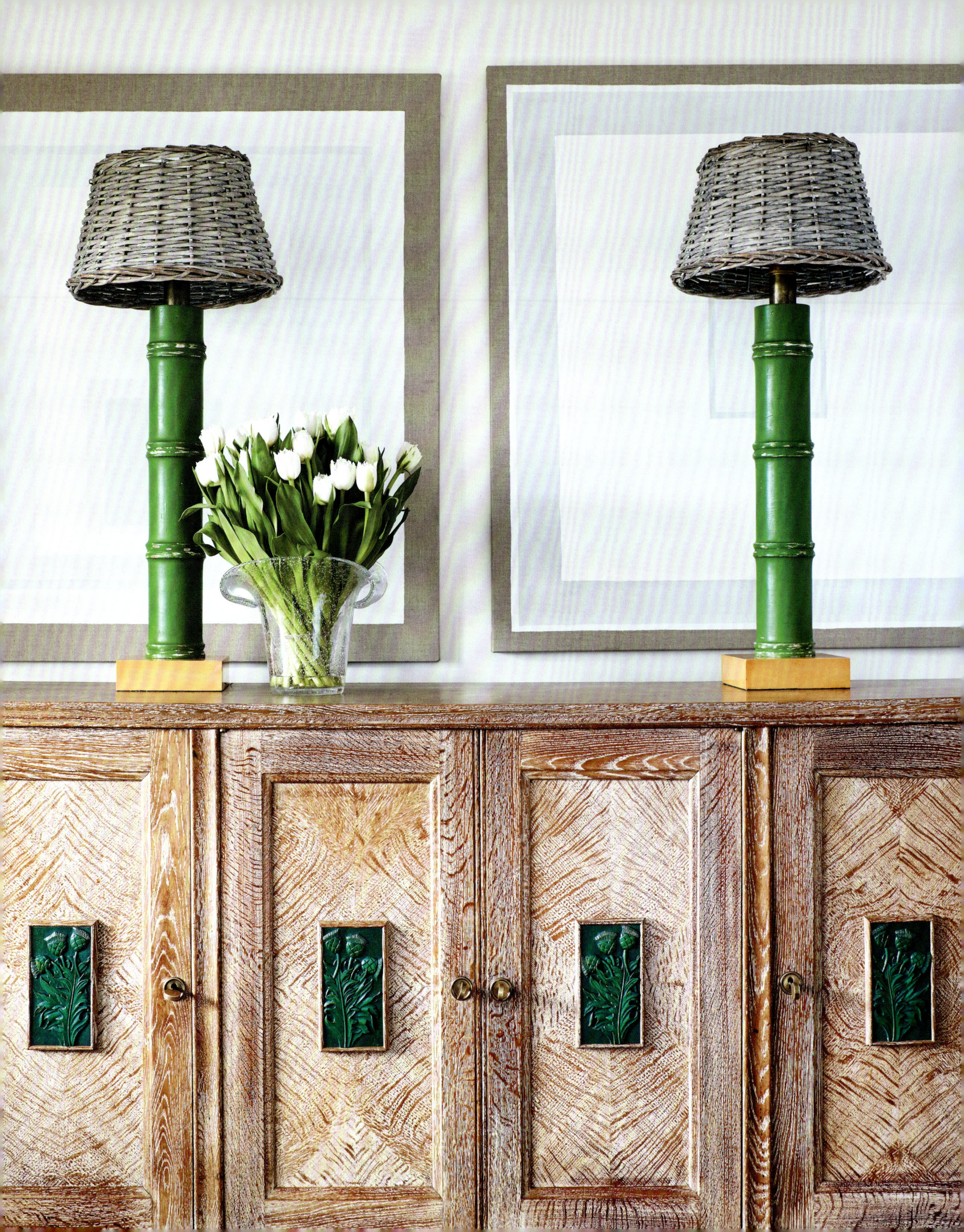

Previous spread (left) - Works by two of our favorite Australian artists – a bronze by Brendan Huntley and a commissioned painting by Daniel Boyd.
Previous spread (right) - Our study, presided over by an antique Flemish tapestry, is full of family treasures. The 1920s American oak desk was a kitchen table in one of our former homes. The little coconut lamp, one of my parents' finds, has been a part of my life since childhood.

Opposite - The verdigris copper inlays of this 1940s Belgian cabinet connect beautifully with the vibrant green of the mid-twentieth-century French lamp bases above.
Above - Another childhood keepsake, the nineteenth-century French carved timber trunk, paired with the timber of a Pierre Jeanneret desk chair. The double shade of the little table lamp was one of those happy accidents that end up being cherished for their quirkiness.

Above - The master bedroom and en suite share a calm, restful palette.
Opposite - In the family bathroom, soft green Murano wall sconces complement the gray Venetian plaster walls and concrete vanity and backsplash.

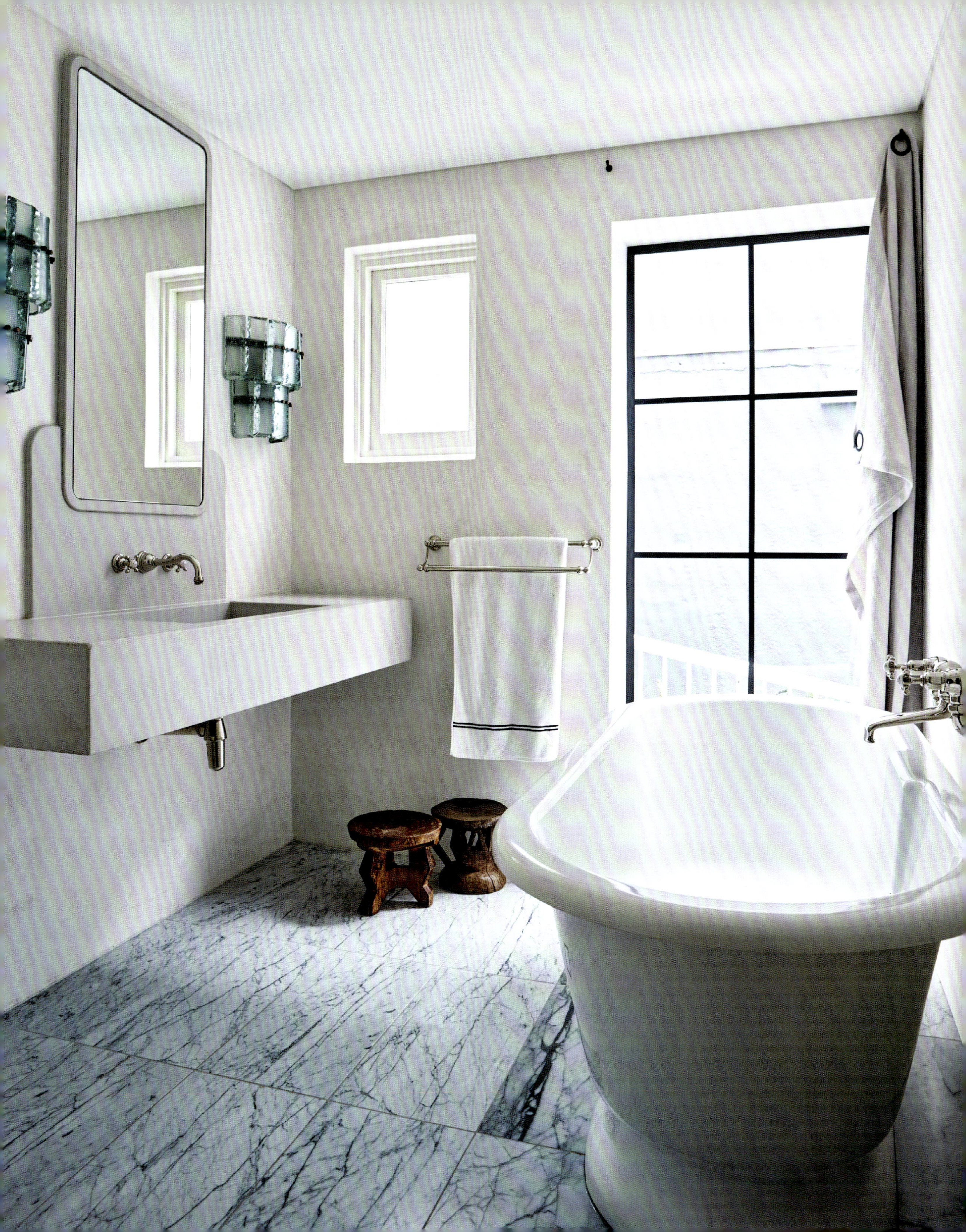

HIDE AWAY

Barrenjoey Road,
Palm Beach, Sydney

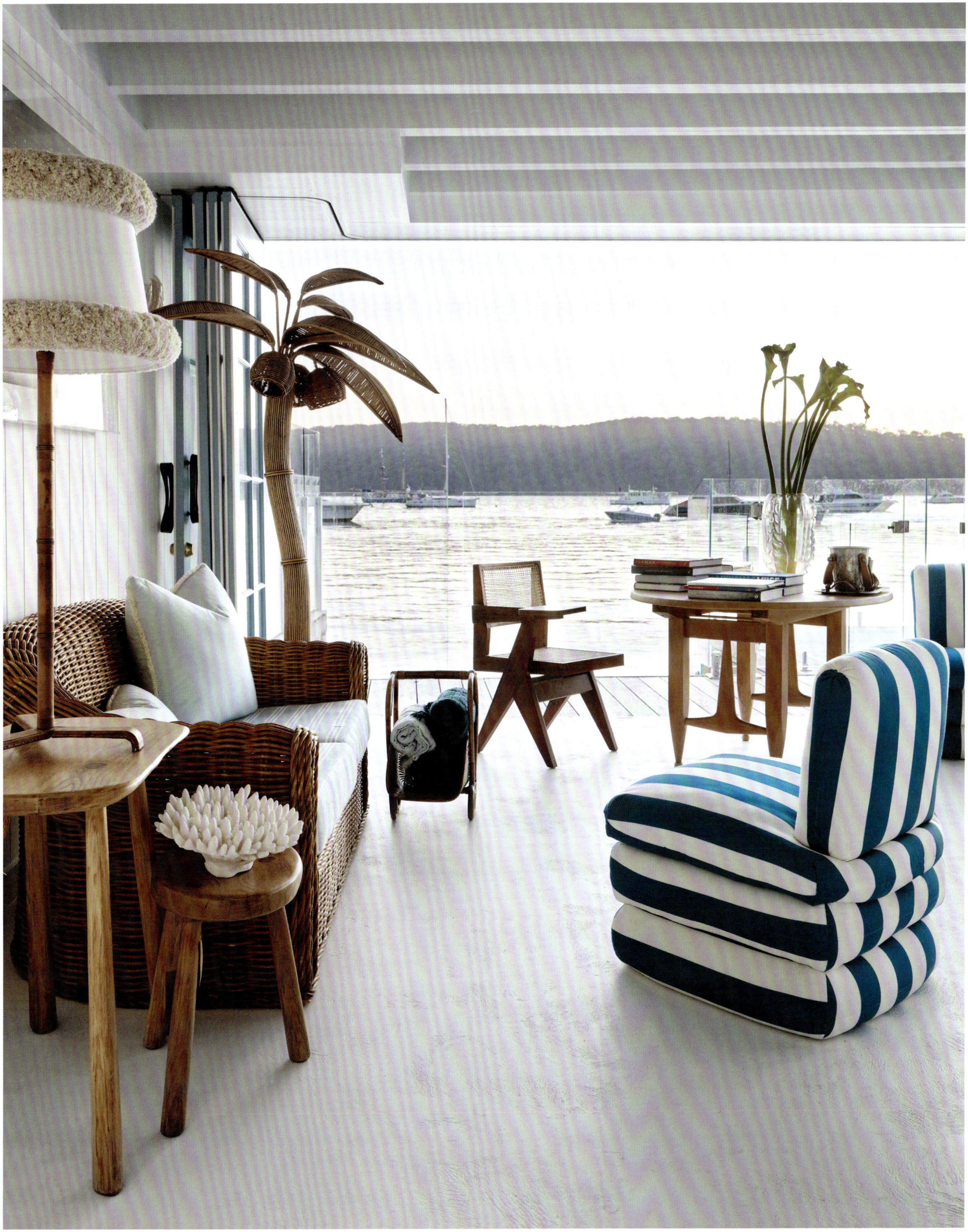

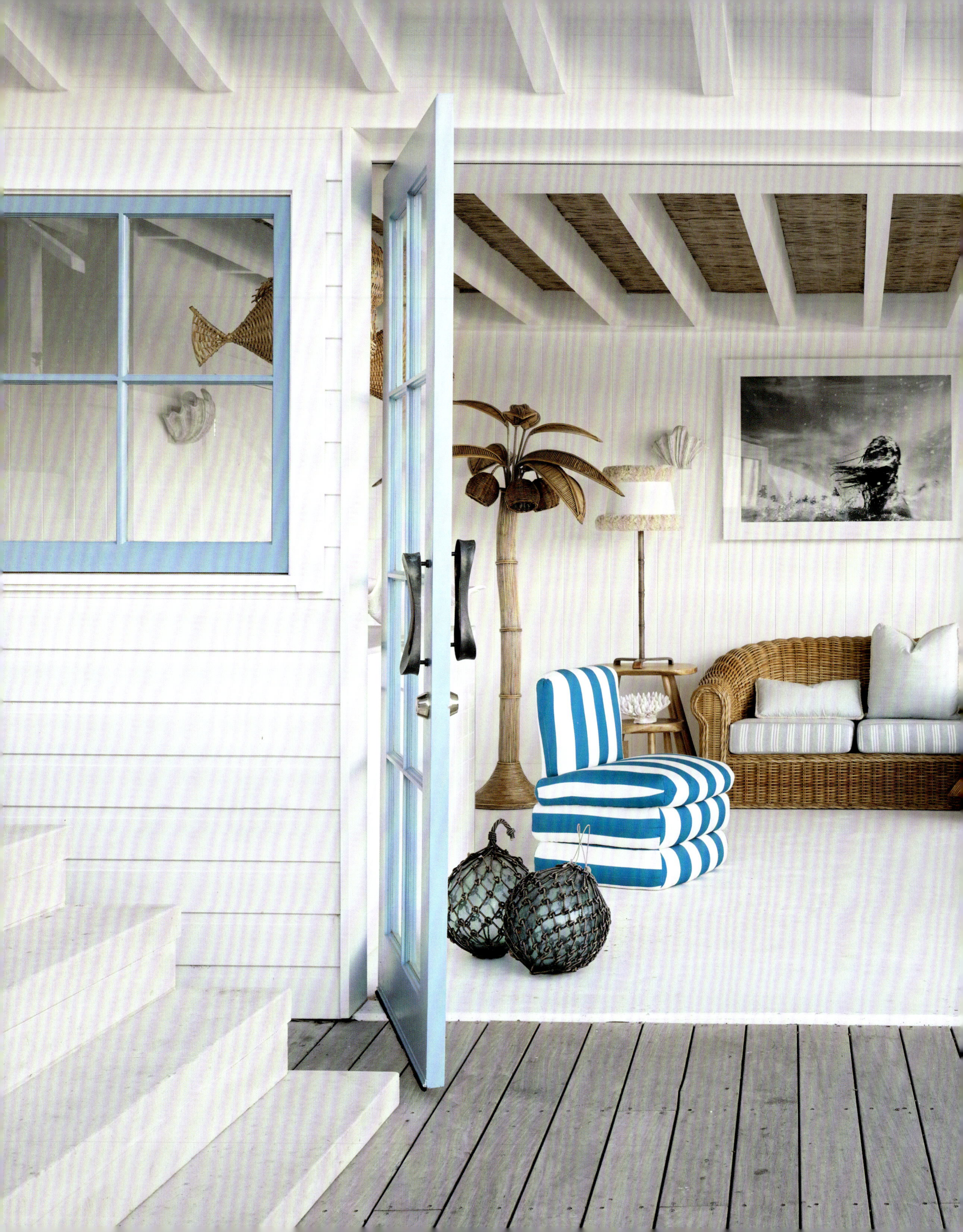

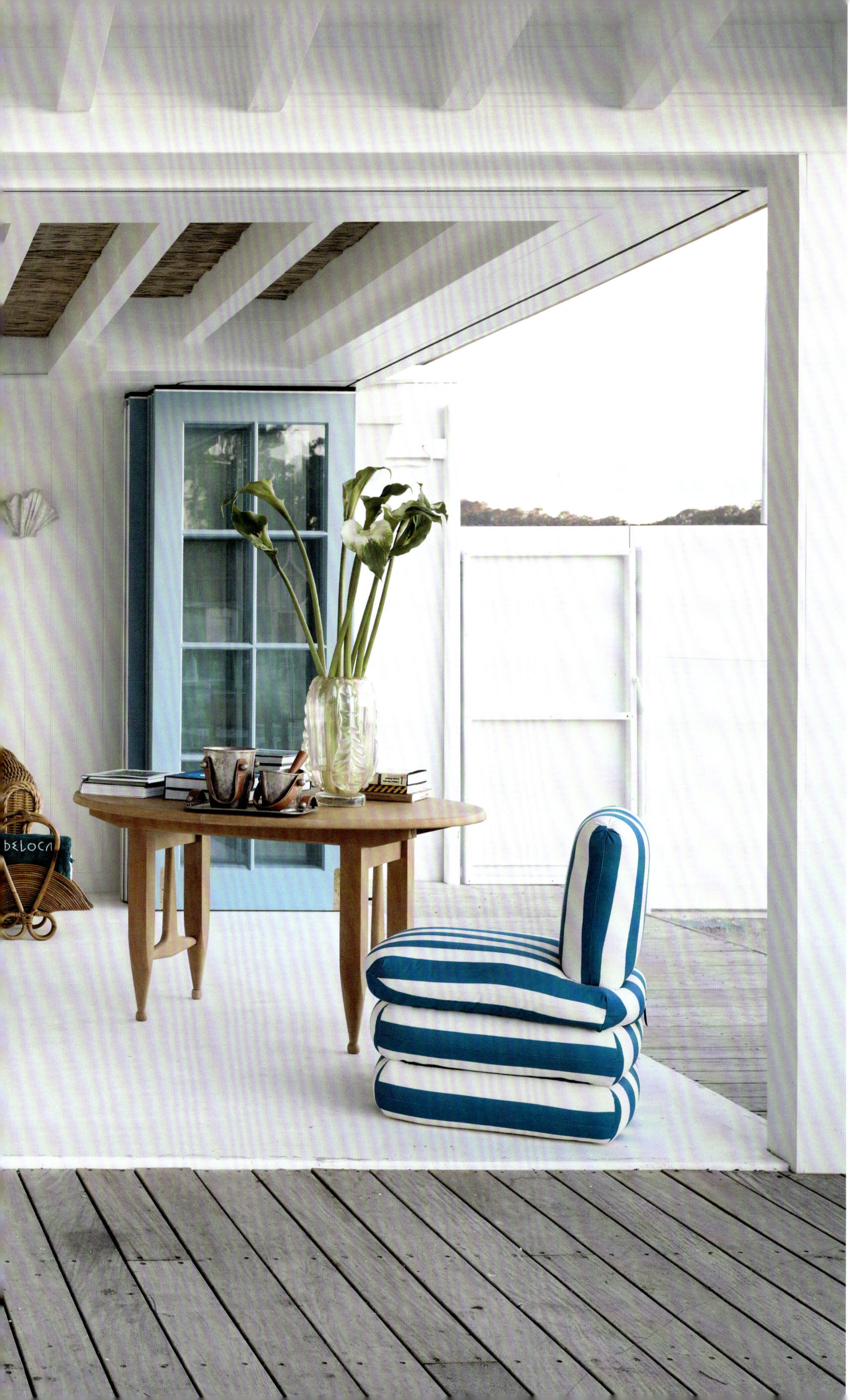

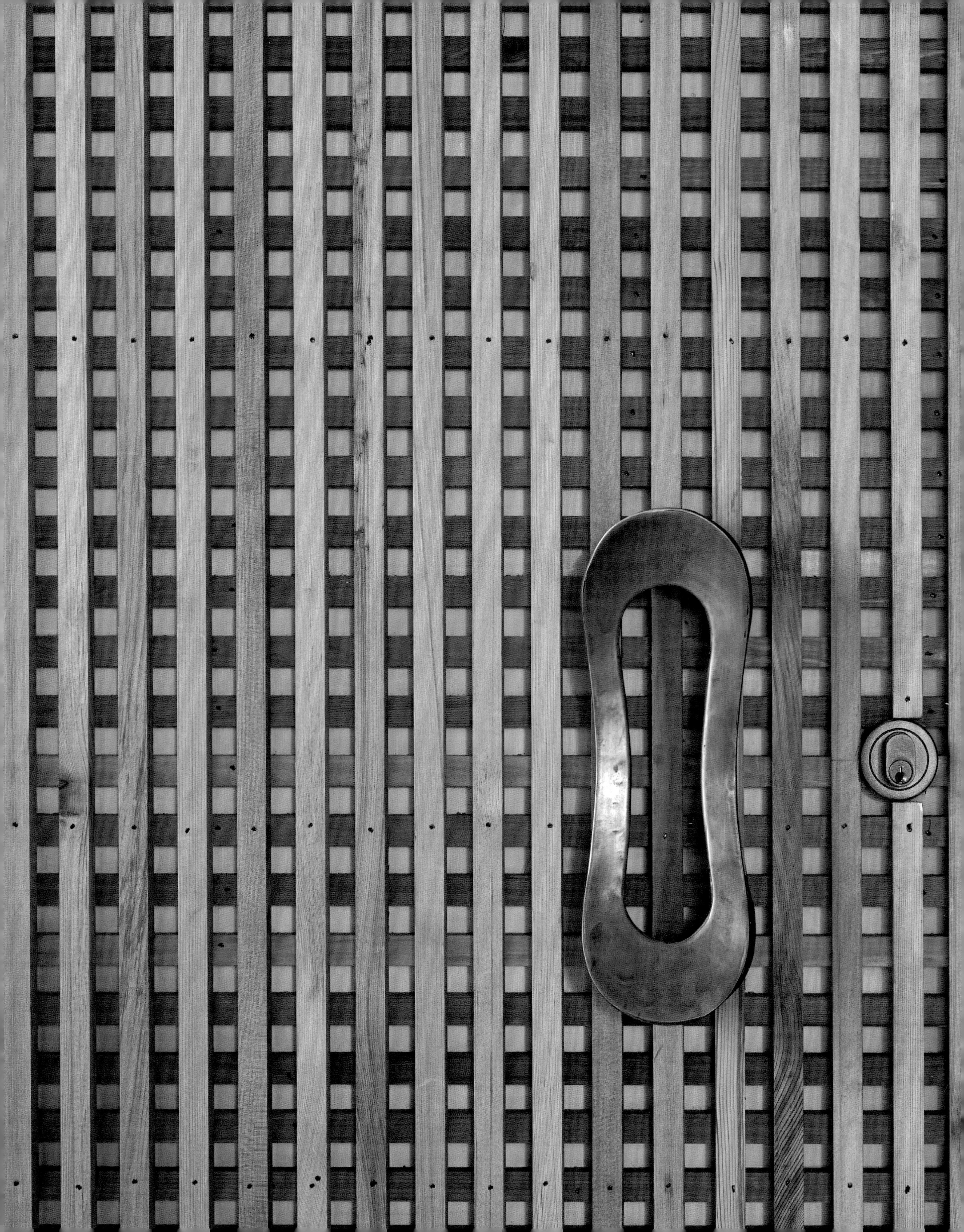

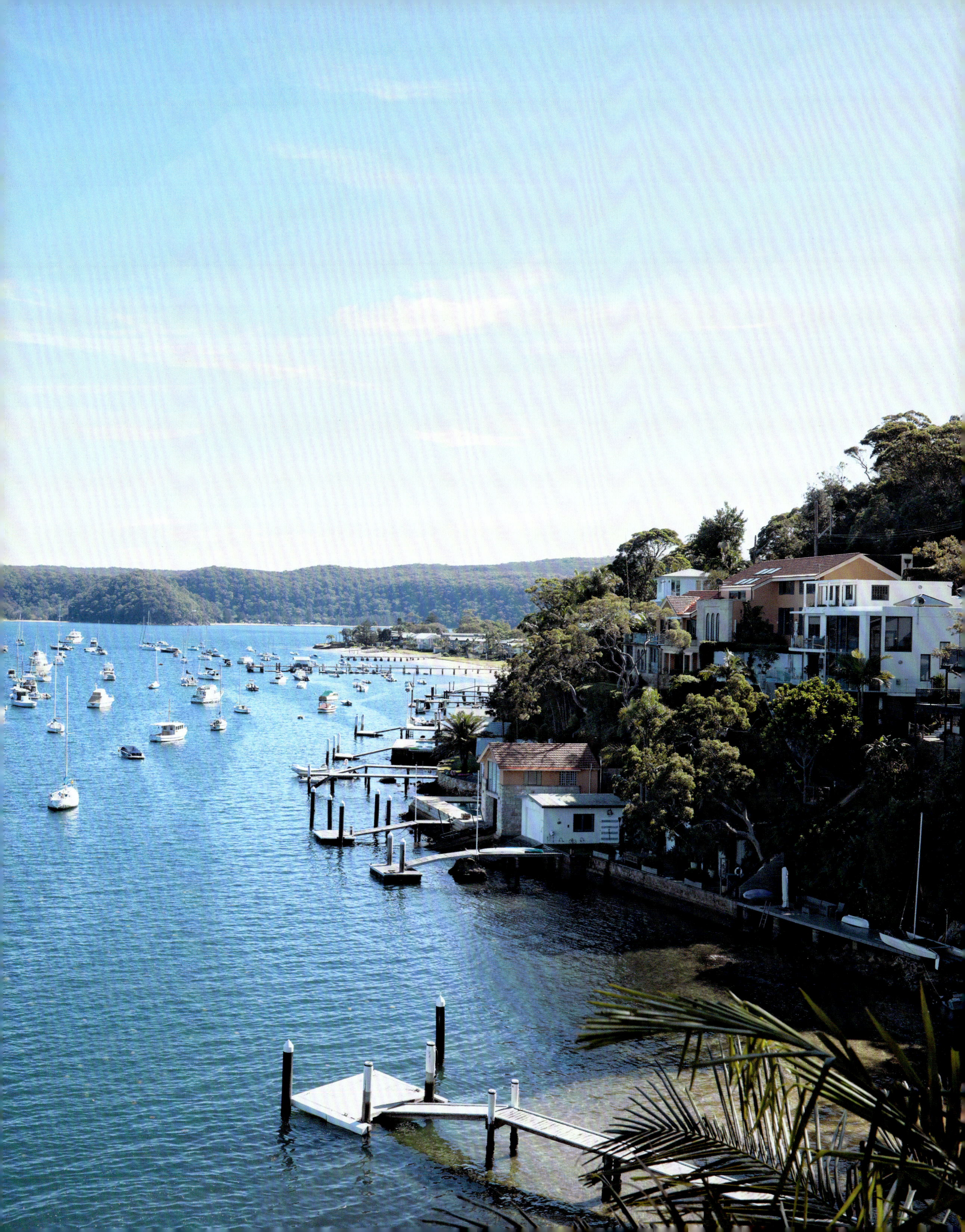

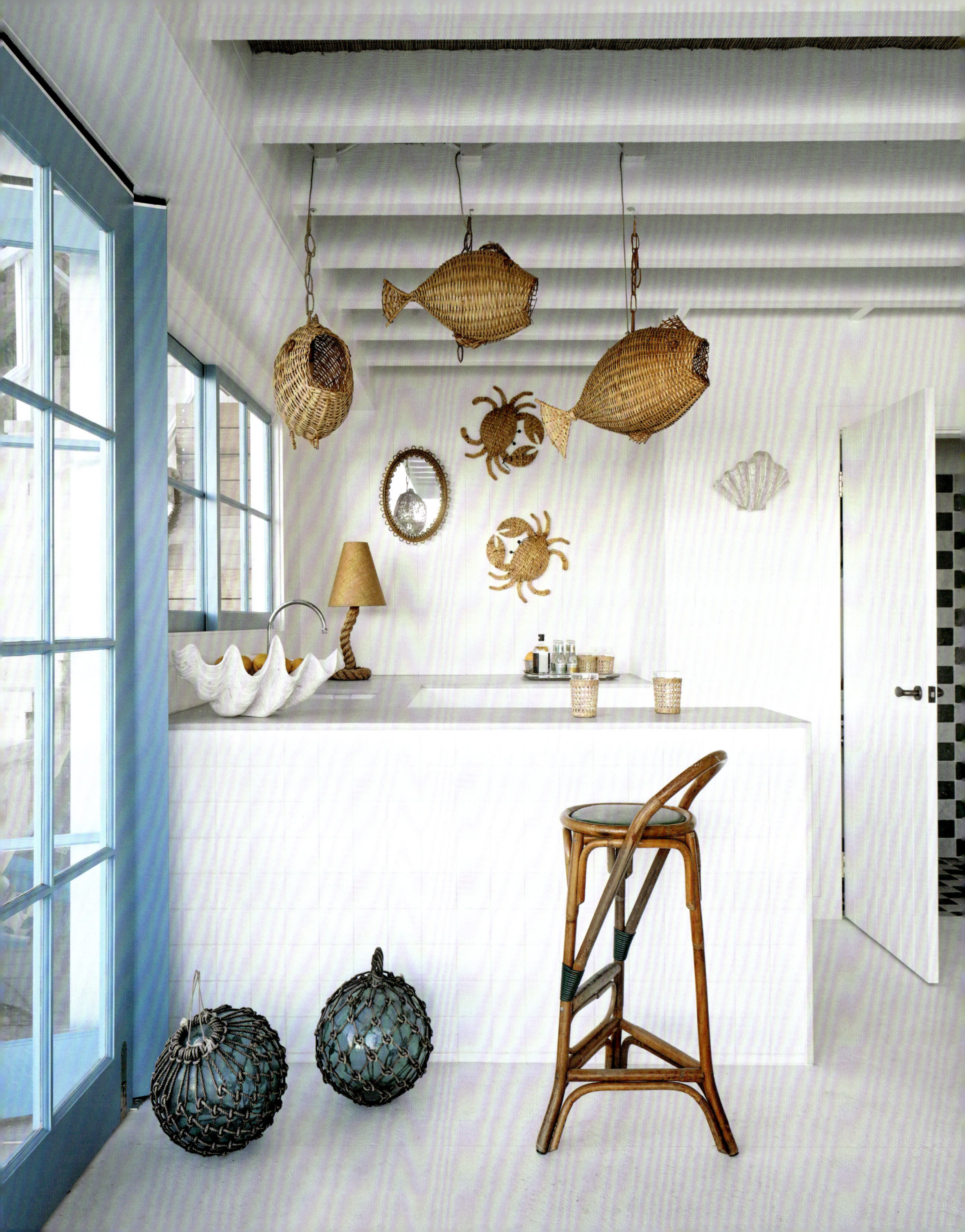

The coastal road that winds its way along Sydney's northern beaches to the renowned Palm Beach peninsula sees a variety of traffic. There are the residents and regular surfers, the day-trippers and tourists here to dine or take a dip, the photography and film crews coming to shoot among the breathtaking scenery, and the city dwellers retreating to their weekend getaways. Among this activity, picture a cavalcade of delivery vehicles arriving to furnish a new house. In this case, the contents included a custom-designed concrete kitchen, driven slab by slab down from Queensland, two forty-foot shipping containers' worth of upholstered furniture from Los Angeles, and another containerful from France, packed with vintage pieces. As furniture deliveries go, it was a fairly large-scale operation. But then nothing about this house is small in scale.

From a street-side garage, it cascades in four levels down a steep slope that plunges to the water. The house enjoys the most spectacular views, looking out over intensely blue sea and bushland beyond. However, when I first saw it, that was the place's only strength. The building itself bore the heavy legacy of 1980s design: drab brown bricks and brown aluminum windows, orange-stained timber floors, and a number of large, awkward rooms that lacked connection and purpose. For its new owners, this would become a weekend and holiday house, where the family could escape from their Sydney home just an hour's drive away. They wanted a durable place, not too formal or precious, that would reflect the pace of their own life when here, whether they were entertaining or simply relaxing. After rendering the exterior, installing new windows, and clearing the interior in preparation for a complete re-furbishment, it was time to unlock the house's potential.

Such is the size of the place — six bedrooms, seven bathrooms, three kitchens — that the interior design needed to take into consideration the various areas and their requirements. With so many rooms, so many spaces, one mood doesn't fit all, and while many areas suit a casual arrangement, some lend themselves to a more formal treatment. Just like the lifestyle of its owners, a house's design needs its own shifting rhythm and energy, and I wanted to ensure this by using the layout of each space to define its purpose. Palm Beach has an appealing duality — the still water of the Pittwater inlet on one side, with its pleasure craft and bayside glamour, and the beach on the other, with its laid-back surfing lifestyle. There is a little of both in this house, which tells its story across each level, beginning, most naturally, with the water.

pp. 43–45 - Mid-twentieth-century furniture and lamps team beautifully with vibrant striped Pillow Chairs from Ash NYC on the polished concrete floor of the boathouse.
Previous spread (left) - The front door, with its woven timber lattice and custom brass handle, presents an elegant preview of the textural layers inside.
Previous spread (right) - The house enjoys a view over the peaceful Pittwater inlet on Sydney's northern beaches.

Opposite - A vintage French bar stool provides a counterpoint to the themed décor in the little boathouse kitchen.

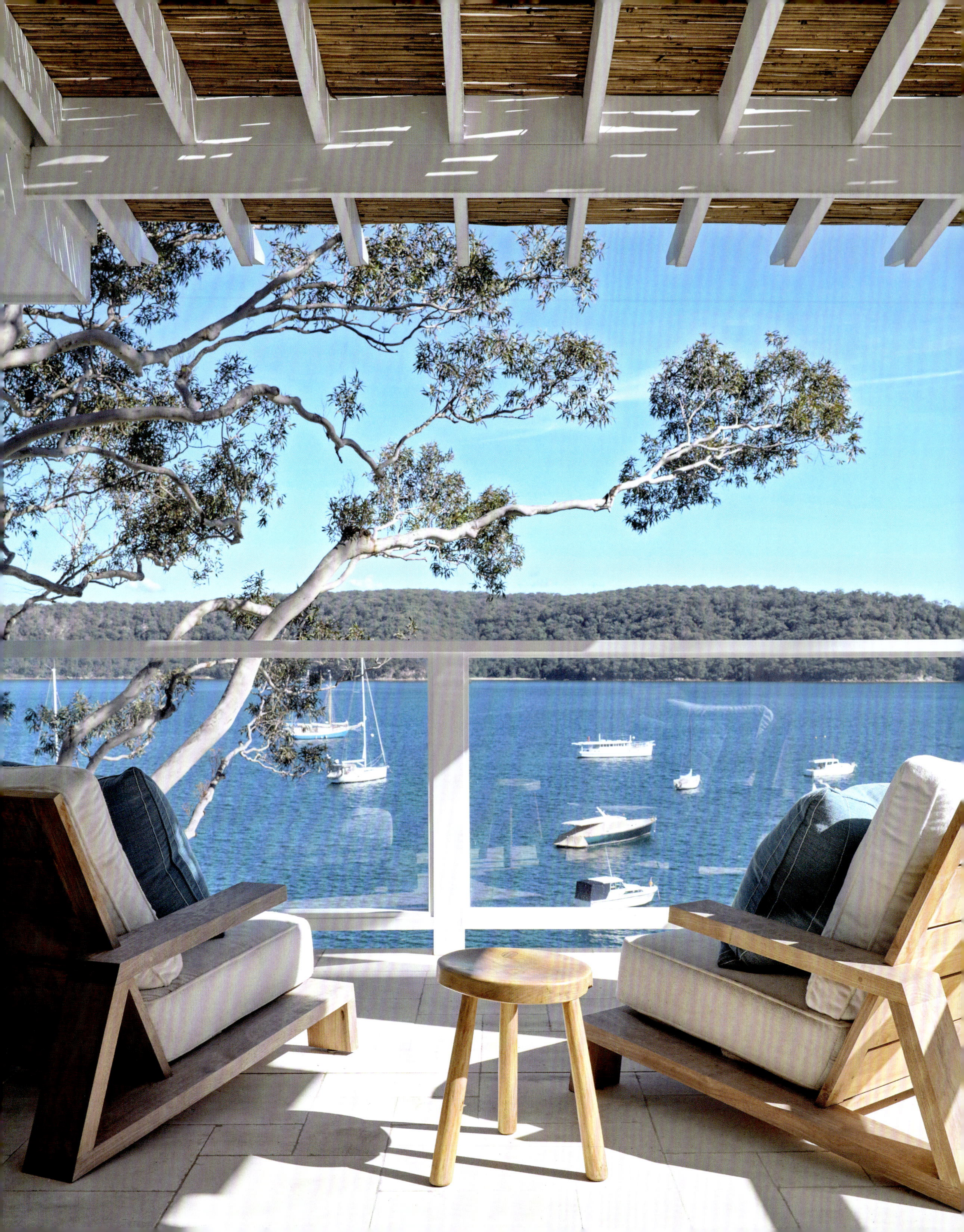

Opposite - Dappled light through the bamboo-clad awning gives this top-floor balcony a Mediterranean feel.
Above - The blue and white palette of the boathouse continues on the pool deck.

The family wanted a colorful beach house that, in terms of style, combined a bit of the Hamptons with a dash of the Mediterranean while encapsulating the luxurious ease of Australian coastal living. Comfort was key, with plenty of natural finishes such as timber, stone, and rattan, and furniture that combined inviting, loosely upholstered seating with one-off antique and mid-twentieth-century finds. Inspiration for the palette came from the surroundings—the blue water, the greens of the eucalypts and other trees, the pink of the sunset, and the unique orange of the sand.

Opening onto the inlet is the boathouse, which leads to a pool deck and private jetty. This space has an endearing identity all its own, with blue-painted window and doorframes, a white polished concrete floor, bamboo-clad ceiling and white timber beams. Playful nods to its setting via rattan fish pendant lights and decorative fishing floats are balanced by distinctive pieces such as a vintage French bar stool. The combination of blue and white continues in a striking pair of striped chairs and, outside, in striped sun loungers and umbrellas, giving this area the vibe of a personal resort. A flight of cliffside sandstone stairs lead up from here to the lowest of three interior living levels, where tumbled sandstone pavers mark a zone for casual living and dining. An extensive pink-cushioned corner lounge provides a chic, cozy link between a sauna and a bar, for more resort-style pleasures, with a colorful kitchenette and casual dining setting nearby. The layout of these spaces is still attuned to seaside pursuits and sandy bare feet, but with the next floor, the interiors evolve in both style and purpose. Here, at the house's entrance, a sense of its scale is powerfully evident in the double height of a split-level space, at the center of which hangs a custom-made rattan pendant over six feet in diameter. I wanted the furniture to play to the drama of the large area, so sumptuous sofas are more than three feet deep and clusters of different seating arrangements feature throughout. Ranged across light oak floors are the main living and dining areas, media room, and concrete kitchen, their vintage and custom pieces merging luxury with livability. One original feature of the house I was eager to keep is an internal stone wall, which anchors the spaces and highlights their scale. Just as the mesmerizing view outside accompanies you at every stage, this wall ascends through the three interior levels, from the casual areas to the top floor. Here, arrayed over seagrass flooring, the master bedroom, en suite, and library create a refined adults' zone, accented by the gleam of antique metal pieces and the detail of beautiful seating fabrics.

High above the lapping of waves, in the canopy of the eucalypts, this is the most formal of the spaces, yet it still evokes effortless coastal style. Looking out to the blue, and hearing the masts of boats gently clinking, the house's story ends, as it begins, with water.

Opposite - An L-shaped, pink-cushioned lounge offers a casual area for post-poolside drinks.

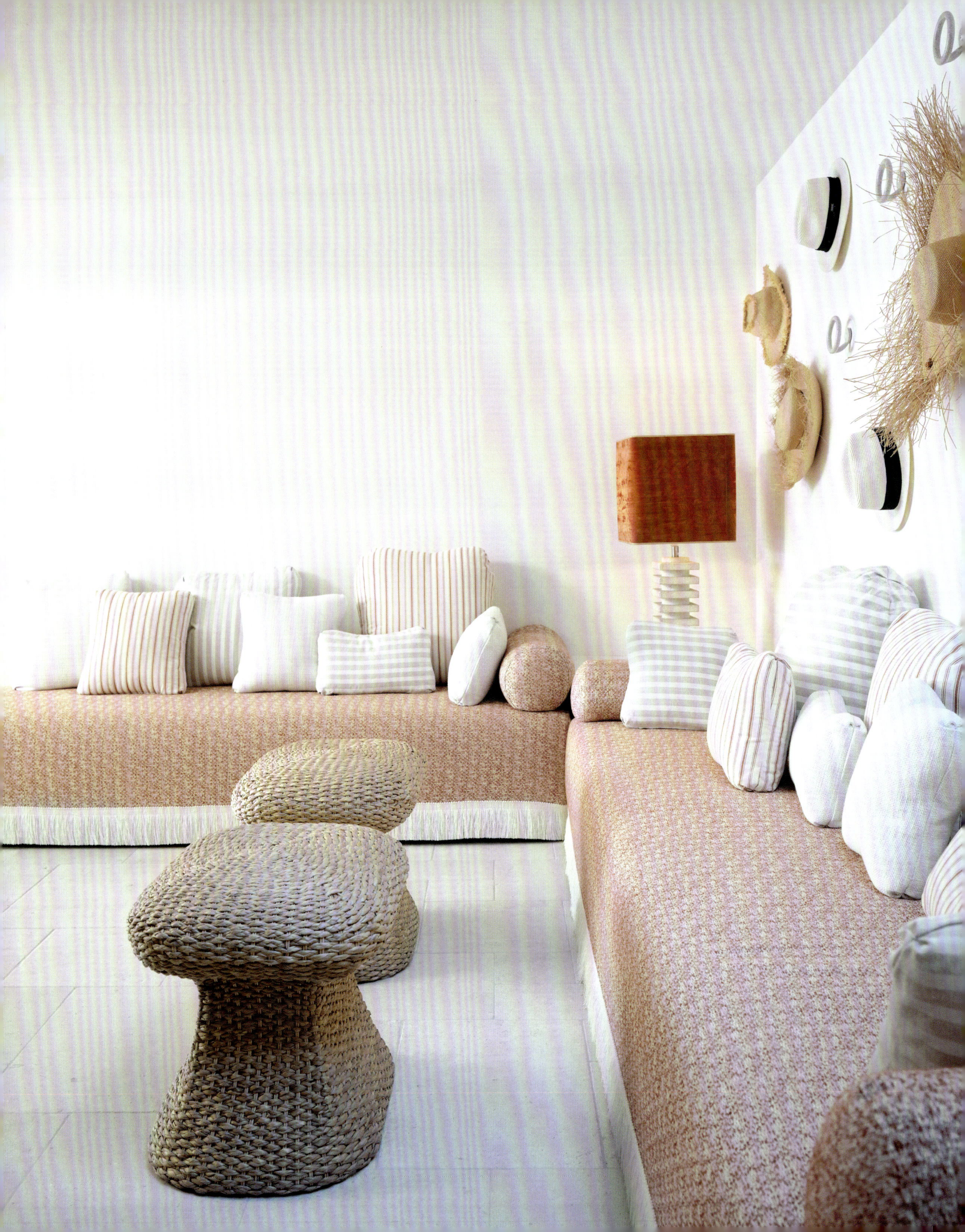

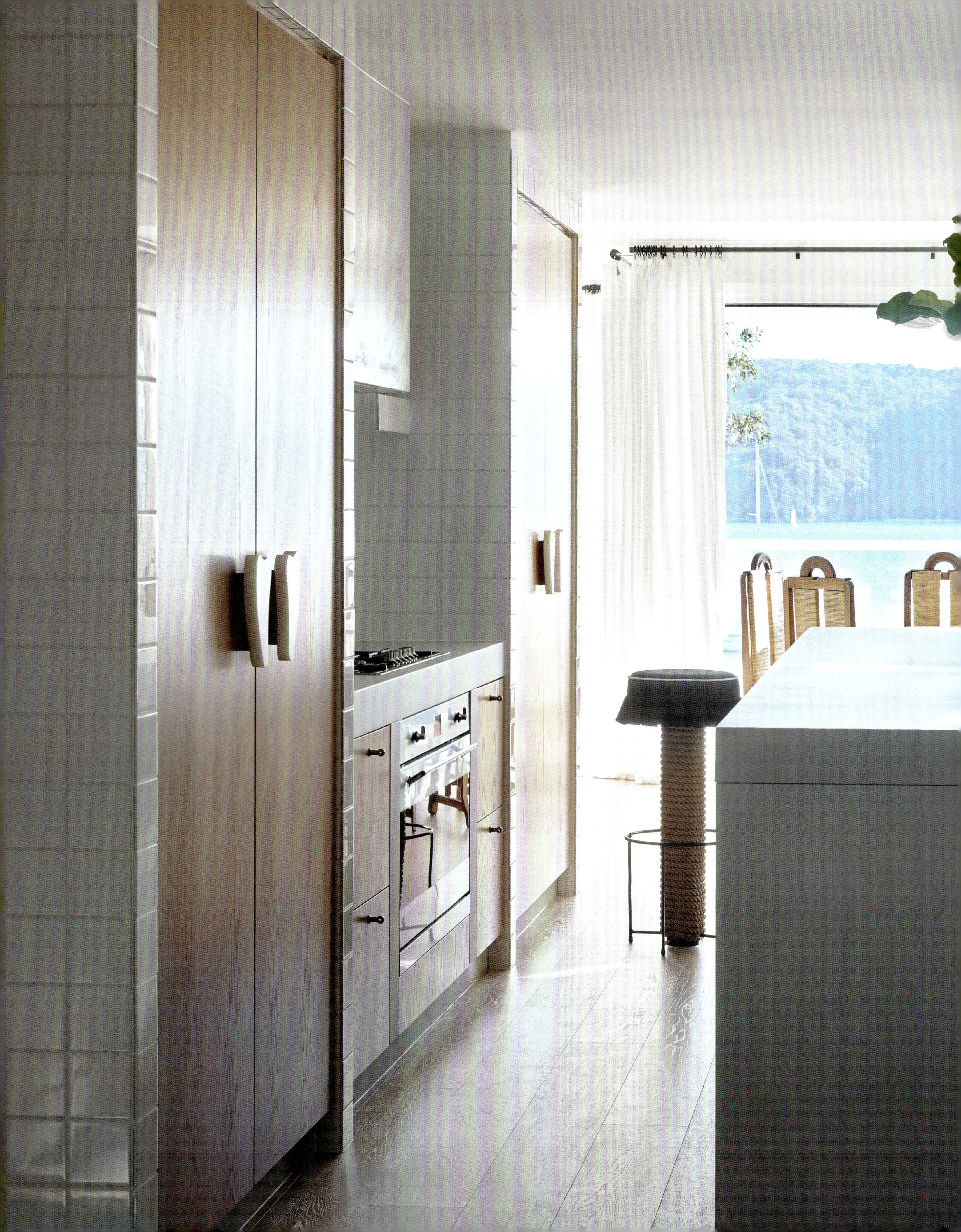

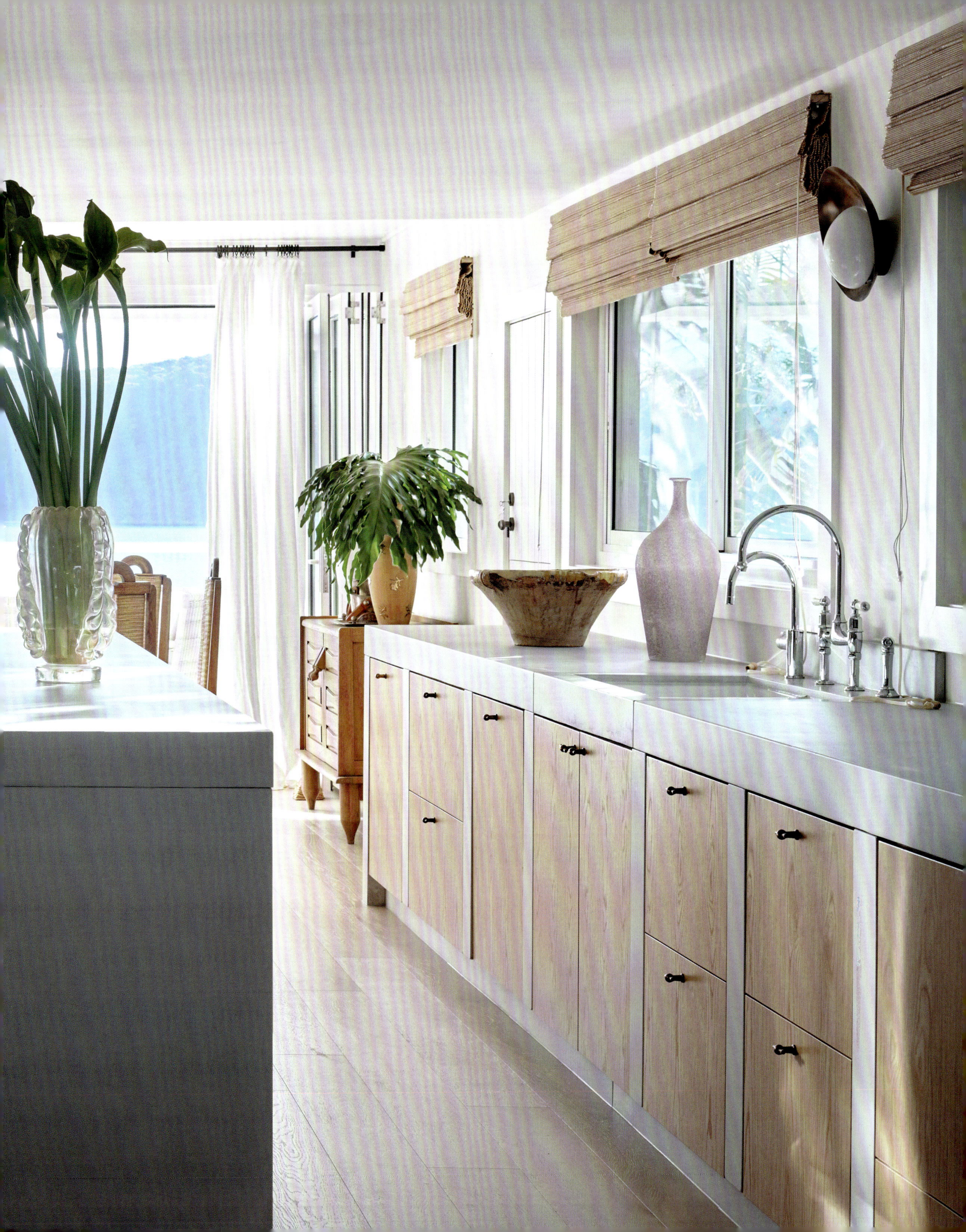

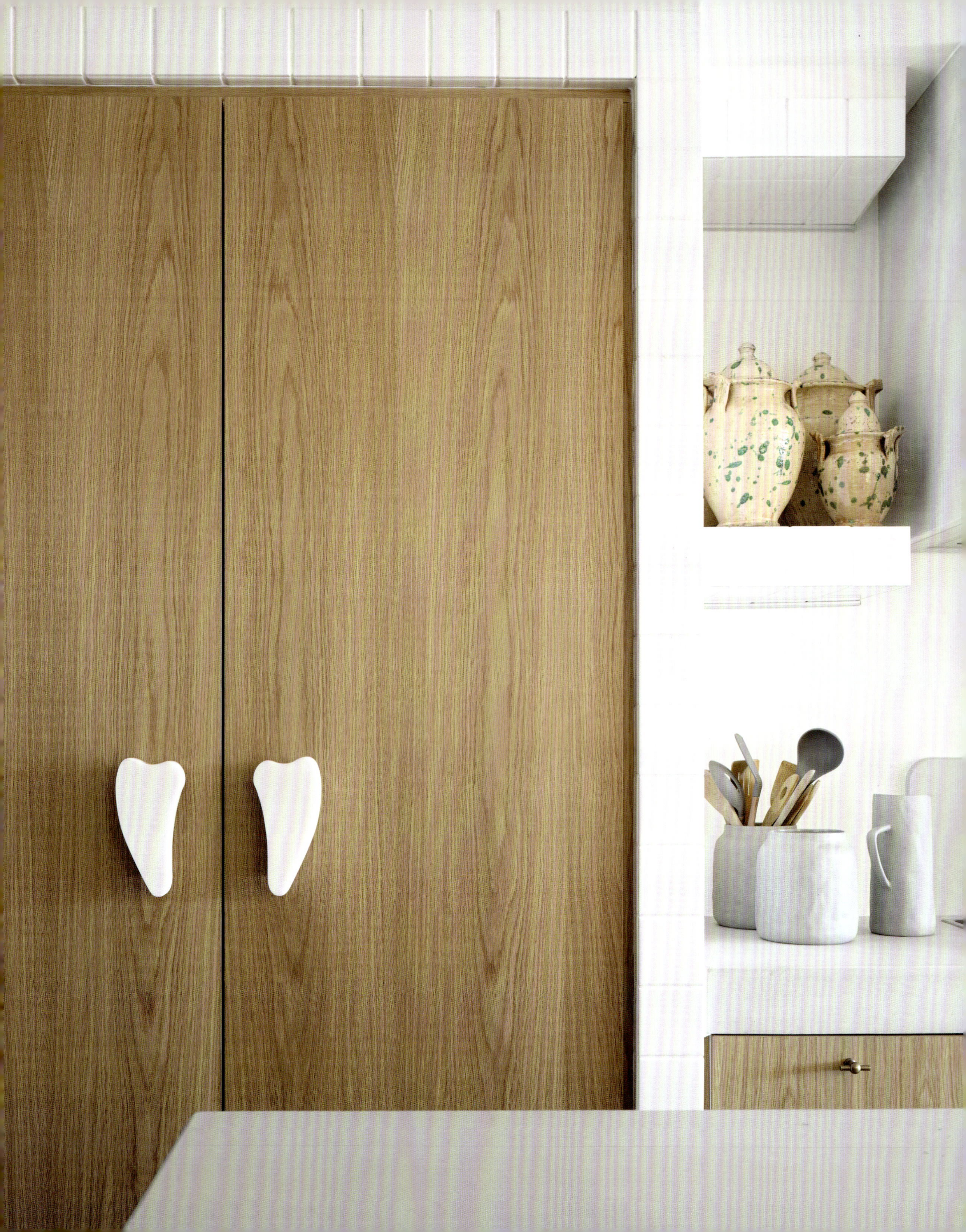

Previous spread, opposite, and above - In the main kitchen, I love the warmth that the oak floors and cabinets bring to the concrete surfaces. The custom-made white acrylic handles were based on a Jean Arp sculpture, while I added new black-and-white upholstery to vintage French bar stools.

Following spread (left) - The internal stone wall, an original feature, acts as an anchor throughout the house.
Following spread (right) - French ladder-back rattan chairs, a travertine table, and a vintage white plaster pendant light make an attractive vignette in the dining area off the kitchen.

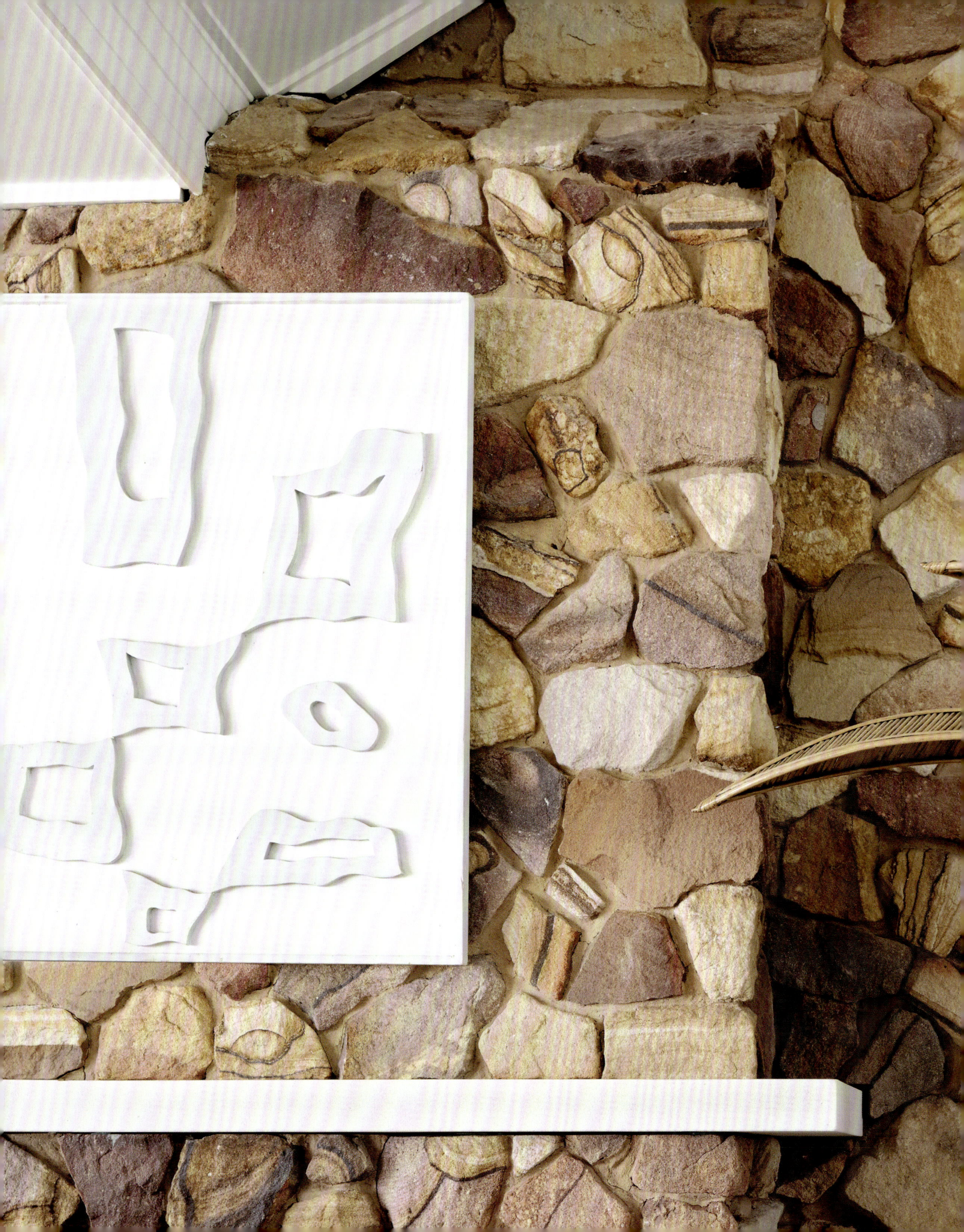

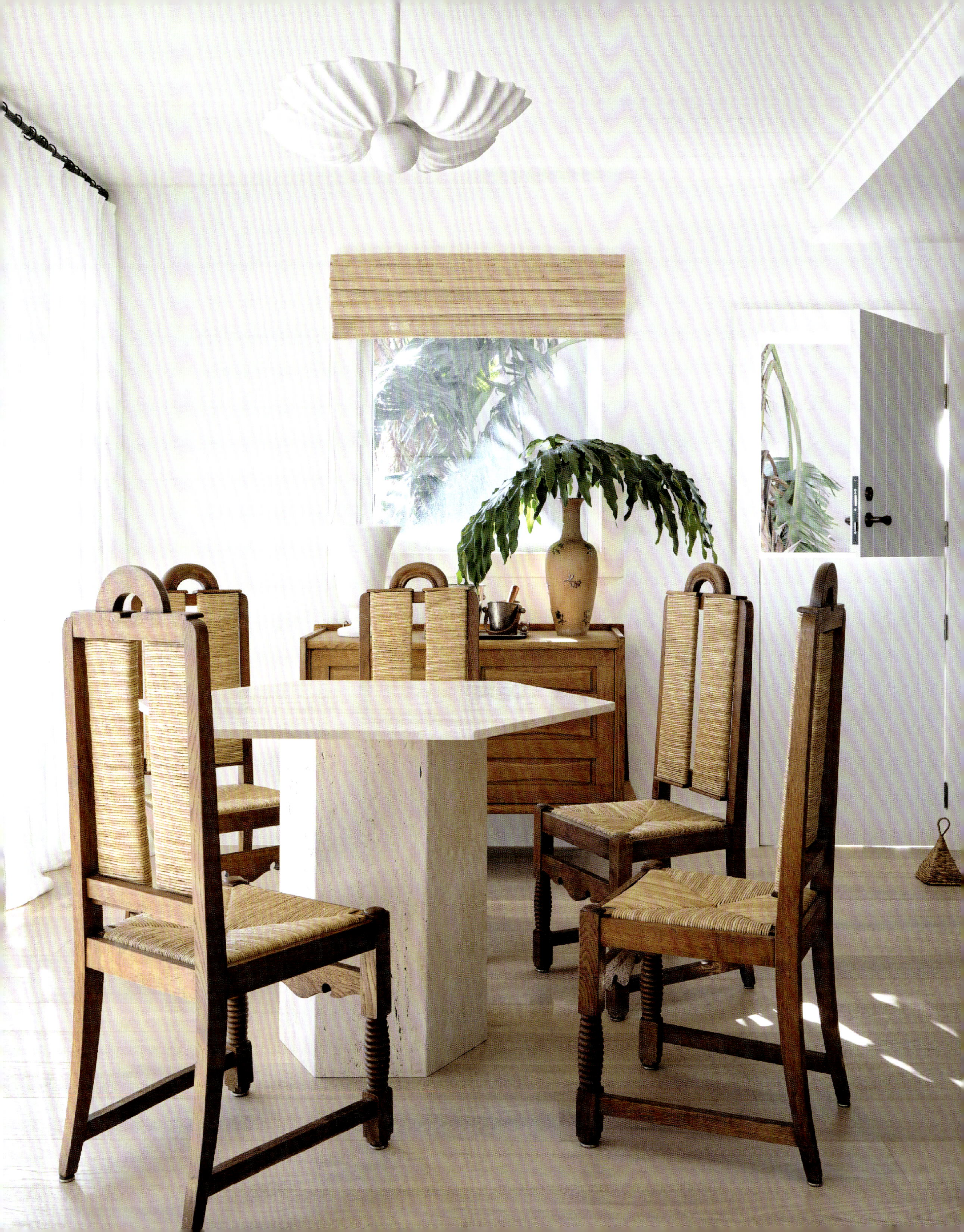

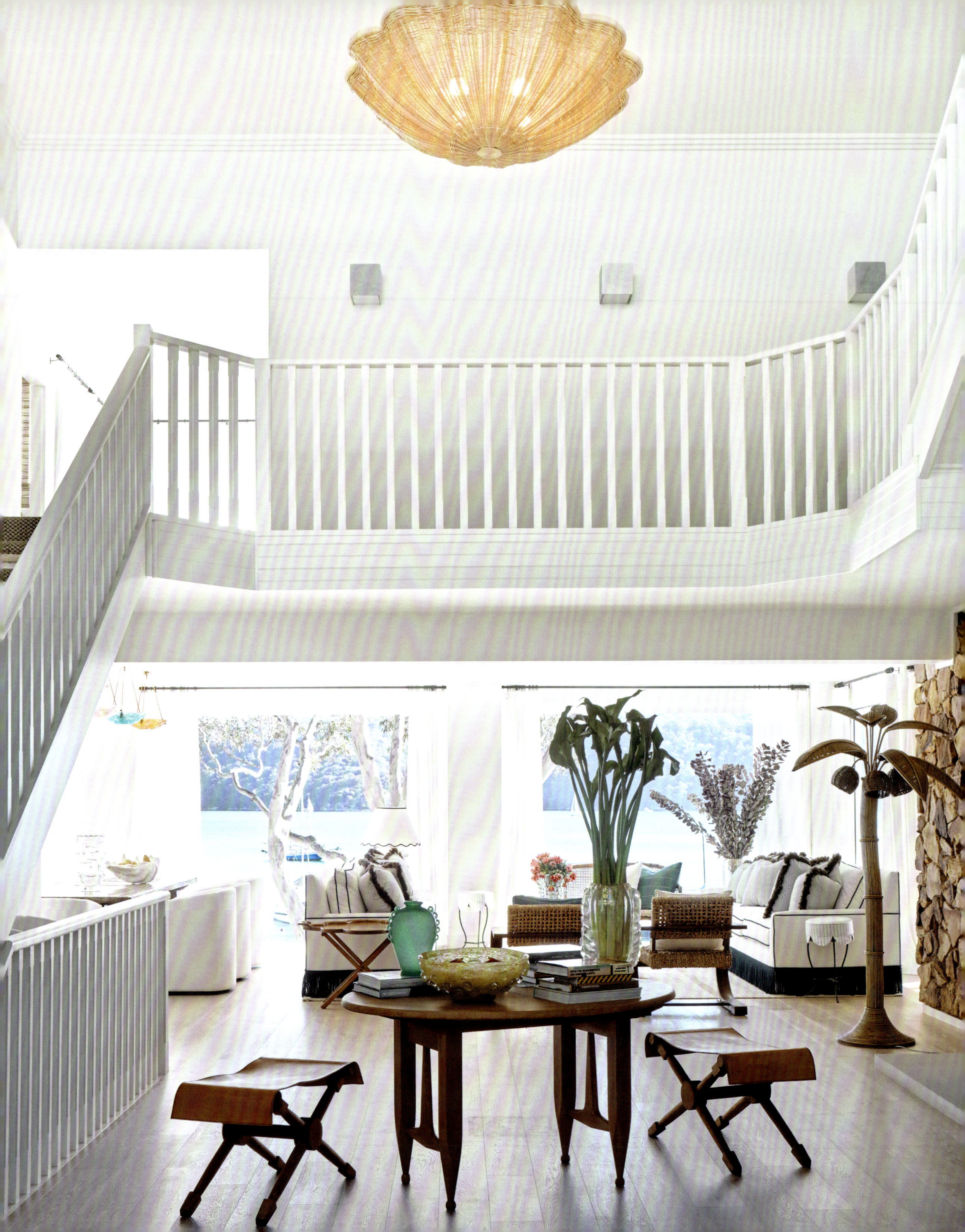

Opposite - The split-level entrance, with a six-foot-diameter rattan pendant, gives an idea of the house's grand scale.
Above - In the foreground of various seating clusters stands a gorgeous 1930s French timber picnic table with a scalloped edge on its removable top.

Above - A trio of 1930s Italian vases and a Kelly Wearstler lamp deliver a study in color and form in the master bedroom.

Opposite - In the media room, the seaside palette of an artwork belonging to the owner set the tone for this relaxed area.

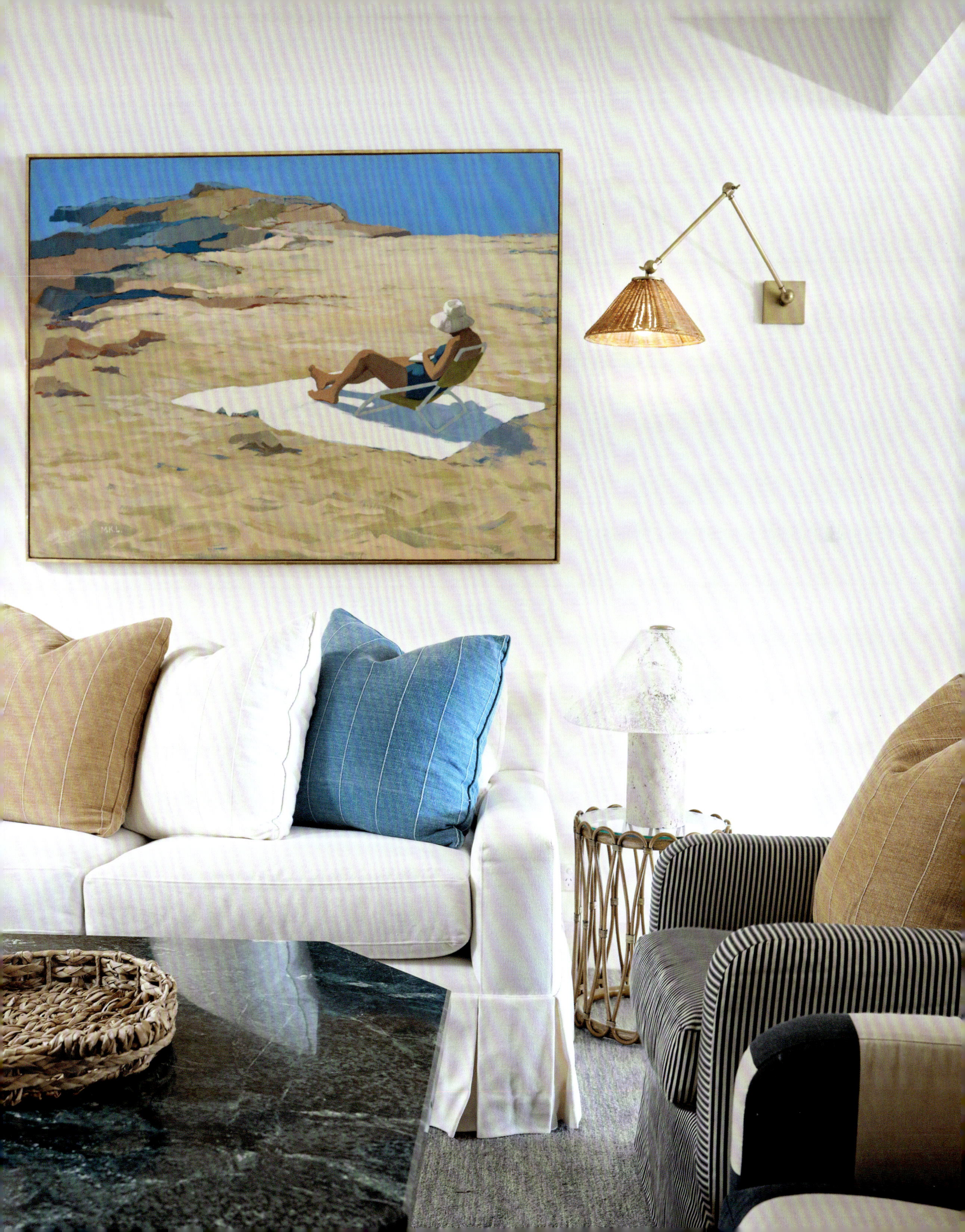

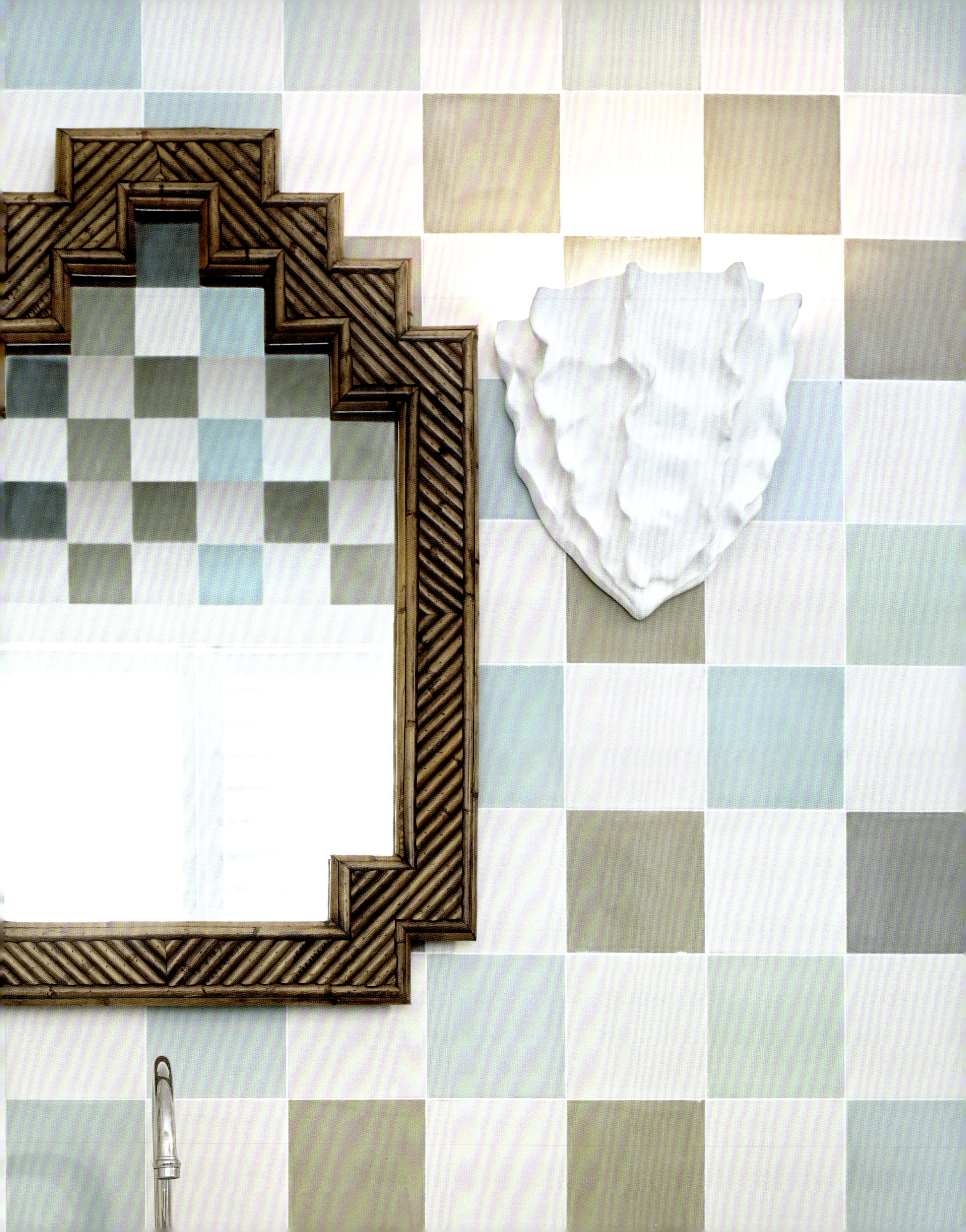

Opposite - Concrete tiles are a striking feature in some of the bathrooms, such as the mismatched checkerboard layout on an en suite wall.
Above - Other tiles form an inlay framing the mirror in a different bathroom.

P. JOHNSON
—TAILORS—

29
Thomas Street

ATELIER

Thomas Street,
Windsor, Melbourne

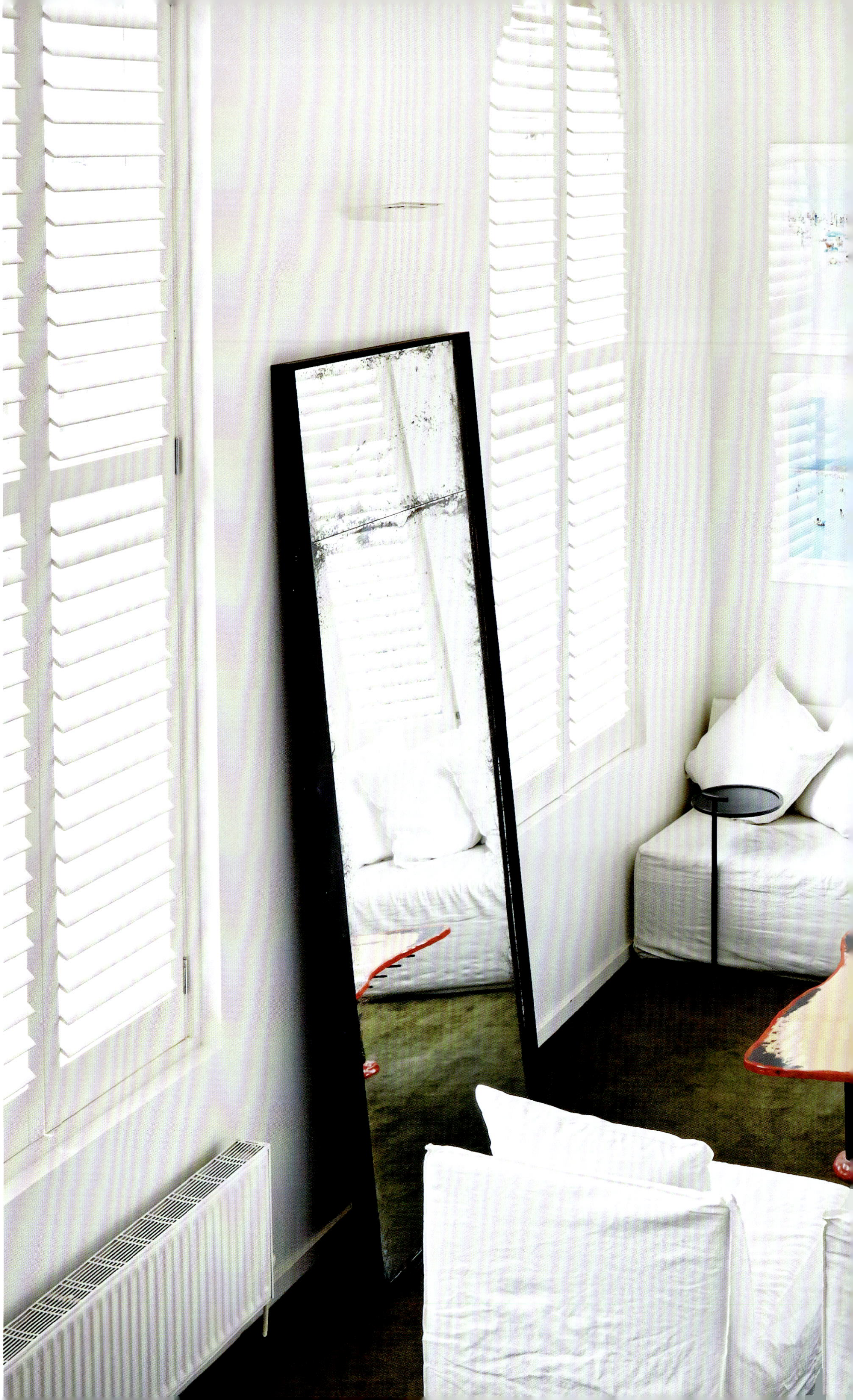

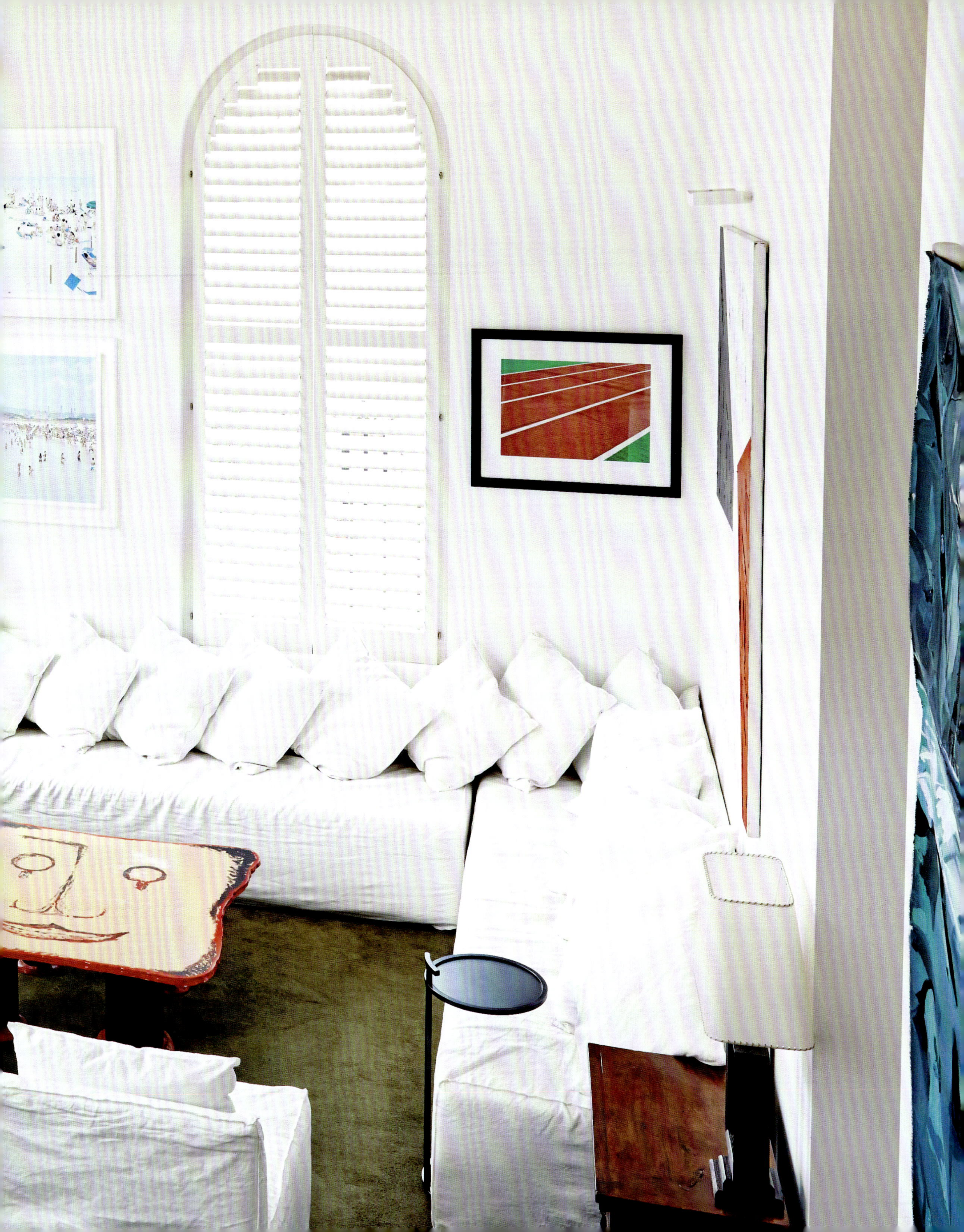

You drop in for coffee and a chat, settling yourself on a divinely comfortable sofa in a living room filled with eclectic artworks and thoughtfully placed tables on which to rest your drink. The setting speaks of easy elegance; the mood is one of relaxed creativity. It's just what you'd expect from a visit to the home of a like-minded friend, only this is not a home but a place of business. Actually, it's a bit of both.

Ten years ago, when my husband, Patrick, and I decided on this three-story townhouse as a showroom for his expanding tailoring company, we were determined that nothing about the space would be like a regular retail experience. The P. Johnson brand, which is known for its fluid approach to tailored clothing, had grown through a series of trunk shows, and we wanted to continue in that spirit, where it feels as if you are shopping in the lovingly curated comfort of someone's house. Merging the retail and the residential is nothing new in my family. My parents, from whom we bought the place, had acquired it several years earlier, renovating the interior to incorporate an antiques store downstairs and family home above. They have always loved dwellings where they could live and work, and I seem to have inherited that penchant. The building, located in the vibrant Melbourne suburb of Windsor, was so familiar to me that responding to its layout, and aligning that with the unique appeal of Patrick's brand, was an enjoyably instinctive process. The antiques store became the showroom and atelier, the house's living areas were transformed into consulting rooms, and its four bedrooms into wonderfully accommodating fitting rooms, their walk-in closets featuring handmade racks of clothing. It's the same generous space that existed before, yet completely repurposed in a way that feels quite natural.

The tailoring business already had a small store in the city, but we wanted a different set-up here— a true destination shop, where nothing is rushed and the experience gradually unfolds for visitors. The exterior maintains an alluring sense of mystery, with a discreet sign and two arched apertures in its soft gray, rendered walls. One of these is a window offering a tantalizing glimpse of the showroom; the other is the front door, with a beautifully rusting metal grill featuring an elephant motif inspired by my father's time in India. As if that weren't enough to announce this as a special space, the entrance confirms it. The first sight to greet visitors is a 1920s Viennese cerused oak desk and classic Thonet bentwood chair, surrounded by a pair of striking photographs, an art deco metal hat stand by Jacques Adnet, and a vintage radiator. This area, at the foot of the stairs and situated by the ground-floor showroom, is in fact the point of sale, but there is not a cash register in sight. Sophisticated yet comfortable, it sets the tone for the place.

Previous spread - The fresh white palette of the first-floor consulting room is balanced by the colors of the olive-hued carpet, the artworks, and a Gaetano Pesce table.

Opposite - A sophisticated setting on the sisal flooring, the point of sale, with its mix of vintage pieces, establishes that this is a unique retail experience.

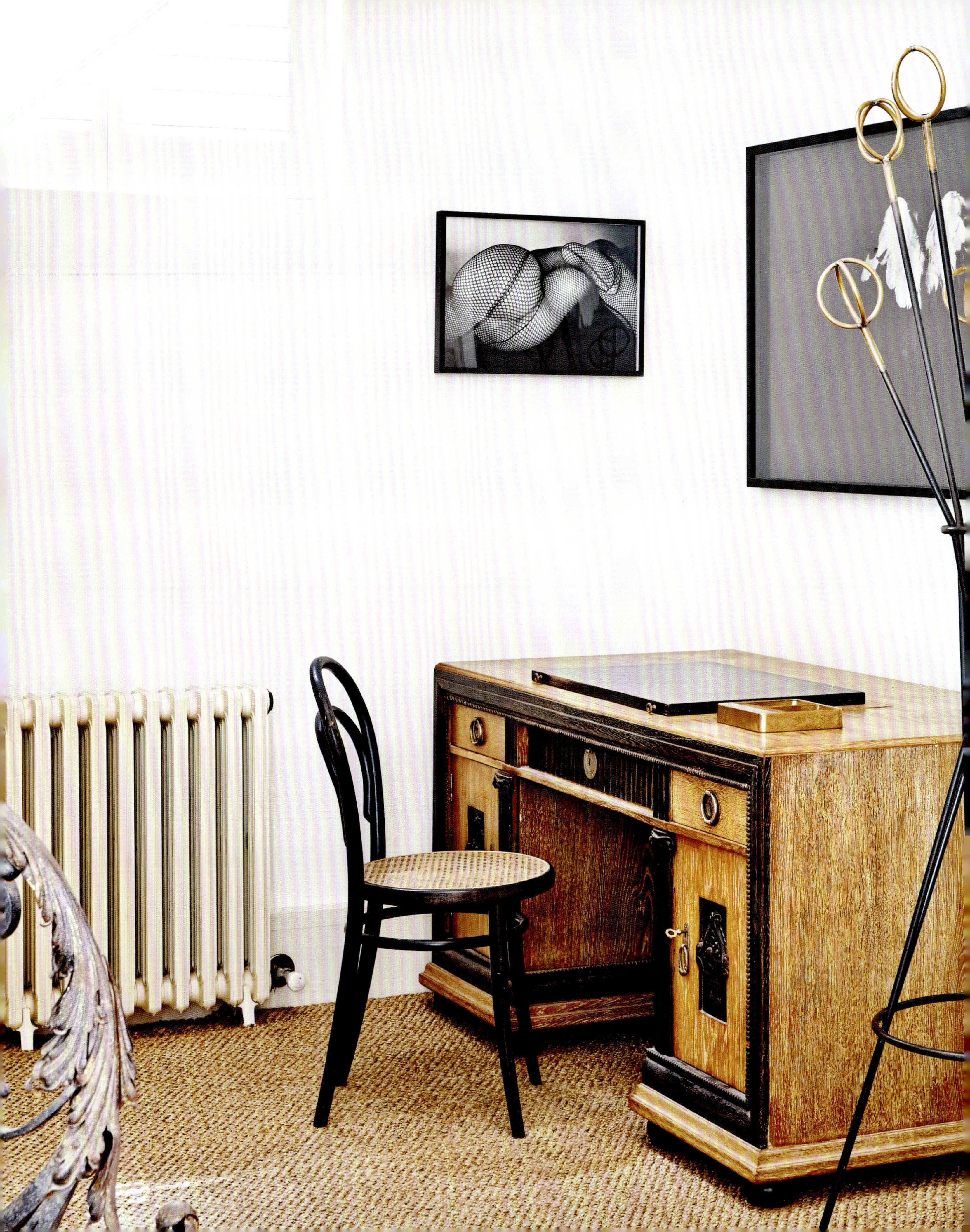

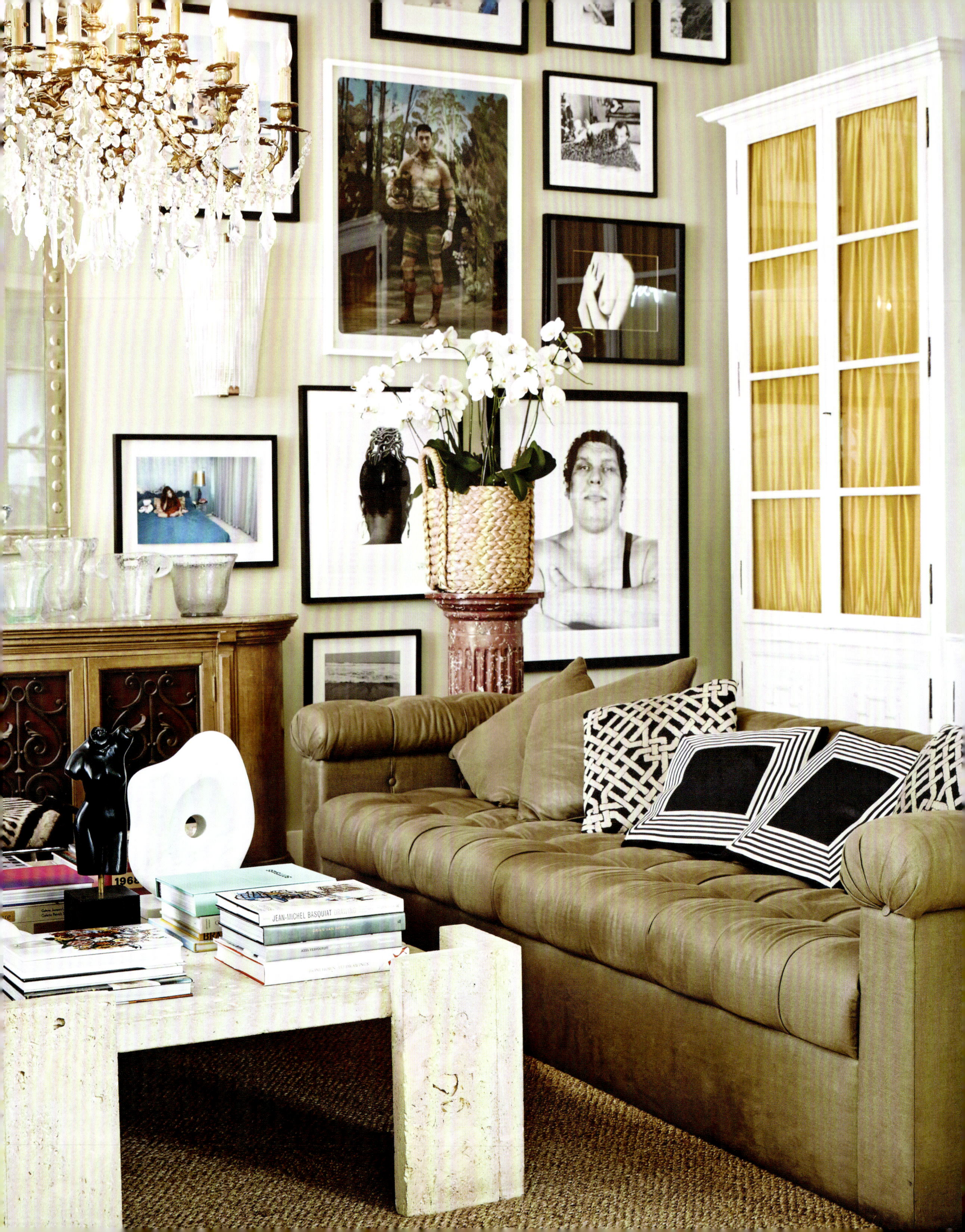
JEAN-MICHEL BASQUIAT
1968

Beyond this and through the showroom lies the hub of the building: the first consulting room on the ground floor. Nothing could feel more welcoming, intimate, and elegant, with soft green-gray walls creating a serene backdrop that is echoed by a traditional-style olive-green buttoned custom sofa, adorned with a few scatter cushions in a mix of plain and patterned fabrics. A travertine coffee table piled with books and sculptures, and a collection of Daum vases and a rattan basket full of orchids heighten the homey factor, while a stunning nineteenth-century French crystal chandelier gives the space a "special occasion" feeling. This is enhanced by the layering of gorgeous pieces, such as an eighteenth-century French oak cabinet with wrought-iron panels, a Venetian mirror and pair of Murano wall sconces, a vintage stool upholstered in zebra hide, and an antique Italian marble pedestal. Here is where visitors discuss their wardrobe requirements with the P. Johnson team before they head to one of the fitting rooms. To store the books of cloth samples, I introduced built-in cabinets with classic paneling and sumptuous lining in yellow Dedar silk moiré. Form and function come together, as the cabinets bring their own attractive façade to the room.

In addition to showcasing significant items of furniture throughout, I wanted this building to function as a gallery space, and so the artworks on the walls offer another layer of interest via a mix of personal and investment pieces. In this room, photography is the focus, with gallery finds sitting beside an old high school project of mine, and subjects ranging from a close-up of waves to André the Giant. In the second consulting room, on the first floor, a pair of Italian beach scenes by Italian photographer Massimo Vitali share space with a track and field photograph and paintings by Australian artists. Together with a quirky coffee table by Gaetano Pesce, they provide splashes of color that contrast with the large white expanse of a custom-built corner sofa and matching chairs. They also reflect the fresh, fun sensibility of the fashion brand in a setting that exudes laid-back luxury. Two fabulous bathrooms reflect the mood of each consulting room. One is rich in color, featuring turquoise Dedar silk moiré wallpaper and a heavenly antique peach-toned glass sconce from Venice above a marble vanity and backsplash in a swirl of rich burgundy, gray, and just a hint of green. The second bathroom features a lighter palette, embellished by details such as tiny travertine wall tiles, olive-shaped bronze cabinet doorknobs, and a quaint brass shell-shaped waste bin.

When Patrick and I are in Melbourne, we often stay here, in an upper-floor bedroom that acts as an office but still contains a walk-in closet and en suite bathroom. We have put so much of ourselves into this place, personally and professionally, that while it is a business, it will always feel like home.

Opposite and overleaf - I wanted customers to feel as if they were shopping at someone's home, and the layers of furniture, décor and artworks make this ground-floor consulting room an intimate, inviting space. Among the collection of personal and investment pieces on the walls is a black-and-white photograph by Australian artist Tom Riley, which sits between two cabinets containing cloth samples.

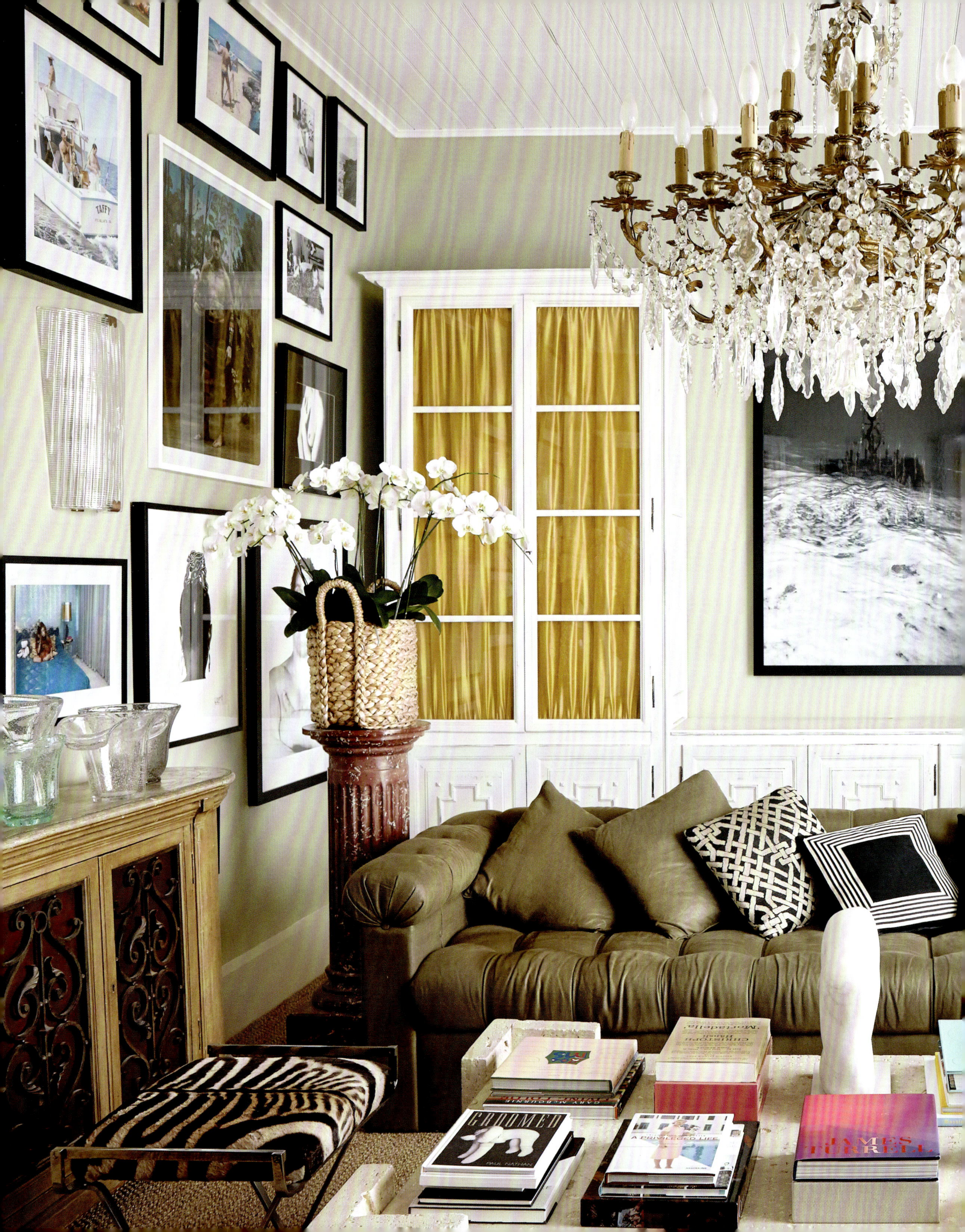

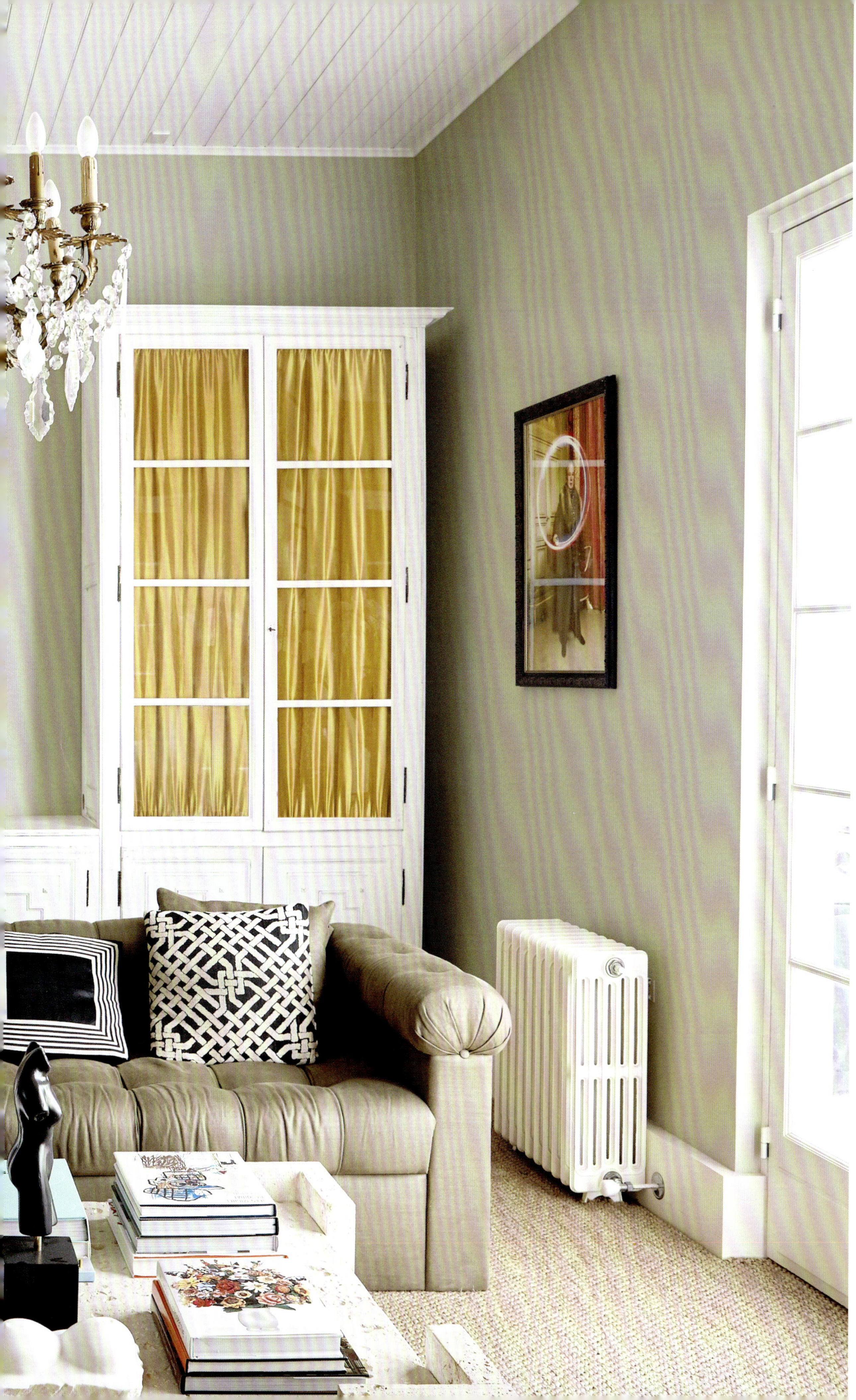

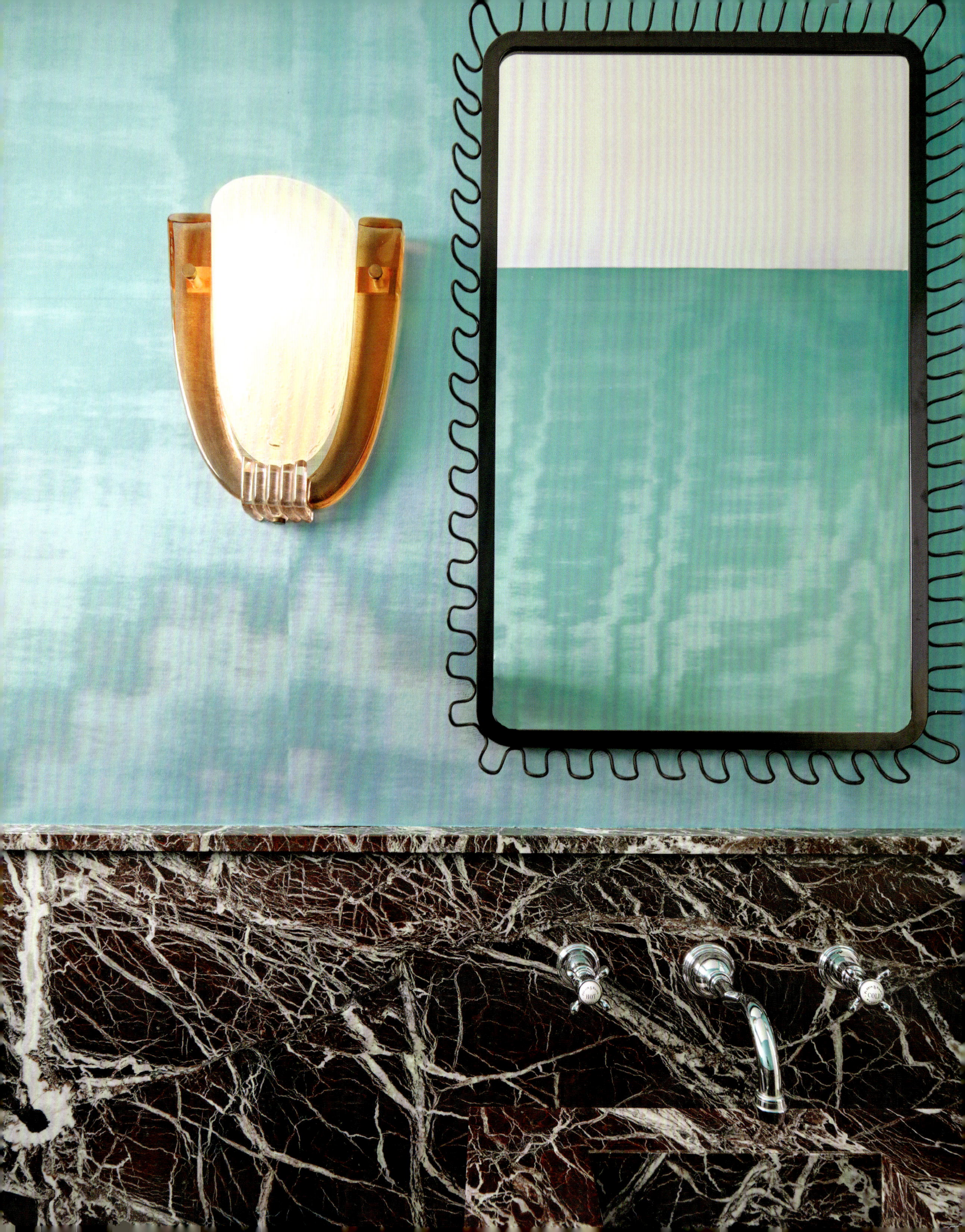

Opposite - In one bathroom, a blackened steel mirror in the style of Jean Royère adds modernist lines to the vivid backdrop of turquoise Dedar silk moiré wallpaper.

Above - Another bathroom features the beautiful finishes of marble floors, travertine tiles, and timber doors in neutral tones, with a brass waste bin that wouldn't be out of place in 1920s France.

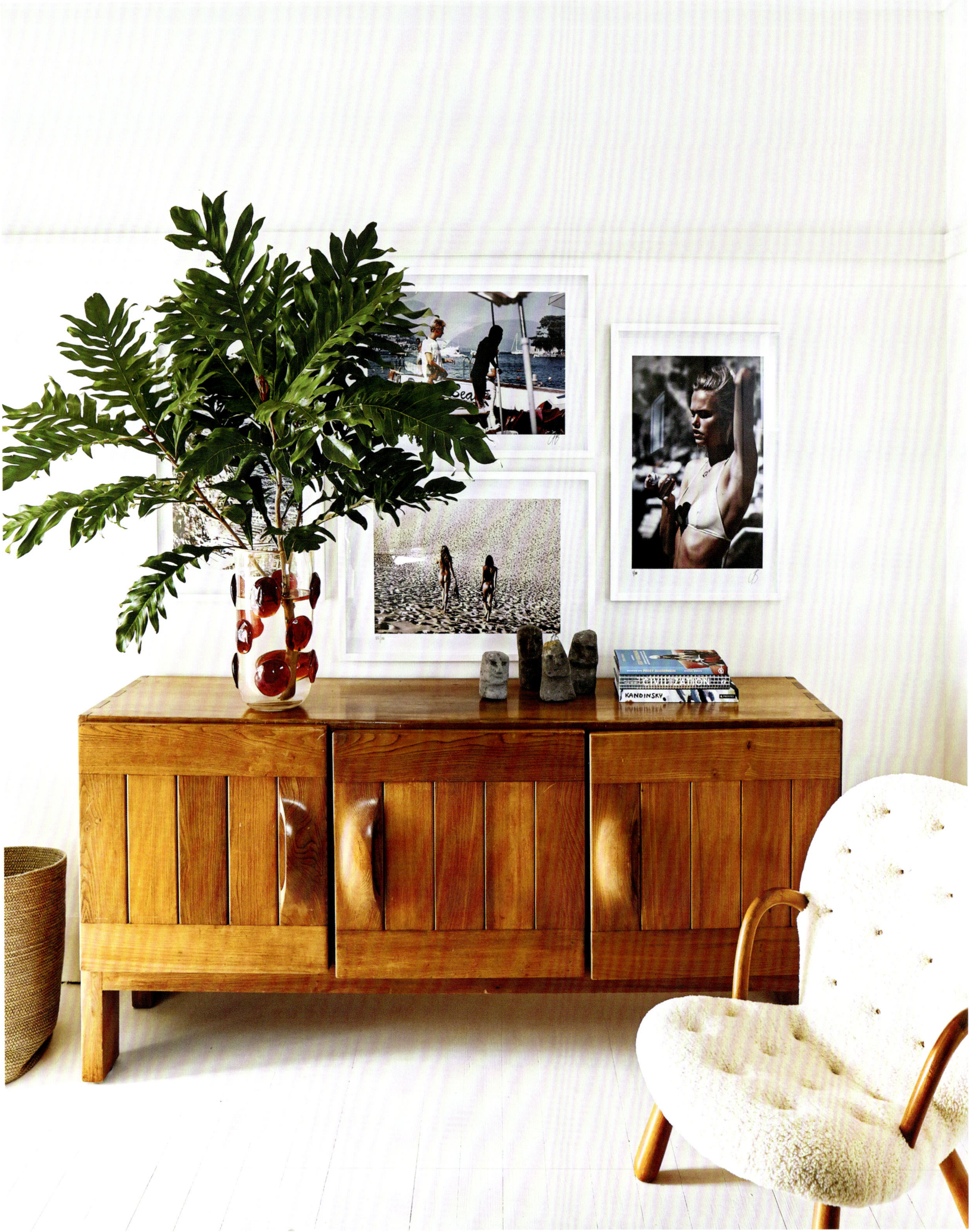
CIVILIZATION
KANDINSKY

BUN GAL OW

Hastings Parade,
North Bondi, Sydney

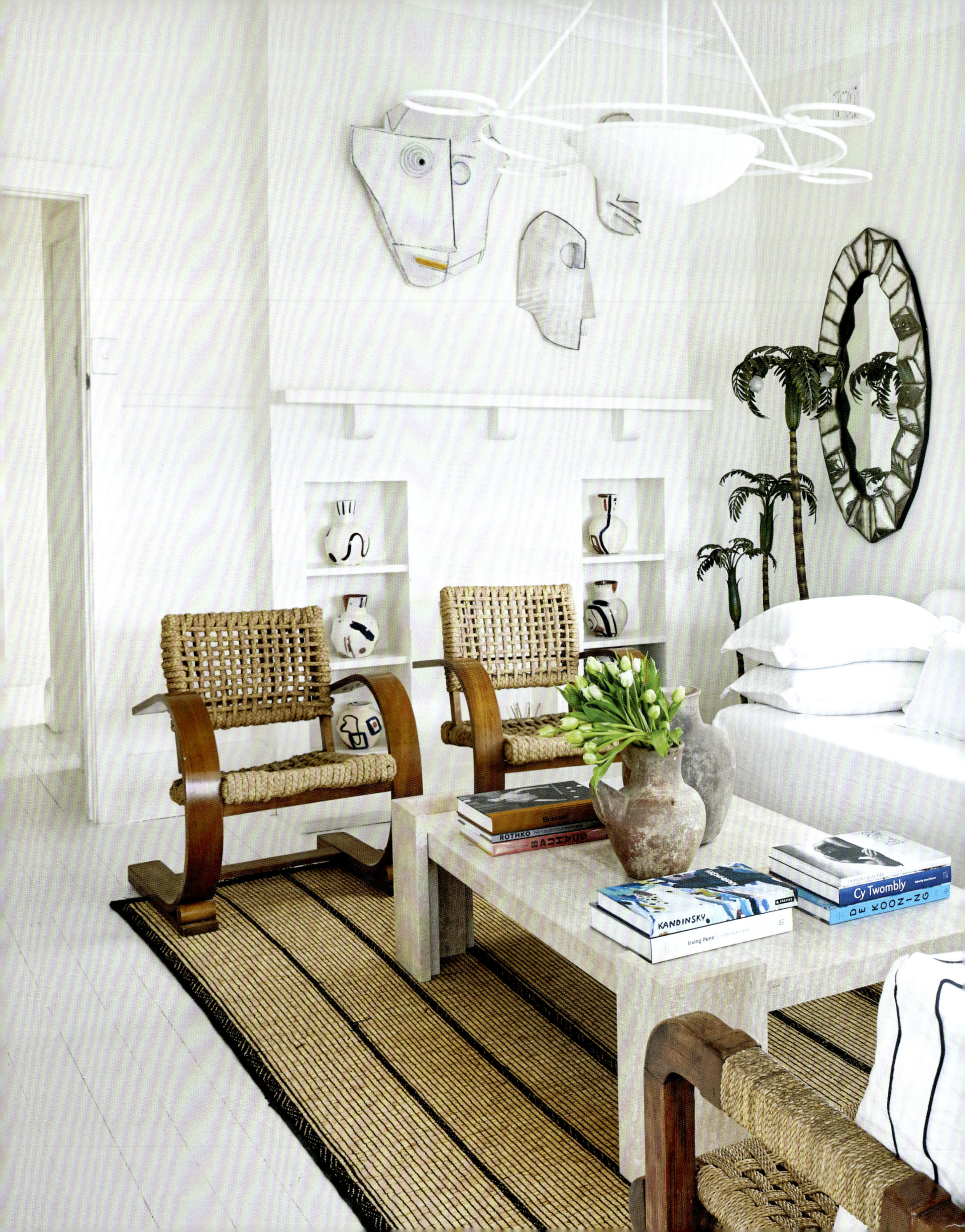
ROTHKO
Cy Twombly
KANDINSKY
Irving Penn

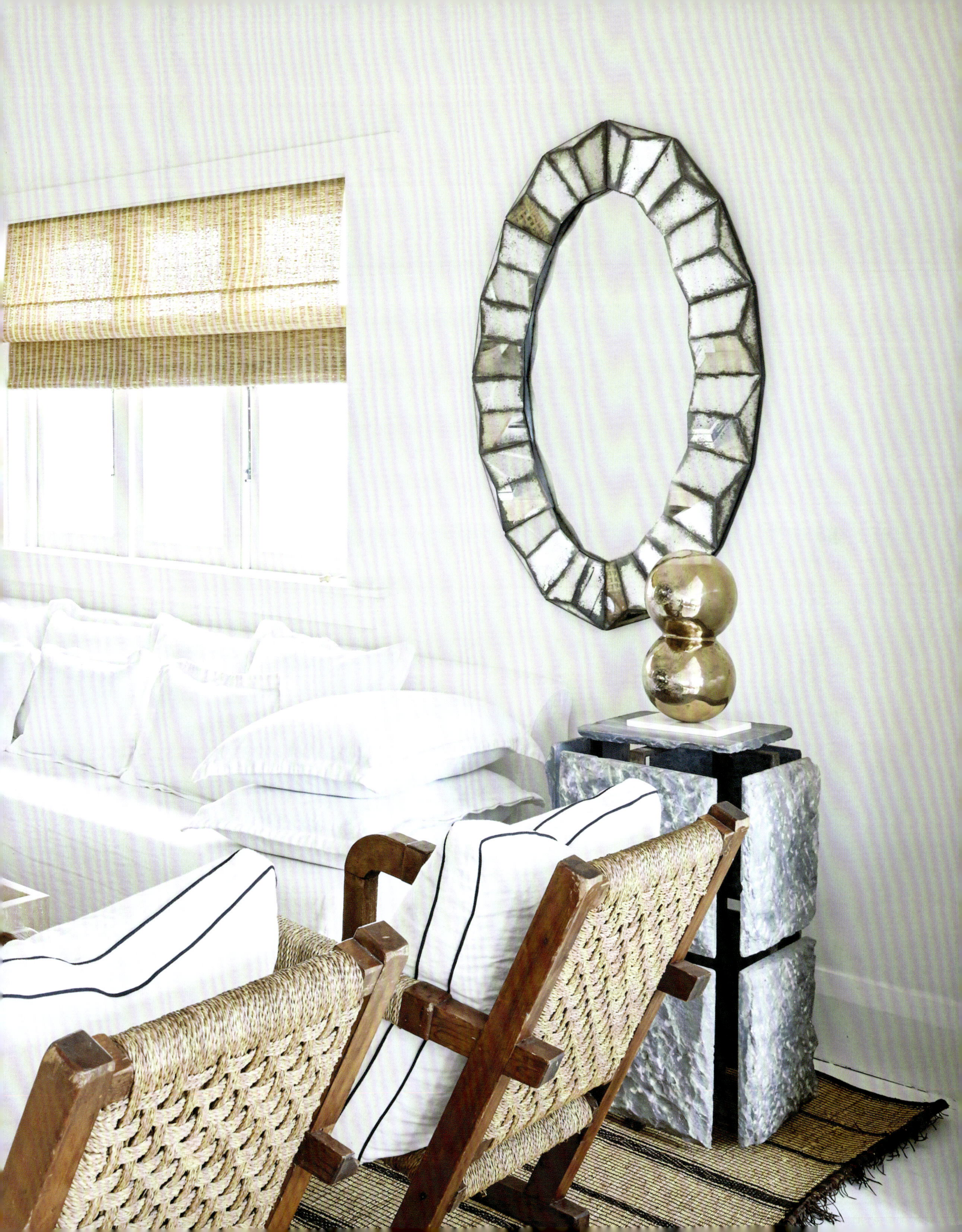

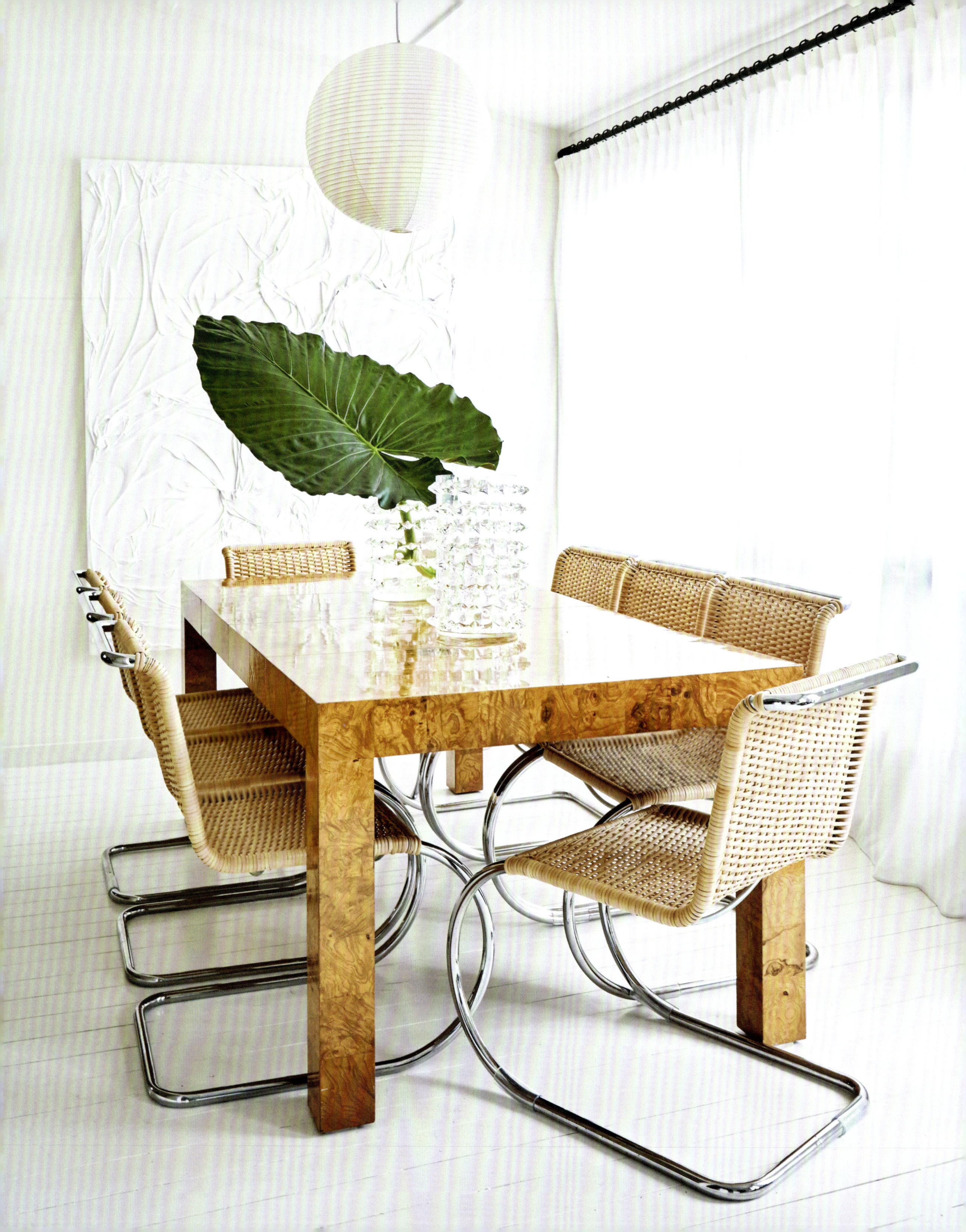

Most of us have some special memory of holidaying at a beach house—the feeling of the cool floor under your feet when you returned after a day of sea and sand; the piece of driftwood you brought back from the beach to display on the coffee table. For me, it was the quirky artworks that filled my family's beach house, located a couple of hours' drive from our home in Melbourne. These were a combination of local finds and pieces collected by my father on his travels, the sort of meaningful layers that build with time in any home. A heavy oil painting of crashing waves, an inevitable beach scene or two, and drawings of kookaburras would sit alongside family photos from long summer days and much-thumbed books, all of which were a little faded from the sun. I'd share a room with my sister and we'd help my parents cook meals in the tiny kitchenette which, like the house itself, was a bit rough around the edges but had everything we needed. The whole experience was understated, low-key, and lovely.

The owners of this Bondi bungalow had a vision of similar simplicity for its interior layout, which I was only too happy to realize. The 1950s-built house, near Australia's best known beach, is the last original building in a street of large, highly developed blocks, a fact that adds to its appeal. Based in Melbourne, the family had bought it so they and their friends could enjoy a little piece of the sunny Sydney landmark from a laid-back base that still felt relatively untouched. The aim with the interior design was to refresh the three-bedroom house and create a bright, cheerful setting adaptable enough to accommodate the different guests who'd come and go, yet imbued with sufficient style to lend it a casual elegance. Structurally, this didn't present any overly complex challenges beyond eliminating one wall to allow an open-plan flow between living and dining areas, restoring the kitchen, replacing the odd broken window or floorboard, and installing new tiles in the bathroom. Where this family did want to invest was in key pieces of furniture and local art—comfortable collectibles that would allow them to begin building the layers of their own beach house story. It was important to find special pieces that were resilient enough to remain in keeping with the purpose of the house, and this is one of the reasons I often opt for mid-twentieth-century furniture—its casual, almost playful functionality seems so well suited to our contemporary lifestyle.

p. 78 - Photographs by Akila Berjaoui establish a retro beach vibe above a Charles Flandre sideboard in the bedroom. Previous spread - The warm tones and textures of rattan and the calm, fresh expanse of white combine to pleasing effect in the living room. A group of white plaster masks from an Italian antiques fair create a dynamic display on one wall.

Opposite - The Milo Baughman table, surrounded here by Marcel Breuer dining chairs, used to be in our New York apartment—another much-loved piece that has found a new home and new life.

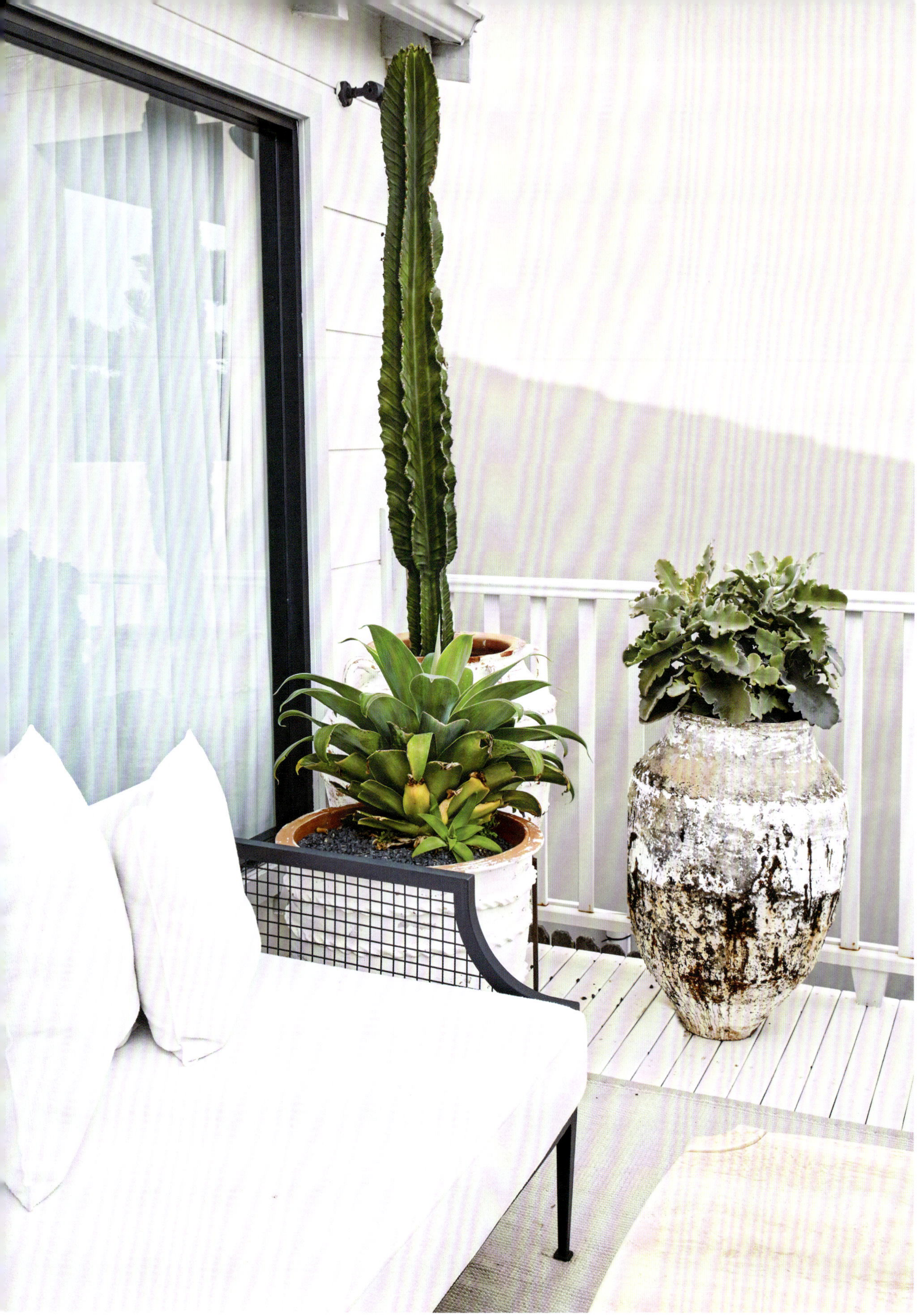

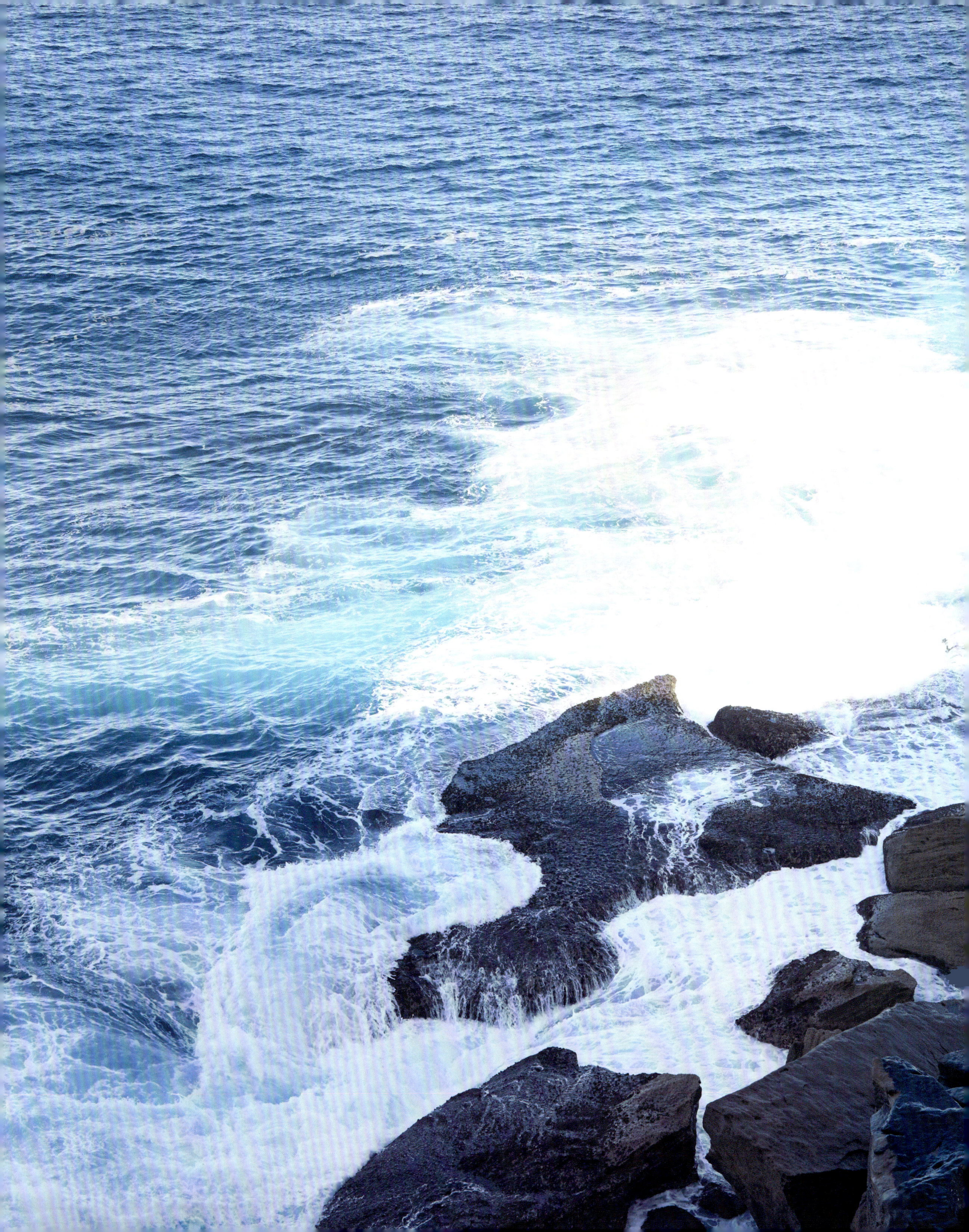

SEAVUE

In the living area, two different pairs of chairs by French design duo Audoux Minet deliver personality and comfort with their textural pairing of rope and timber. Beyond, gathered around a Milo Baughman dining table with a burl veneer, rattan appears in a set of Marcel Breuer dining chairs, the curved steel legs of which deliver an unexpected gleam among the natural finishes. Elsewhere, two iconic Philip Arctander Clam chairs combine an inviting softness with a unique shape befitting their seaside location. Between these pieces, the predominance of white keeps the interiors neutral and relaxed. White paint wields a transformative power, reinvigorating everything from walls and ceilings to the original pine floors. Throughout the house, white sheer curtains create a delicate, breezy effect and Noguchi pendant lanterns bring their own warm light and soothing ambience.

In the kitchen, white timber joinery and open, floating concrete shelves offer a clean, unobtrusive layout. A white concrete custom vanity in the small bathroom fulfills a similar role, with a little striped linen curtain underneath to hide storage for beach-going necessities. In the living area, a white sofa melts serenely into the house's palette, allowing the warm, sandy tones of other pieces to anchor the scene. The leather and straw of an African Tuareg mat introduces some more textural interest, with touches of glamour appearing in a 1940s painted iron palm floor lamp and 1930s Venetian glass mirrors from France. Two mid-twentieth-century pieces up the glamour ante, while still being agile enough to work in this beachside setting. A French ebonized oak bar cabinet creates a stunning zone for drinks beside the kitchen, its delicately lit mirror-lined interior introducing a gorgeous element of theater to the room. In the master bedroom, a 1950s Charles Flandre elmwood sideboard adds a beautiful solidity and detail of line. Above the sideboard, there is a collection of beach scenes by Australian photographer Akila Berjaoui, known for her sultry retro images of seaside life around the world. The theme continues in the kitchen, via the colorful brushstrokes of paintings by local artist Gabrielle Penfold, and at the entrance, in a print of the iconic black-and-white photograph *Sunbaker* taken by famous Sydney native, the late modernist Max Dupain, at another Australian beach.

Different takes on a shared experience, these are part of an art collection that largely features Sydney artists or locations, and set the scene for holiday memories to come. The walls still have many spaces, the special furniture plenty of surfaces, for the owners to gradually accumulate layers of their own as warm recollections of summers past.

Previous spread - Simple furnishings and resilient greenery are all that is needed on this beachside balcony with such a dramatic view on offer.

Opposite - A white exterior reflects the strong Australian light and connects to the clean white walls inside.

Above - In the kitchen, colorful paintings by Gabrielle Penfold continue the beach theme.
Opposite - A 1930s Venetian glass mirror, one of a pair, provides beautiful detail above the relaxed living room setting.

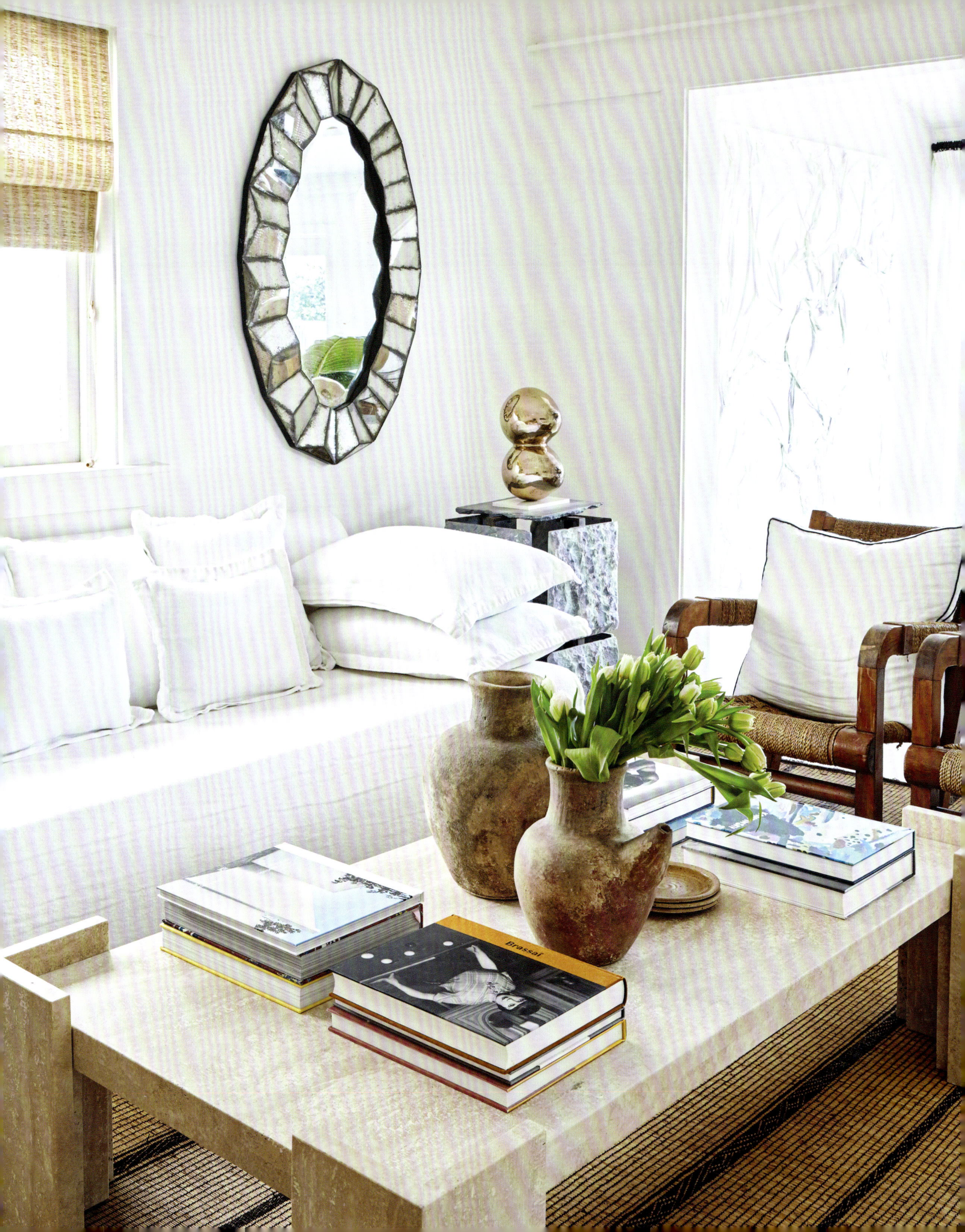
Brassaï

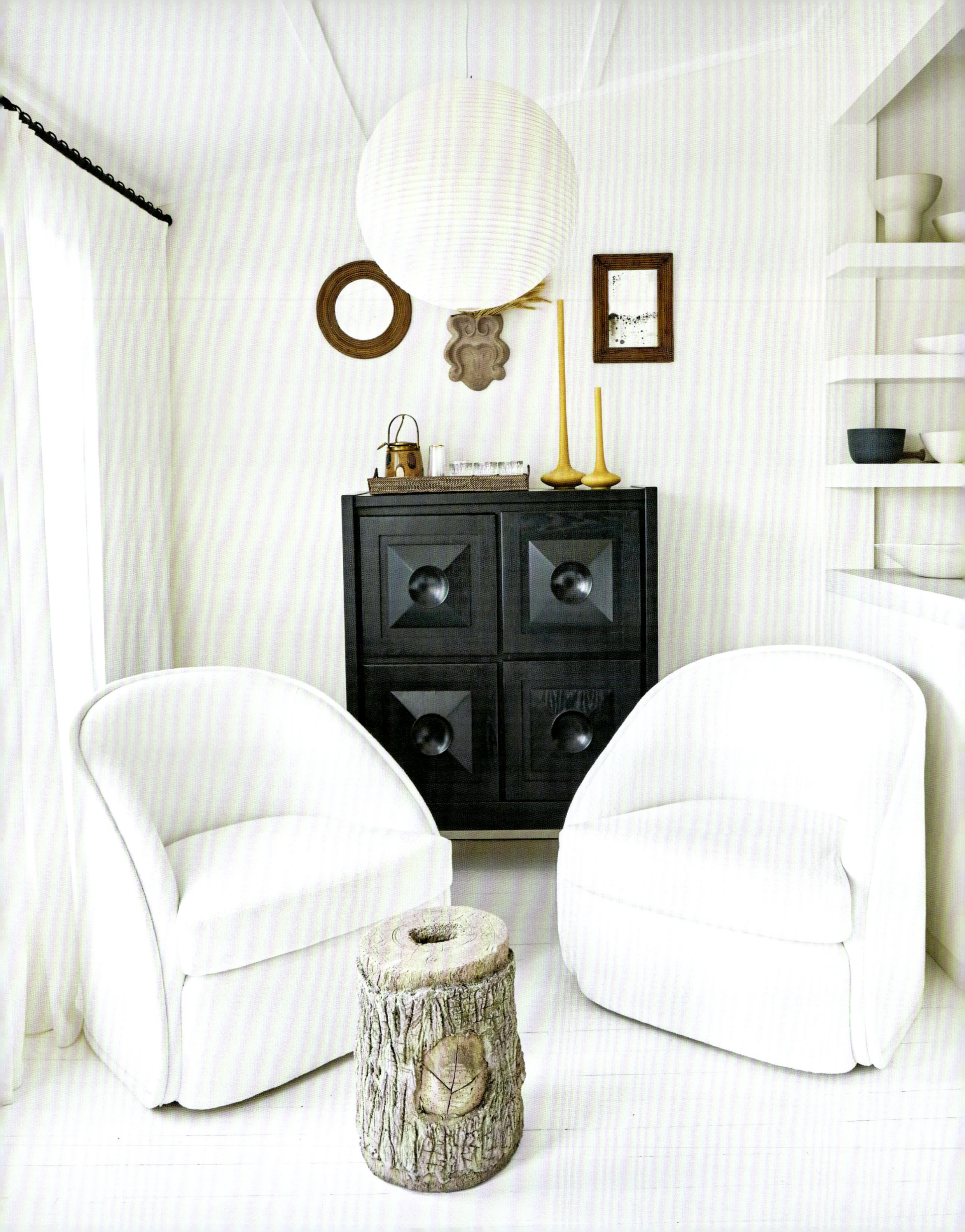

*Opposite - With a pair of white custom chairs upholstered in bouclé fabric as anchor,
an antique faux-log side table and ebonized oak bar cabinet make a dramatic impression.
Above - Ceramics from Mud Australia add their shapely forms to the kitchen's floating shelves.*

*Above - A pair of Audoux Minet rattan mirrors and a wall-mounted vase create an appealing group above the bar cabinet.
Opposite - In the master bedroom, with its black-and-white bedding, a 1930s French tapestry may seem an unusual choice,
but its palette fuses perfectly with that of the bungalow.*

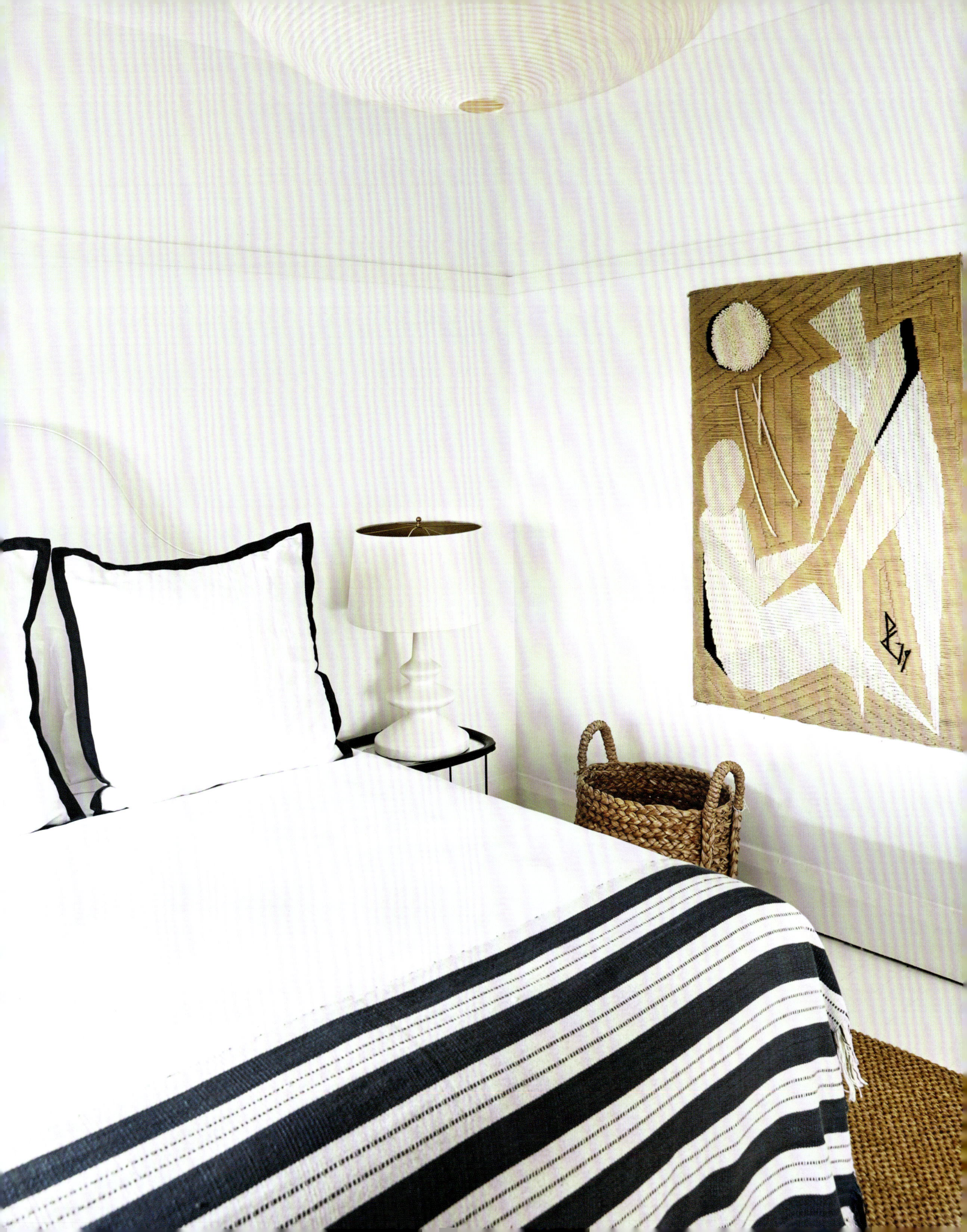

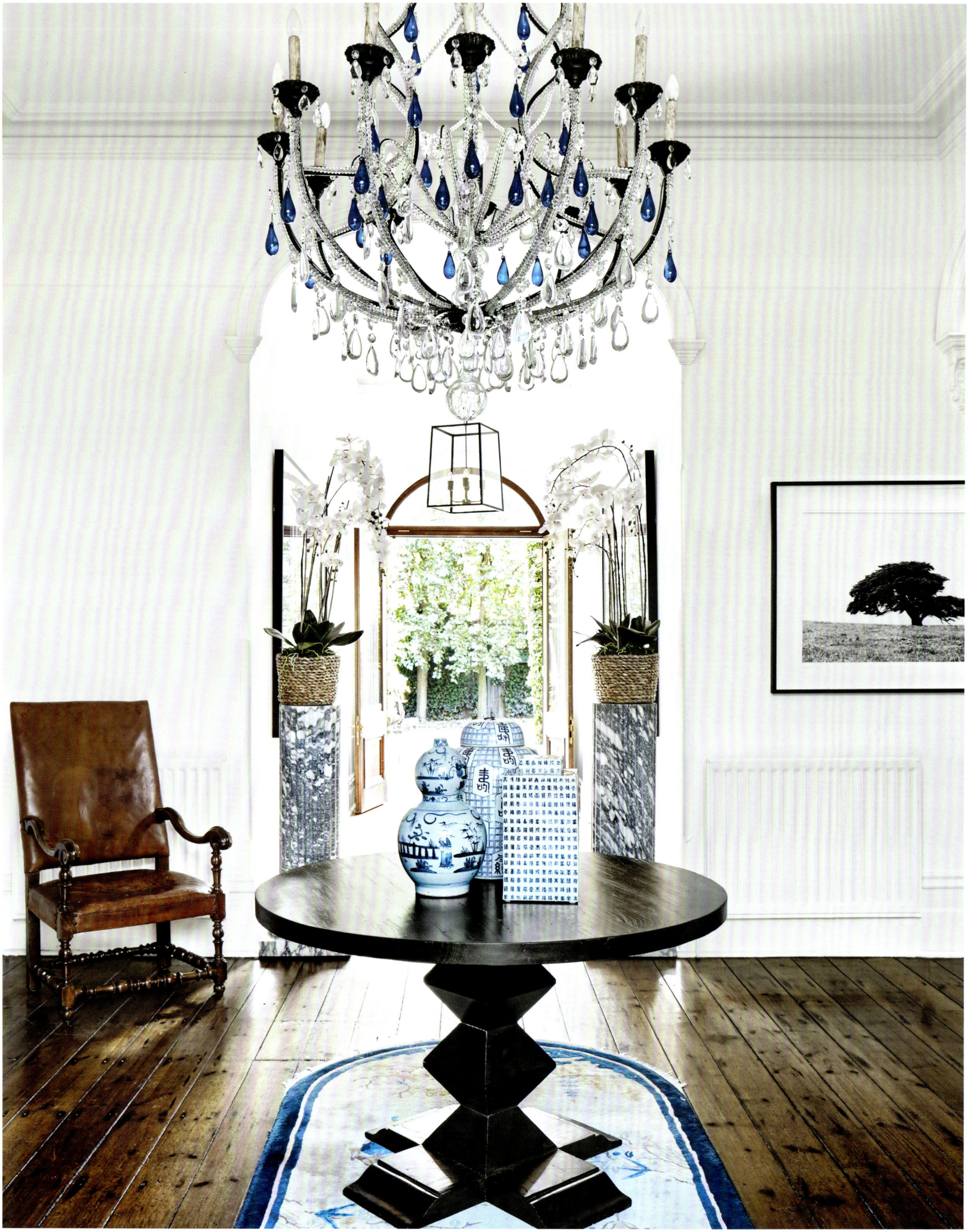

VILLA

*Avondale Road,
Armadale, Melbourne*

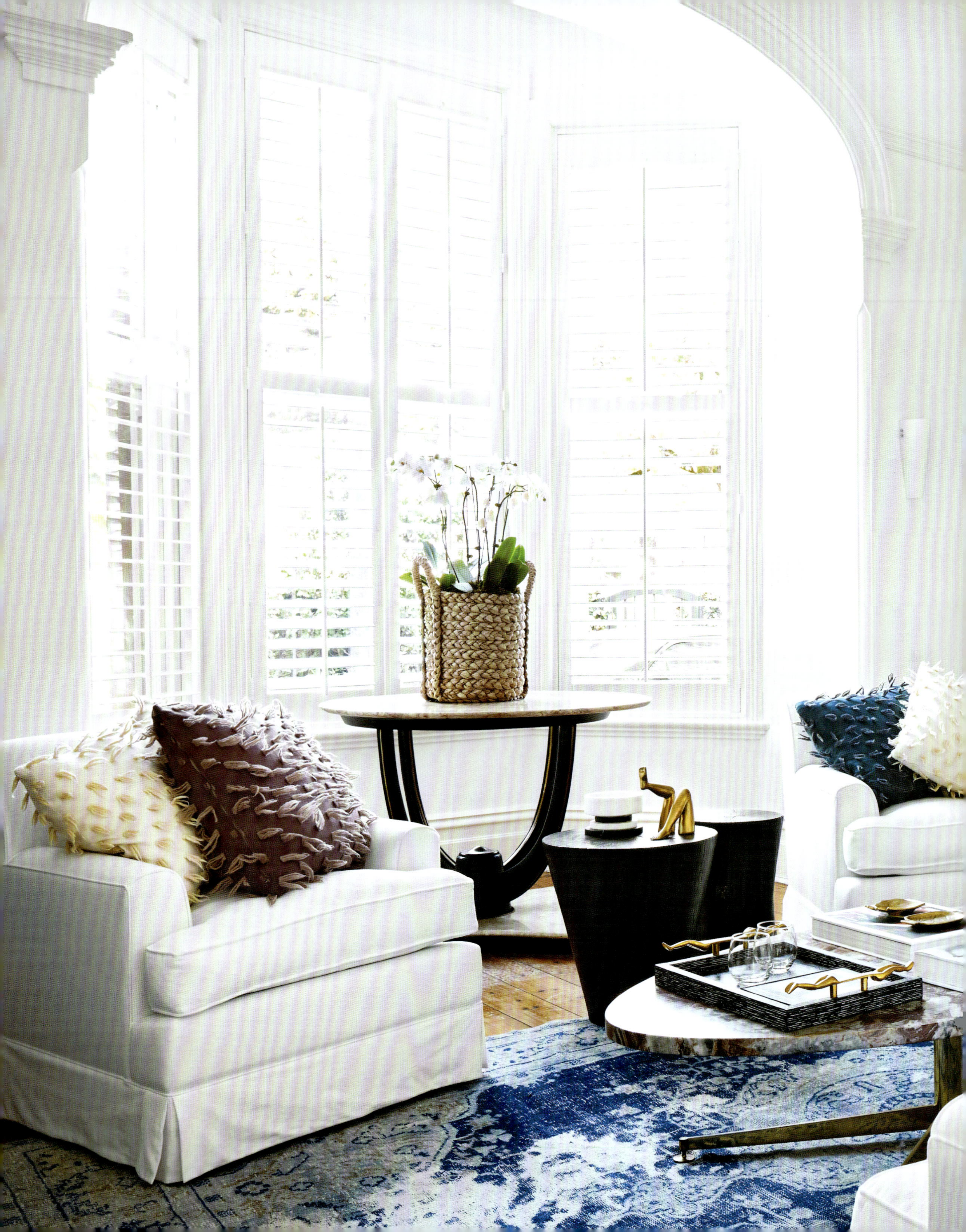

97

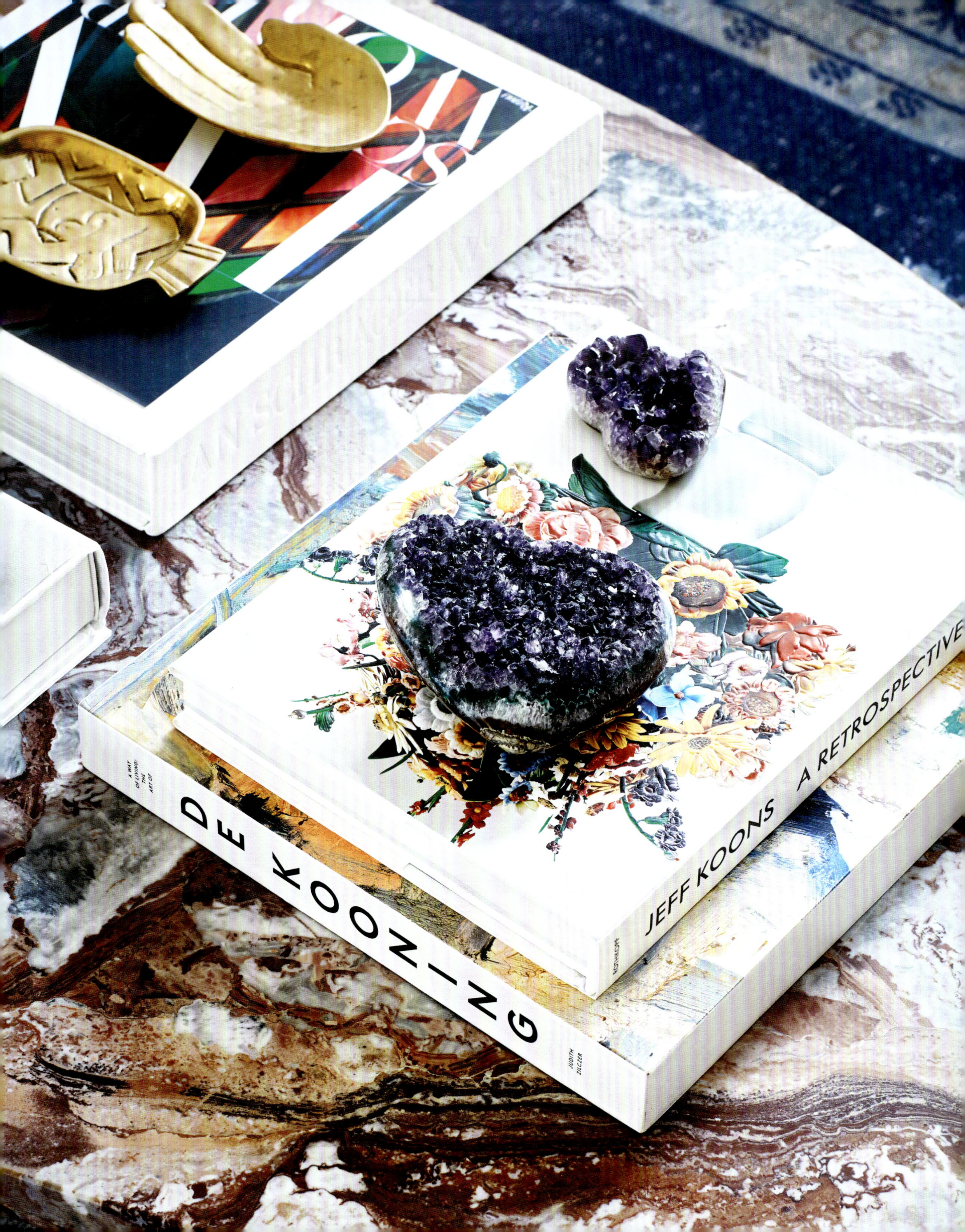
DE KOONING
JEFF KOONS A RETROSPECTIVE

There's something so captivating about a grand entrance: a jaw-droppingly fabulous chandelier at the center, a curated display of objects beneath it to anchor the setting, a mirrored arrangement of pieces along a hallway to lure you inside. It presents an enticing glimpse of what's to come, yet also politely requests that you pause to appreciate what is before you. That sense of arrival, and the suggestion of timelessness that accompanies it, is something I think old houses can do so well. The interior design of this Victorian-era house, in the elegant Melbourne suburb of Armadale, was always going to lean towards the formal. Its owners, a young family with two children, wanted a grown-up dwelling that would be theirs for the long term, a true family home. Furnishing this residence became a fusion of the beautiful and the functional, featuring pieces that suited the traditional look of the house yet were still comfortable and easy to maintain. Here was a place for classic rather than quirky choices, with a mix of old and new delivering elements of surprise.

When it comes to the classics, I find blue such a calming and versatile color—with a wide range of tones, it is pleasing to all parties. Blue permeates the story of the entrance to this house, which begins with a gorgeous Chinese art deco rug that I found at the online site *1stdibs*. Inspired by the rug's palette, I added a collection of antique blue-and-white Chinese porcelain, which sits on an ebonized round entry table in the middle of the rug. The strong, sculptural lines of the table balance the softer colors and patterns above and below, and completing the picture is a huge 1920s Murano glass chandelier, with electric blue drops dotted like jewels among its clear crystals. From this centerpiece, the rest of the décor evolves quite naturally across the lacquered Baltic pine floorboards. A couple of antique pedestals in solid Calacatta Viola marble frame the arched hallway, supporting rattan planters filled with orchids that seem to bend gracefully forward to welcome visitors. Old and new inhabit either side of the hallway, in the form of an antique Louis XV chair in its original cognac-colored leather upholstery, and a simple black-and-white modern photograph. Another wall recalls this mix, with more blue-and-white Chinese porcelain arranged on an antique French pharmacy console with a marble top and low mirrored back. The contemporary and the classic create a dramatic combination above, with two architectural photographs by Sydney-based artist Felix Forest sitting between a pair of eighteenth-century Italian carved timber wall sconces. Gothic in feel, their smooth parchment shades contrasting with the textural wood, these lights give another moment for pause.

p. 94 - The Murano glass chandelier, the ebonized table, and the art deco rug form the centerpiece of the grand entrance. Previous spread - Flooded by light from the bay windows, the living room merges comfort and style, with the blue tones of a kilim rug continuing the palette from the entrance.

Opposite - Crystals, brass accessories by Kelly Wearstler, and all-important books make an attractively tactile arrangement on the marble-topped coffee table.

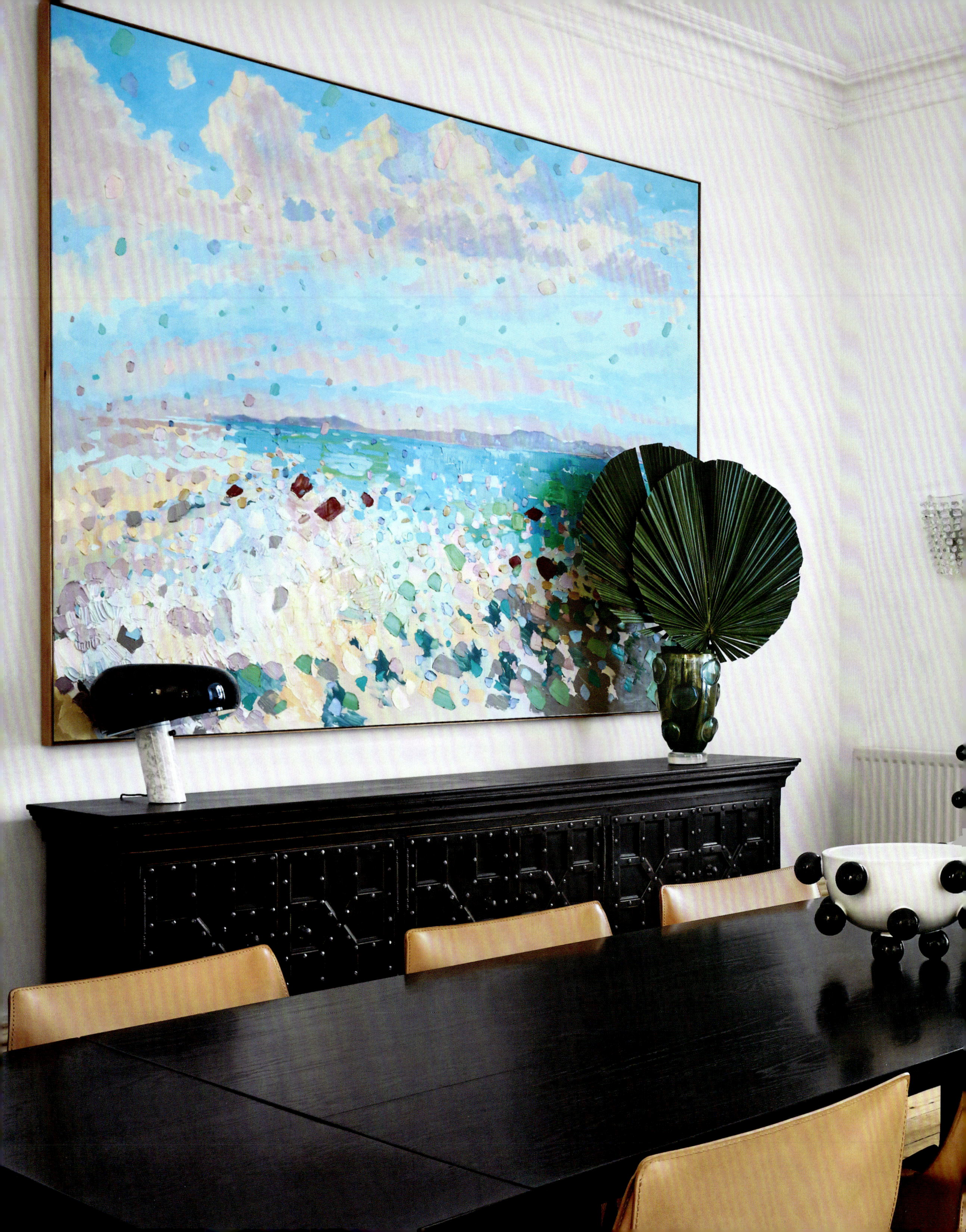

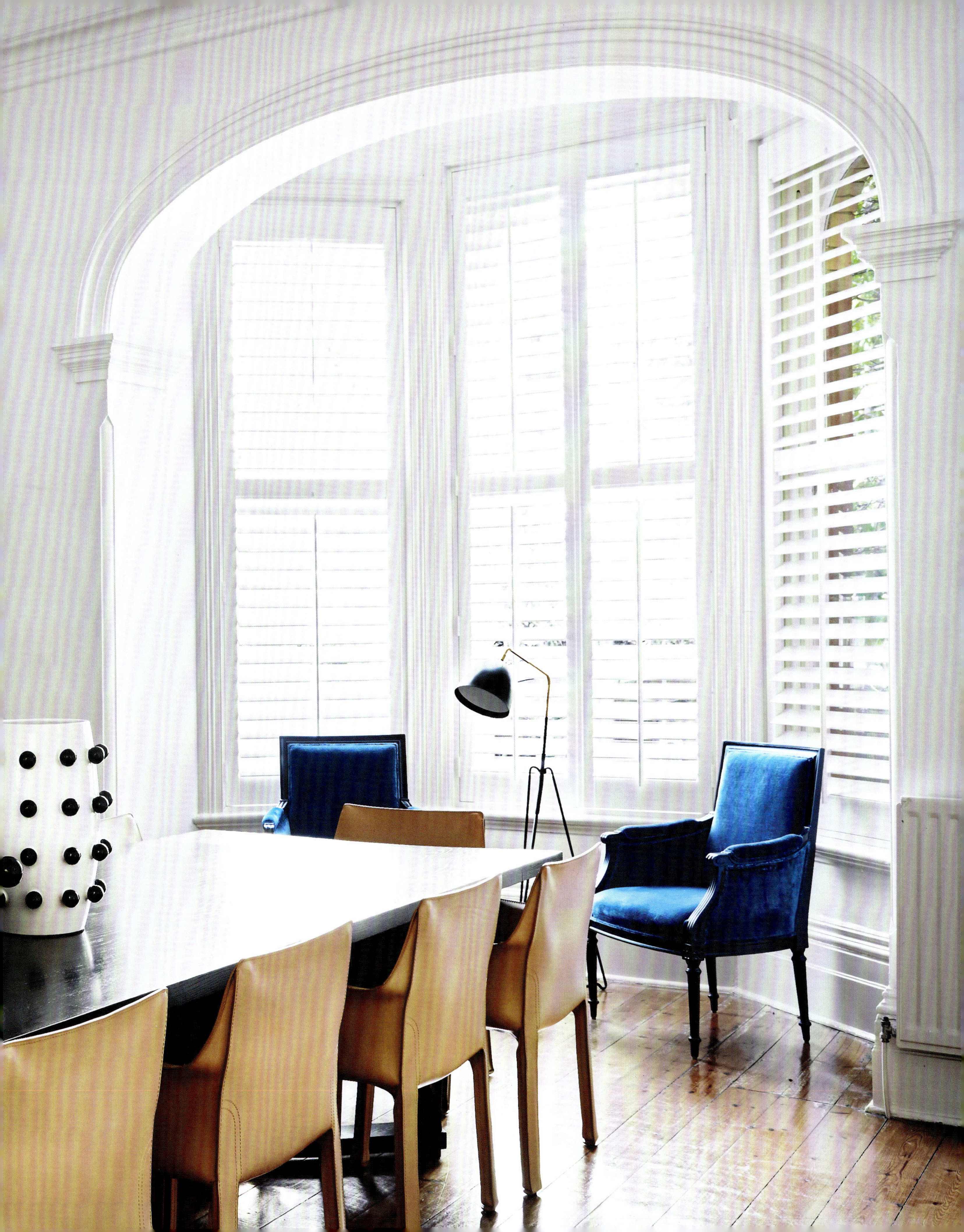

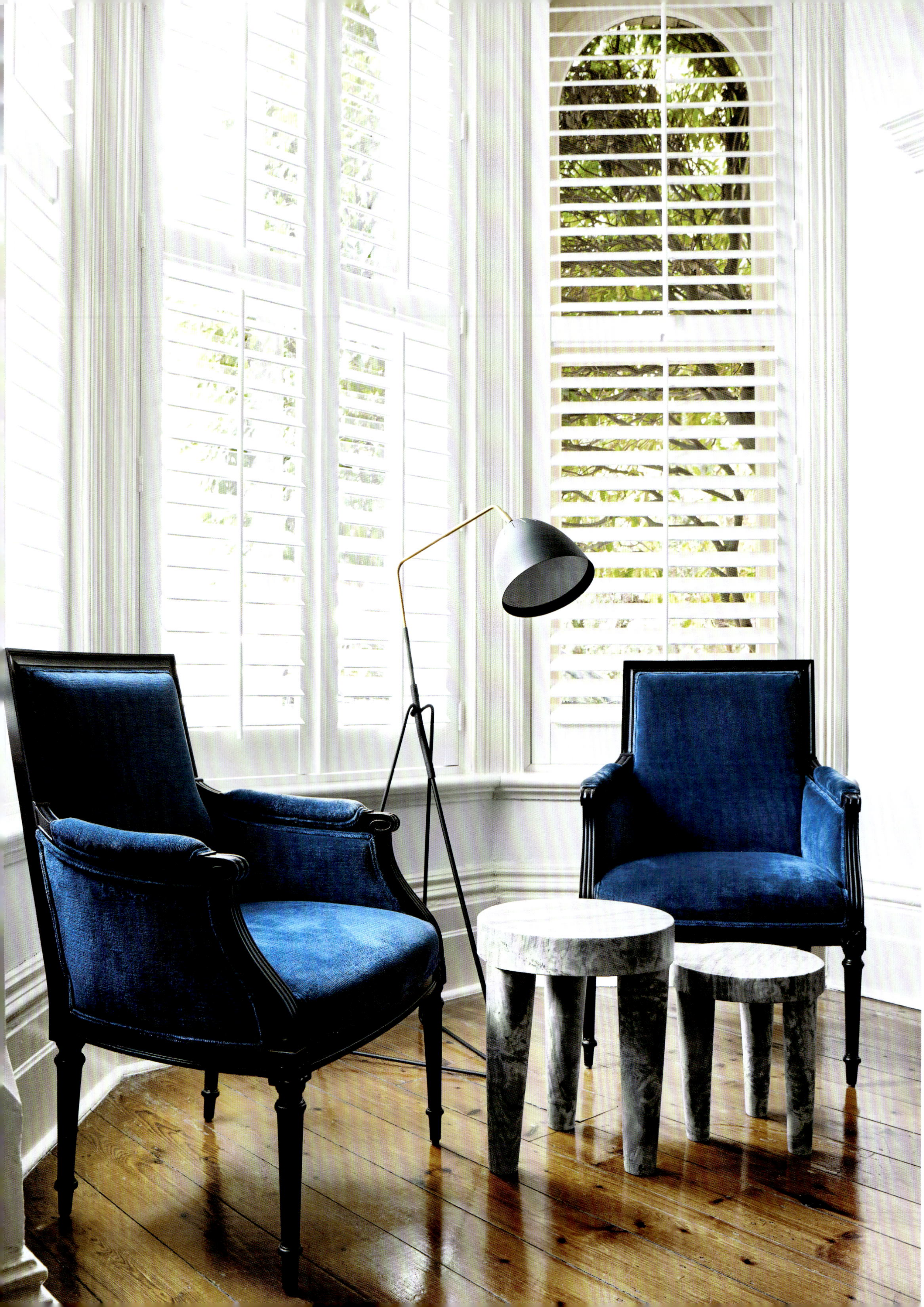

For every grand statement like this, there is one of practical sophistication, particularly in the living and dining rooms. The house's traditional layout has these situated on either side of the entrance, with both featuring generous bay windows that flood the spaces with light. In the living room, a custom white sofa and armchairs piled with tufted cushions speak of easy luxury and comfort. Tables are attractive yet accessible, including a mid-twentieth-century Italian marble-topped coffee table and an Italian side table with curved legs as well as a pair of small, solid ebonized timber pieces. A nineteenth-century French Beau Ivorie bookcase with gilt detailing and dark green shelves presents a graceful melding of form and function. Here, blue appears in the patterns of an antique Turkish kilim rug, whereas in the dining room, on the opposite side of the house, it delivers a rich pop of color via a couple of Louis XVI armchairs. Reupholstered in Dedar mohair velvet, the chairs encapsulate the blend of old and new that continues throughout the house and finds happy synthesis in this room. Modern pieces such as an extendable black-painted oak dining table and tan leather Cassina Cab chairs share space with an antique ebonized sideboard, which echoes the table's lines while adding its own intricate details. Black-and-white accessories, including Kelly Wearstler vases and a Flos *Snoopy* table lamp, provide fun decorative touches, while a landscape painting by Irish-born artist Colin Pennock gives the room another burst of color.

A variety of artworks also bring a layer of personality to the bedrooms, ranging from contemporary photographs to an Andy Warhol print of Mick Jagger. The Warhol's modern look presents a playful juxtaposition against the classic pairing of blue and white that appears in the boldly striped upholstery of a Louis XV armchair and the bedding with its Hermès throw. I love how vintage luggage can be repurposed to create interesting furniture, and this guest bedroom also features a pair of vintage Louis Vuitton suitcases as a chic storage option, as well as an antique French trunk as a bedside table. Both pieces pick up the warm tones of the sisal flooring, while a custom headboard in gray bouclé linen, here and in other bedrooms, offers a cool, neutral backdrop.

In the master bedroom, where the bed lies between two large windows, a headboard would have distorted the proportion, so the wall plays that role instead. To avoid an empty space above the bed, I added a couple of light, Matisse-style sketches and a Calder-style mobile. Their delicate lines display just enough detail without dominating the space, while low-profile furniture provides balance in the form of two custom black-lacquered bedside tables featuring little book holders, and a pair of antique French footstools at the end of the bed. Like the rest of the house, the interior is aesthetically appealing without being overworked. Just as contemporary pieces complement classic ones, style and comfort work together, and the balance established in the entrance, with its symphony of blues, sets the tone for this harmonious family home.

Previous spread - The glossy black finishes of a custom dining table and antique sideboard draw warmth from tan leather Cassina Cab chairs and a brightly colored Colin Pennock painting.

Opposite - Old and new come together in the corner of the dining room, which features Louis XVI armchairs reupholstered in Dedar mohair blue velvet, a Grasshopper-style lamp and robust gray marble side tables by Kelly Wearstler.

Above - Classic and contemporary meet with a Louis XV chair and a Warhol print of Mick Jagger.
Opposite - Chinese porcelain continues the palette of blue and white that runs through the house,
while gothic-looking timber wall sconces make a dramatic statement.

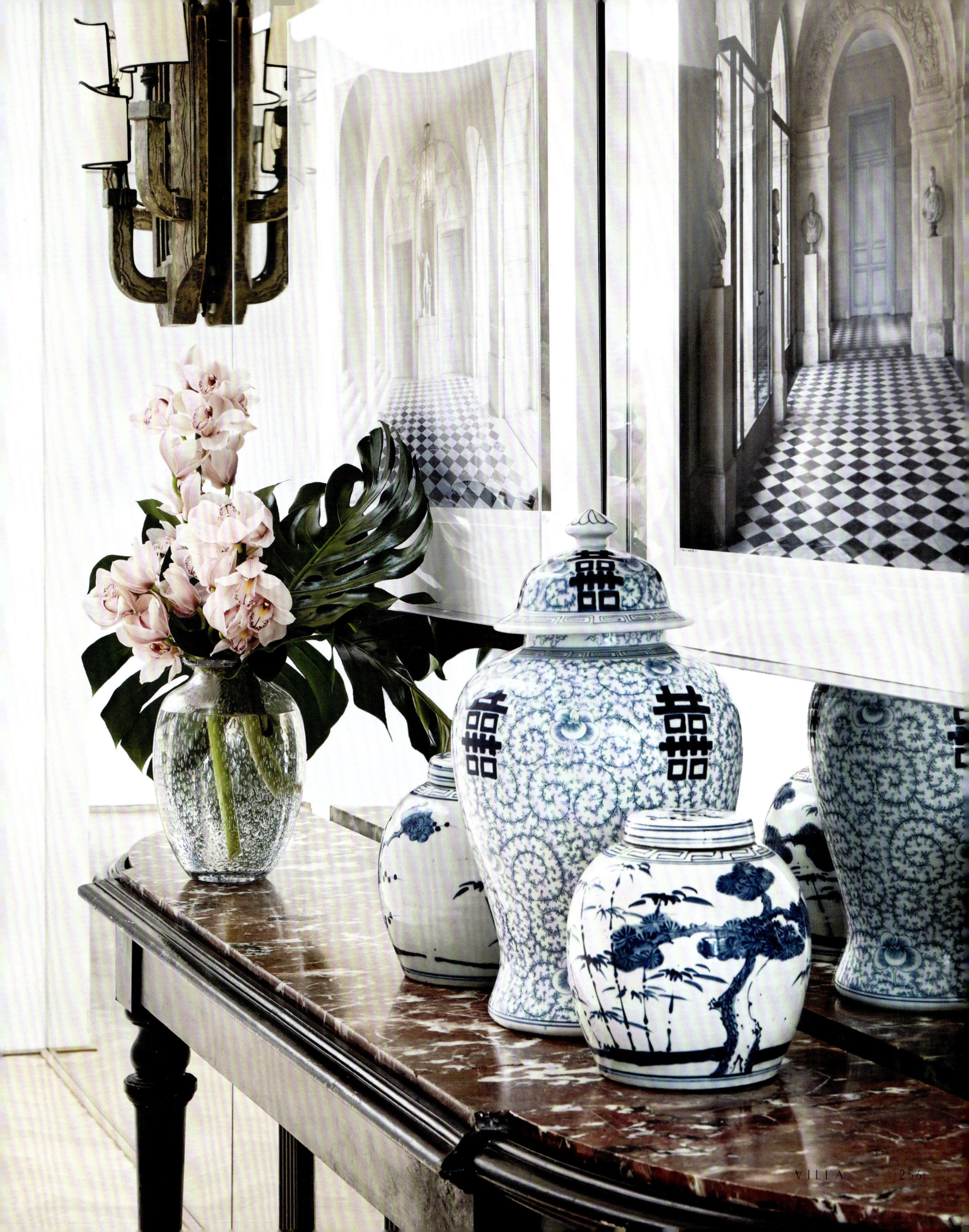

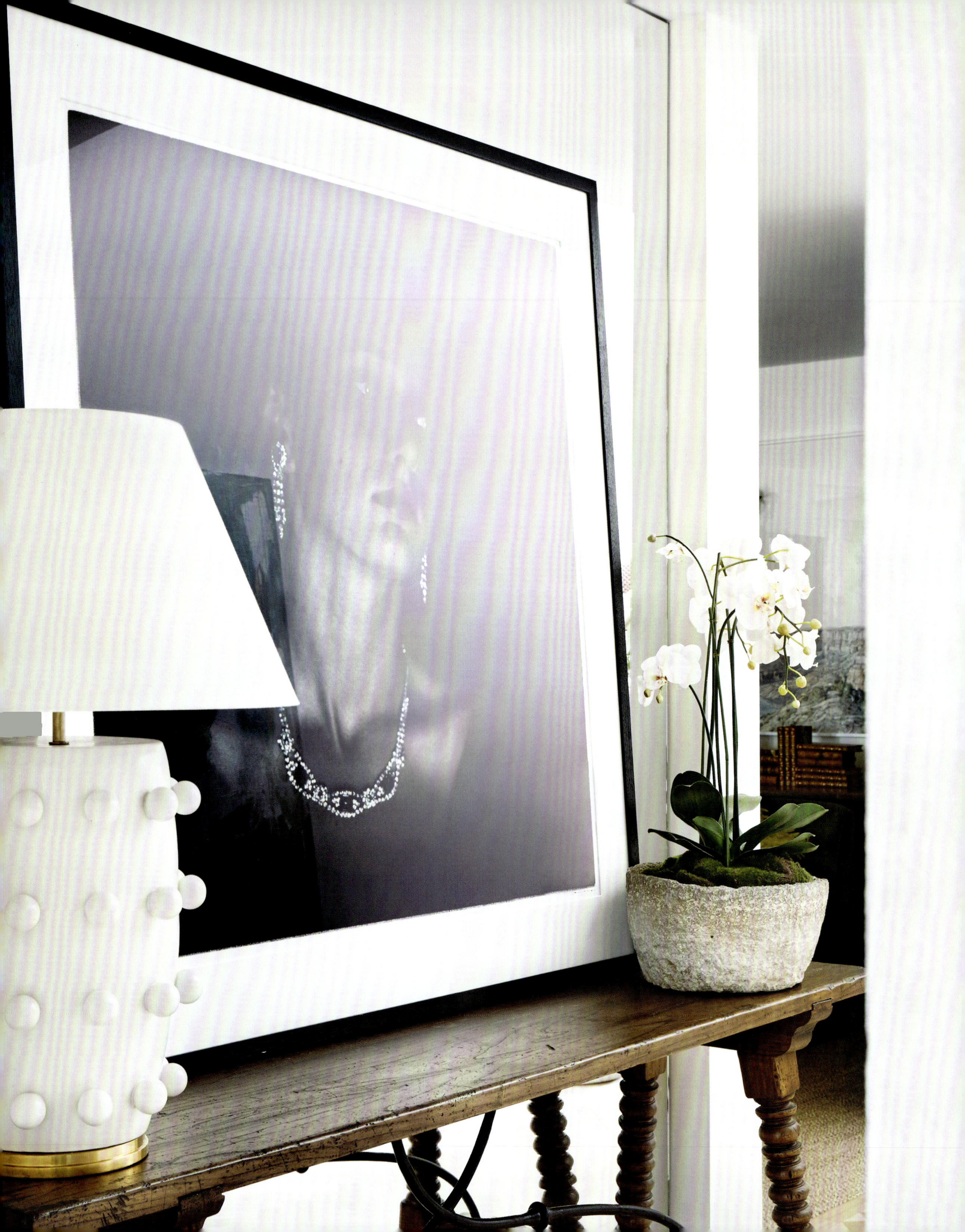

Opposite - A Bill Henson photograph delivers a sultry modern mood above a nineteenth-century Spanish walnut console table.

Above - The cool neutral tones of the bedroom receive a hit of color from a blue Hermès throw and a Massimo Vitali photograph above the antique French trunk that serves as a bedside table.

Above - In another bedroom, the metallic gleam of a brass reading light breaks up the monochrome palette.

Opposite - The master bedroom presents a composition of symmetry and harmony, where artworks deliver a delicacy of line.

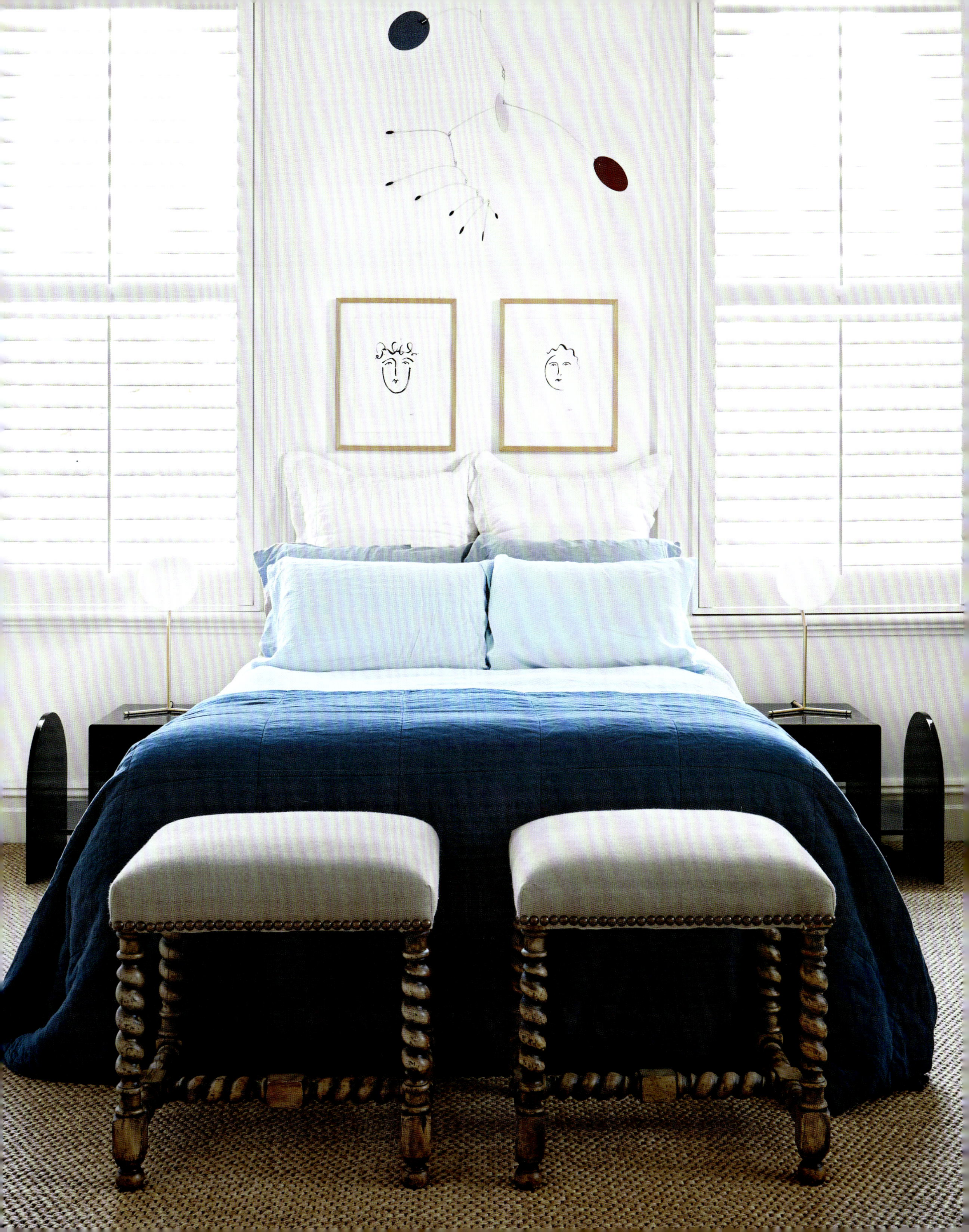

TREE HOUSE

*Domain Road,
South Yarra, Melbourne*

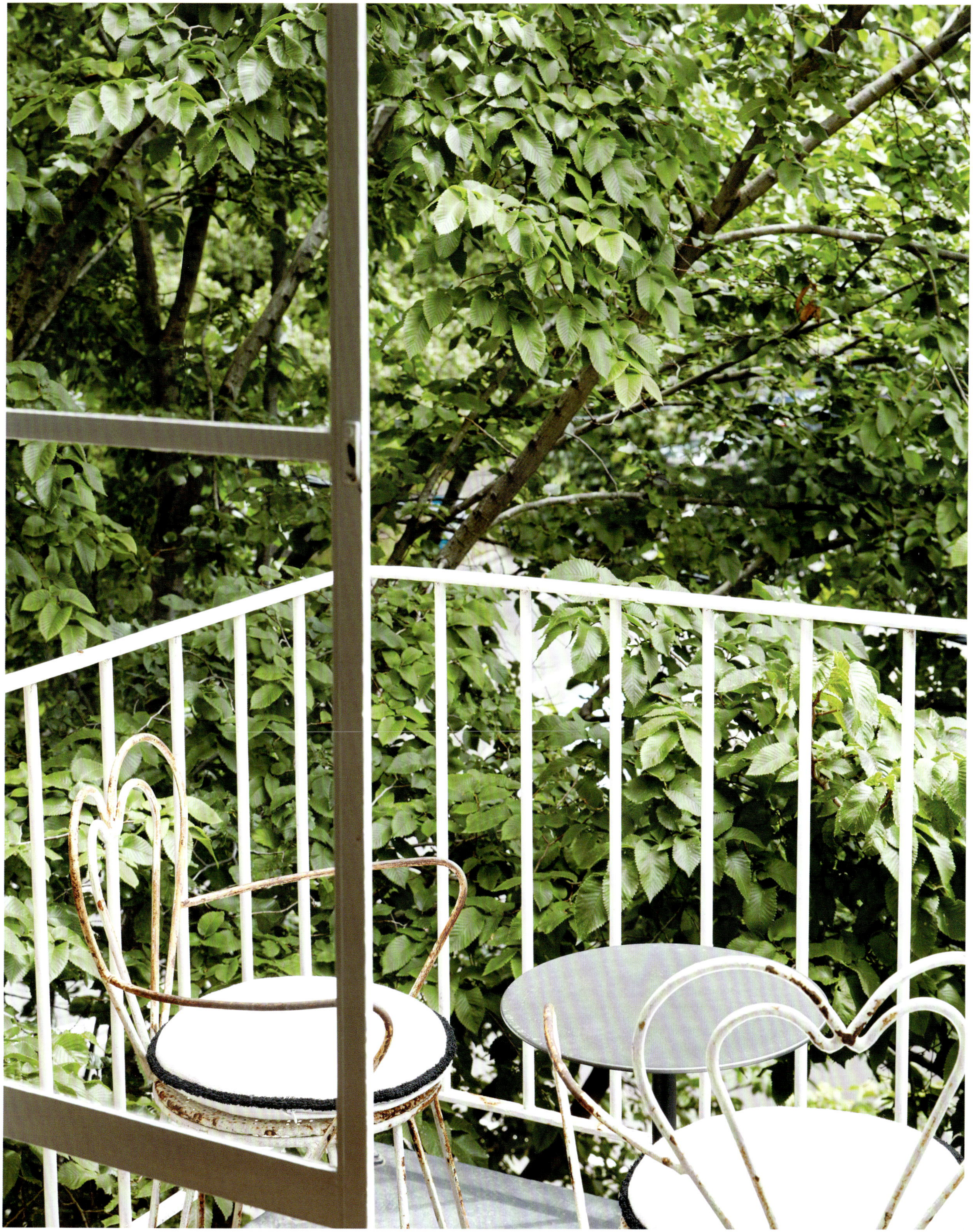

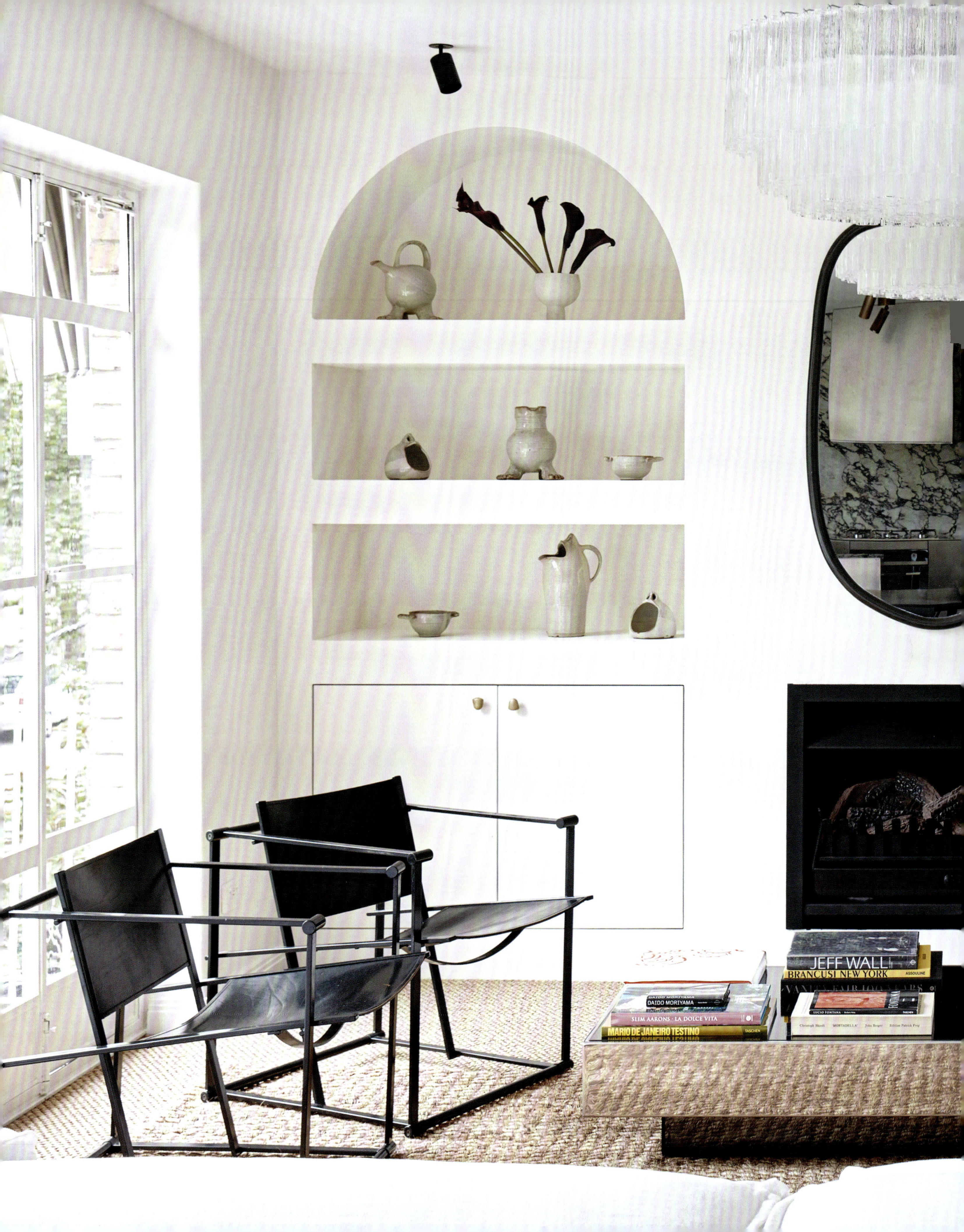

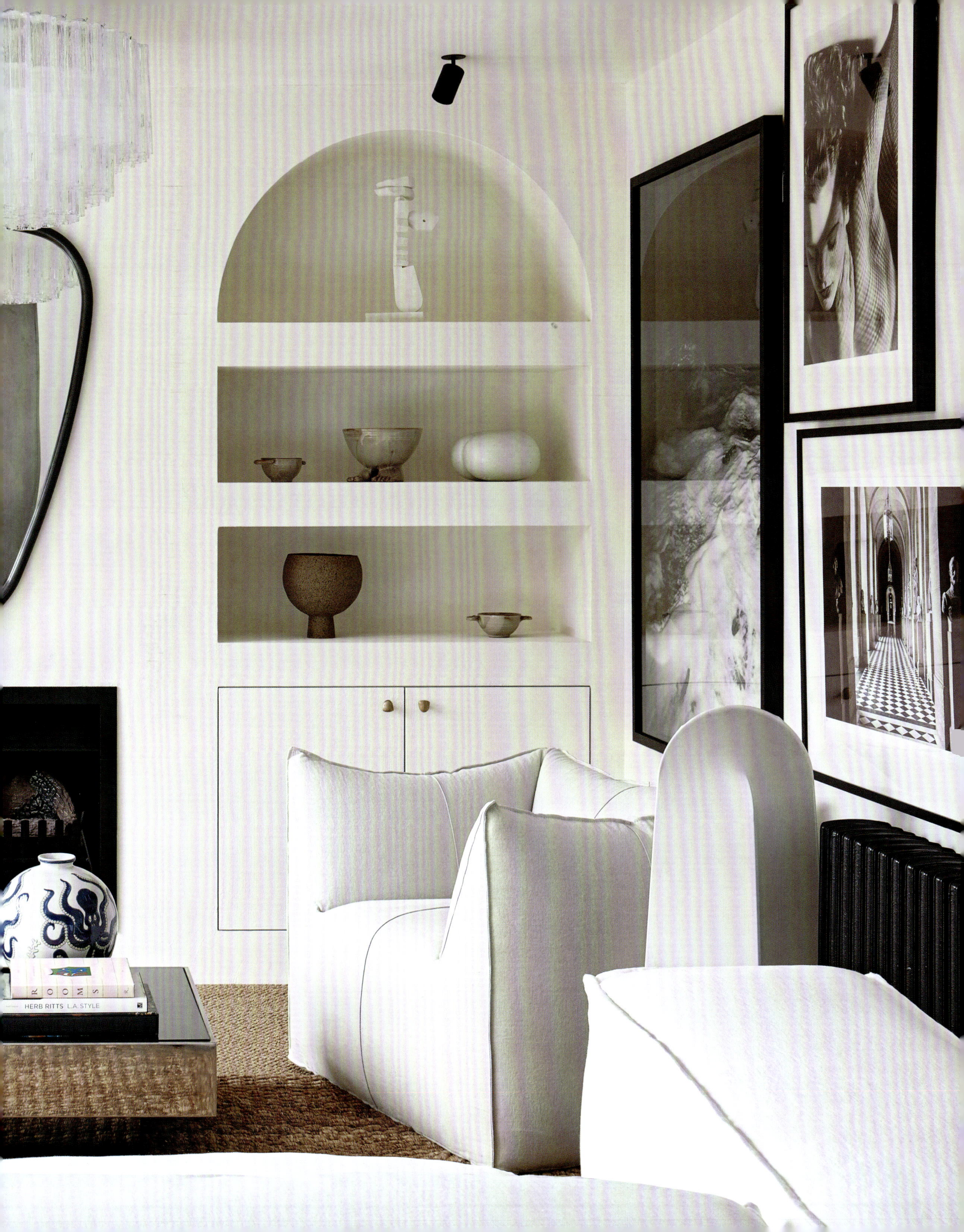
ROOMS
HERB RITTS L.A. STYLE

"Let your imagination run wild!" It's not often you receive a brief like this as an interior designer. Yet these were the owner's words, on a note that had been left for me under the mat when I went to see her apartment for the first time. She'd been called away for work unexpectedly and was keen for me to begin the process of transforming her home. We wouldn't end up meeting in person until nine months later, when the transformation was complete.

In the stylish Melbourne suburb of South Yarra, this three-bedroom apartment, at the top of a four-story art deco building, has the unique pleasure of looking out over the city's Royal Botanic Gardens. A profusion of windows along one side follow the line of the tree canopy, their original steel frames capturing each delicate verdant vista. Even the other side of the apartment faces neighboring greenery, so you really do feel as if you're perched amid the treetops. Inside, the ambience was a lot less airy. The tired, old rooms looked very much the worse for wear, from shabby cupboards and carpet to major limitations such as a poky hidden kitchen, two tiny bathrooms, and a narrow entry hall leading to the living room via a gloomy solid door. "Gutting" may not be a pleasant word but it certainly conveys the scope of renovation needed here. I reconfigured the kitchen, opened up and joined the two bathrooms to create a larger one, and made more of a landing at the front to create a better sense of entrance. For starters. After treating the steel-framed windows to a little restoration—and restorative white paint—I replaced the solid door with a pair of steel-framed glass doors. Not only are they in keeping with the style of the windows, they also create a more elegant transition between the entrance and living room, making the latter appear cozier, its own separate space, while also letting in plenty of light. Their black frames give the doors definition and a sleek modern look that suits the owner's lifestyle.

Given her equally demanding work and social calendars, her home needed to act as both retreat and entertaining hub, and I wanted it to feel contemporary yet timeless, almost like a Parisian apartment with its elegant urban edge. The greenery outside provided enough color to allow for a strong monochromatic interior design, which is most fully realized in the living area.

p. 111 - On the balcony, iconic Mathieu Matégot chairs with cushions in an outdoor fabric reward sitters with a canopy view. Previous spread - On the living room wall, a graceful picture of curves is created by the black-framed mirror and the arched, recessed shelves, which display a collection of quirky French ceramics.

Opposite - Black steel frames make a feature of the internal glass doors and tie in beautifully with the nearby artworks.

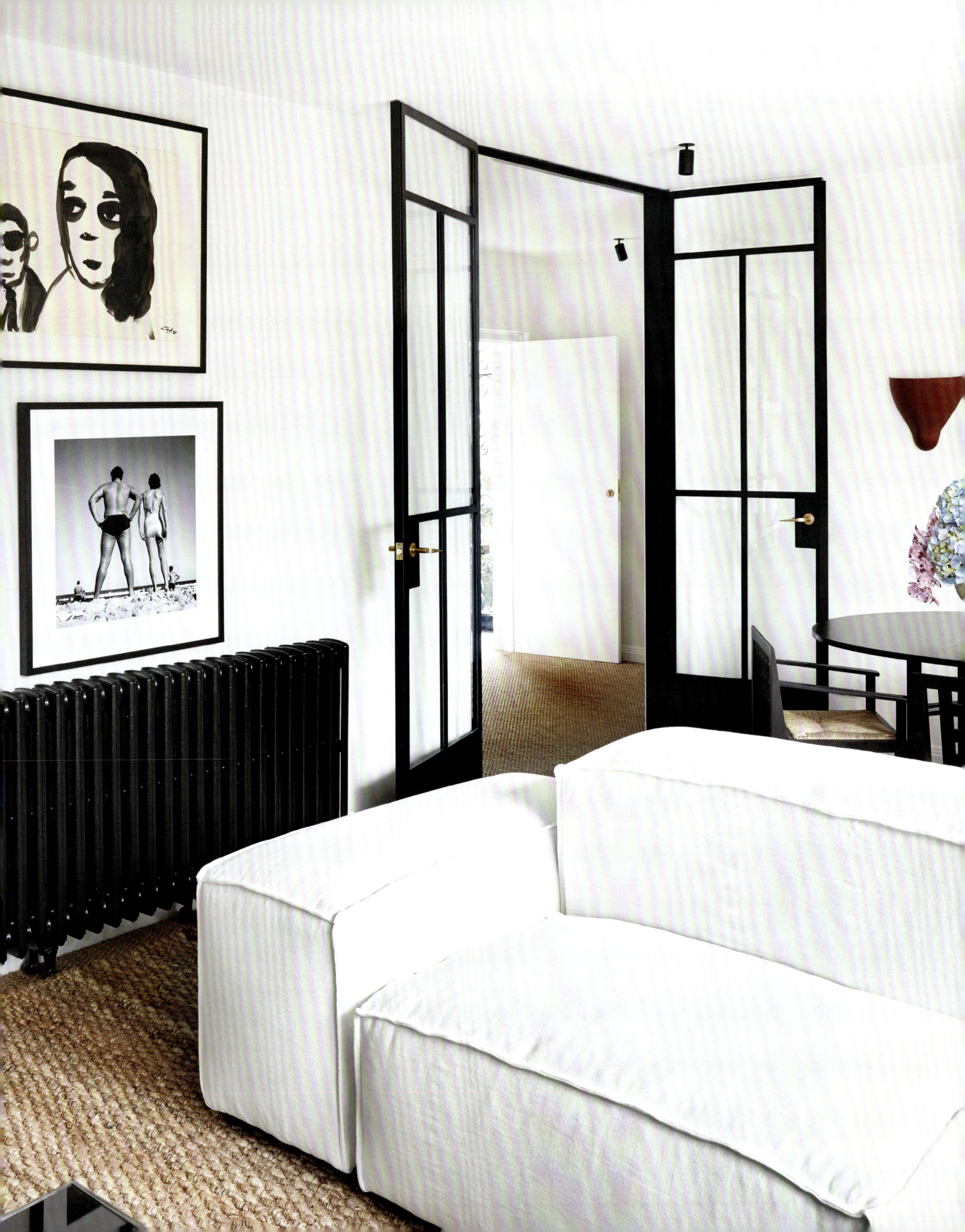

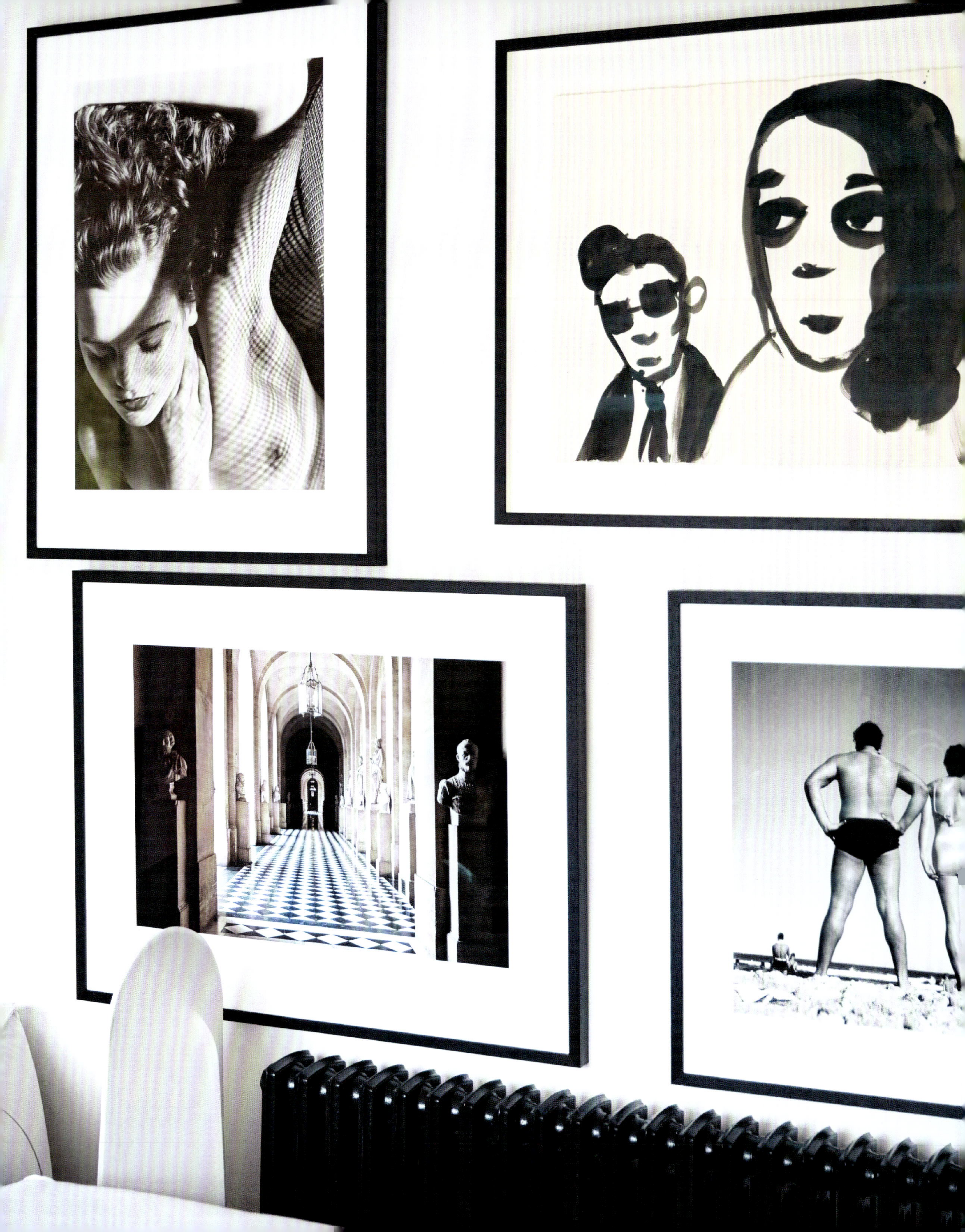

On one wall, four artworks present a vibrant grouping in black and white: a drawing by Australian actor and artist Noah Taylor, two photographs by the late Australian modernist Max Dupain, and one by Sydney-based French photographer Felix Forest. The angles of their black frames echo those of the doors and meet a shapely contrast in the organic curves of a black-framed mirror on another wall. On either side of the mirror, I added more curves in the form of arched, recessed shelves in the white walls. The arches bring a little art deco element to the room and have a softening effect on the sharper angles elsewhere. Below, the furniture presents another picture of contrasting shape and tone. The precise lines of a pair of 1980s Mario Botta black leather chairs echo the frames of the artworks opposite. Distinguished by their different silhouettes are the yielding, sumptuous folds of their neighboring pieces: a Living Divani sofa in white brushed cotton and an iconic 1970s Le Bombole chair by Mario Bellini, upholstered in oatmeal linen. At the center, the box-like design of a coffee table in stainless steel by Willy Rizzo is tempered by the natural texture of the new sisal flooring. That frisson between strong and soft, black and white, lines and curves plays out through the apartment, in different vignettes. There is a sense here that no aspect is either wholly feminine or masculine, that anything is possible.

In the arched shelves sits a wonderfully unusual collection of 1920s French anthropomorphic ceramics, each with little feet and featuring a different facial part. I discovered them in Paris's Clignancourt flea market and knew that the owner, whom I'd been in touch with regularly via phone and email, would love them as much as I did. It was a delight to send her a picture from the market and see her immediate shared enthusiasm for this unusual find. I think it is moments like this and creations like these that show what can happen when we let our imaginations run wild. Speaking of which, I have always wanted to design an entirely stainless steel kitchen. I find the material beautifully understated and here it is a fitting accompaniment to the owner's streamlined lifestyle. In this kitchen, seamless planes of stainless steel envelop the countertop, rangehood, and even the floating shelves, with the pantry, fridge, and other appliances all concealed behind stainless steel doors that open via push latches. With no handles and a glamorous brushed finish, the hand-molded joinery becomes an artwork in itself.

Here, the softening elements are the parquet floor, with its warmth of tone and detail, and backsplashes in Calacatta Viola marble, its pinks, purples, and browns bringing a ripple of color into the space. I used some leftover marble to create the top of a small console table, balancing it with a blackened steel base. This sits in the new entrance space with an eclectic mix of objects arrayed on top: two glass vases, a spiky Murano and a smooth Daum one, alongside a bold white marble breast sculpture and a black concrete torso, both by Kelly Wearstler. More plays on form and finish, in a place whose nuances extend far beyond the black and white.

Opposite - Photographs by Max Dupain (top left and bottom right) and Felix Forest team with a drawing by Noah Taylor in a powerful grouping of black and white.

Above and opposite - A dining setting by Charles Rennie Mackintosh brings its striking black lines to the monochromatic mix, while a custom wall sconce hand-painted in Le Corbusier's Rouge Vermillon delivers a dramatic punch of color.

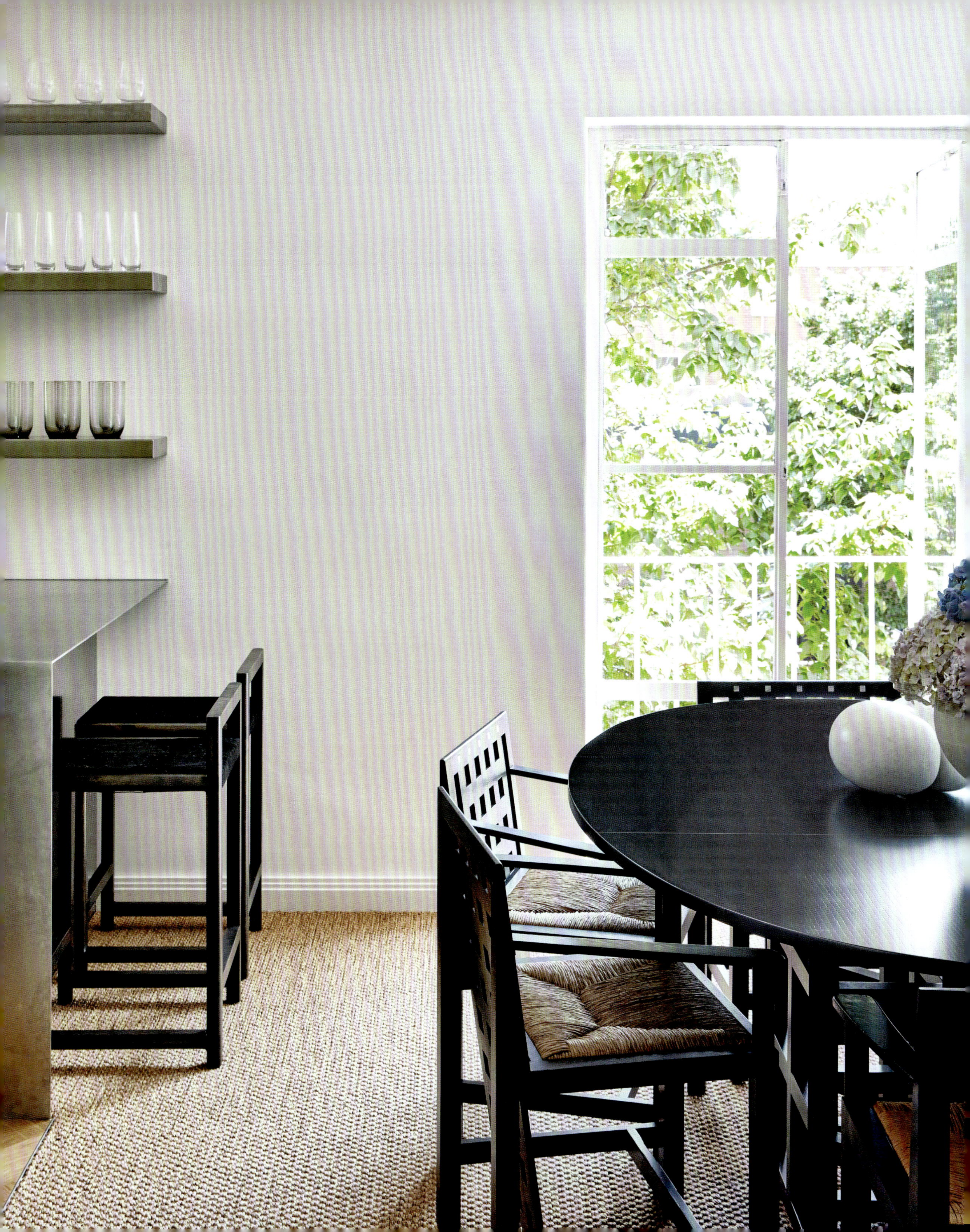

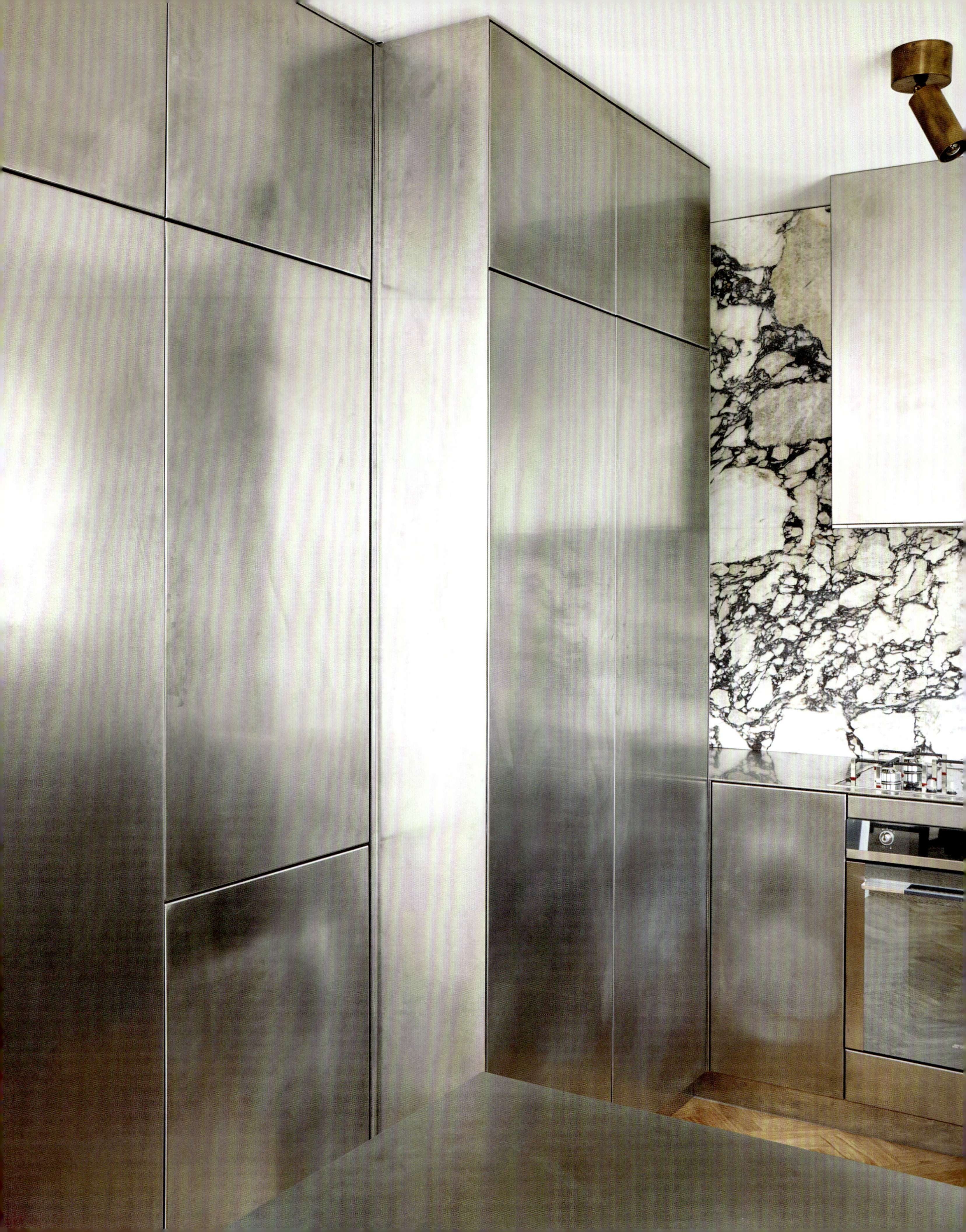

Opposite and above - Brushed stainless steel gives a seamless sheen
to the kitchen surfaces, softened by ripples of Calacatta Viola marble.

Following spread - The bedroom features soft neutral pieces such as a custom headboard in gray velvet
and a 1970s Le Bombole chair, one of a pair upholstered in oatmeal linen (the other is in the living room).

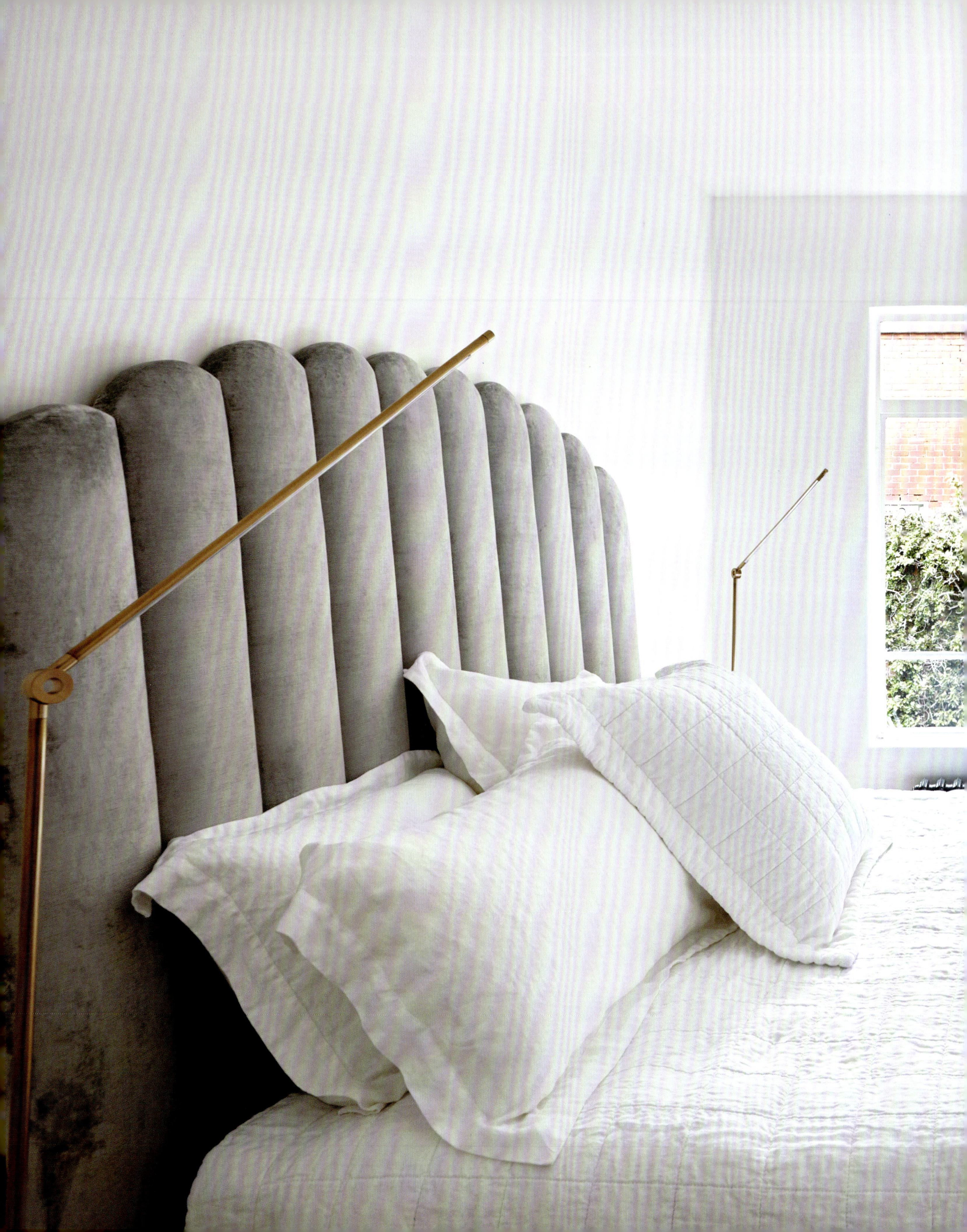

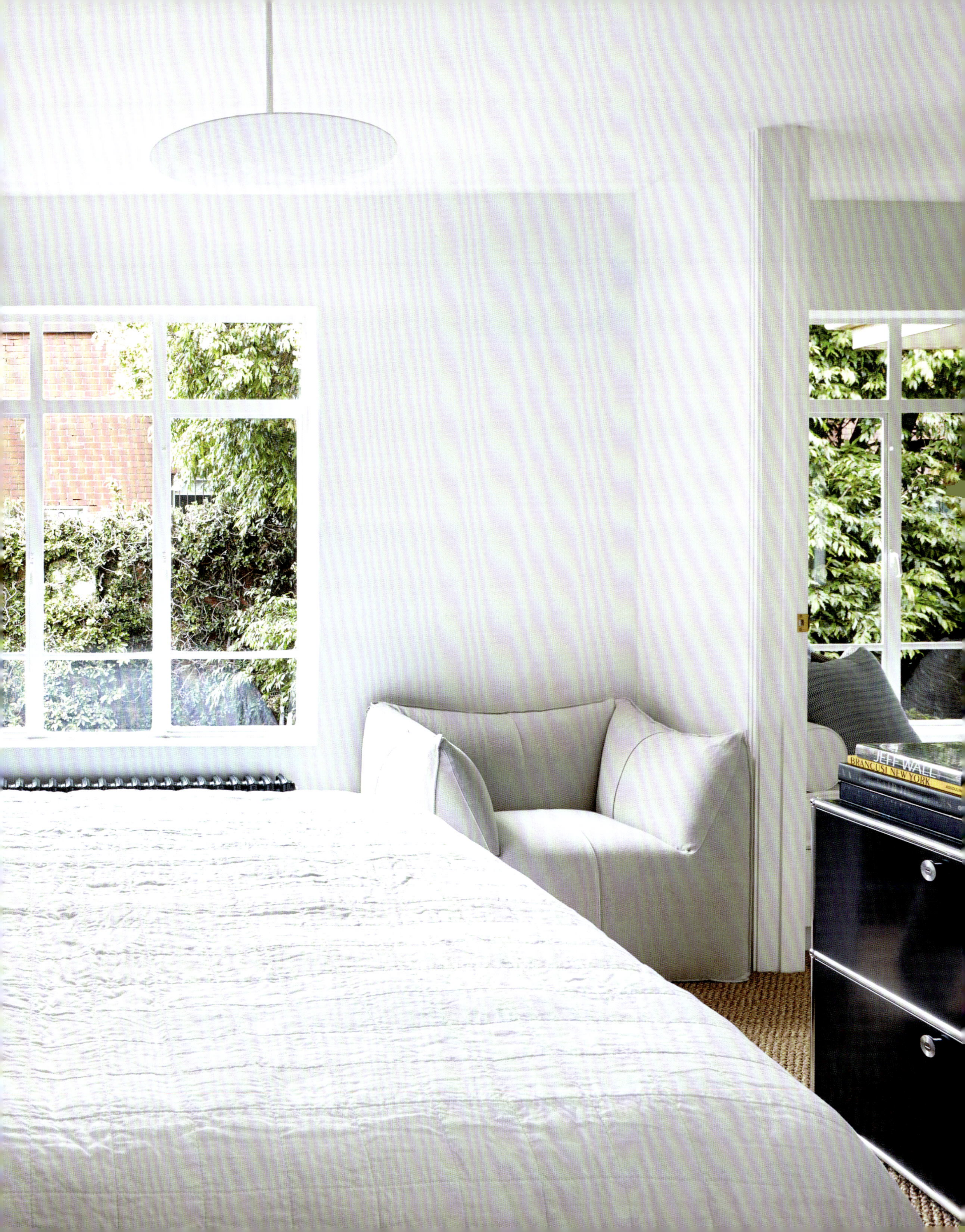
JEFF WALL
BRANCUSI NEW YORK

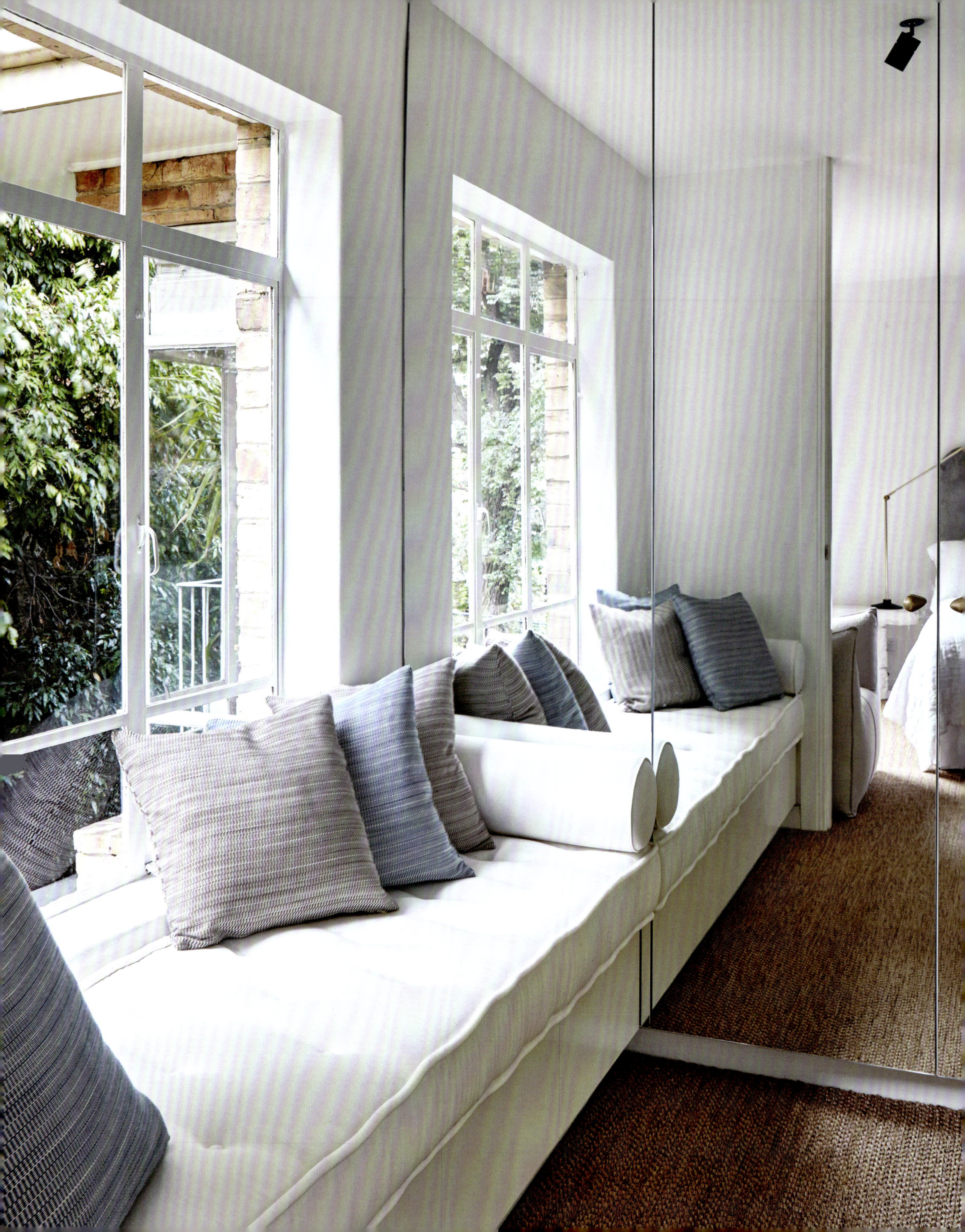

*Opposite and above - An unused bedroom became a walk-in wardrobe with a banquette window seat.
On the mirror-fronted cabinets, sculptural brass handles like little watermelon pips add glamour to the space.*

Above - Gray Tadelakt plaster gives a sumptuous finish to the bathroom walls, offset by a distinctive Murano glass sconce.

Opposite - The console table, made from some leftover Viola marble, displays a bold blend of forms.

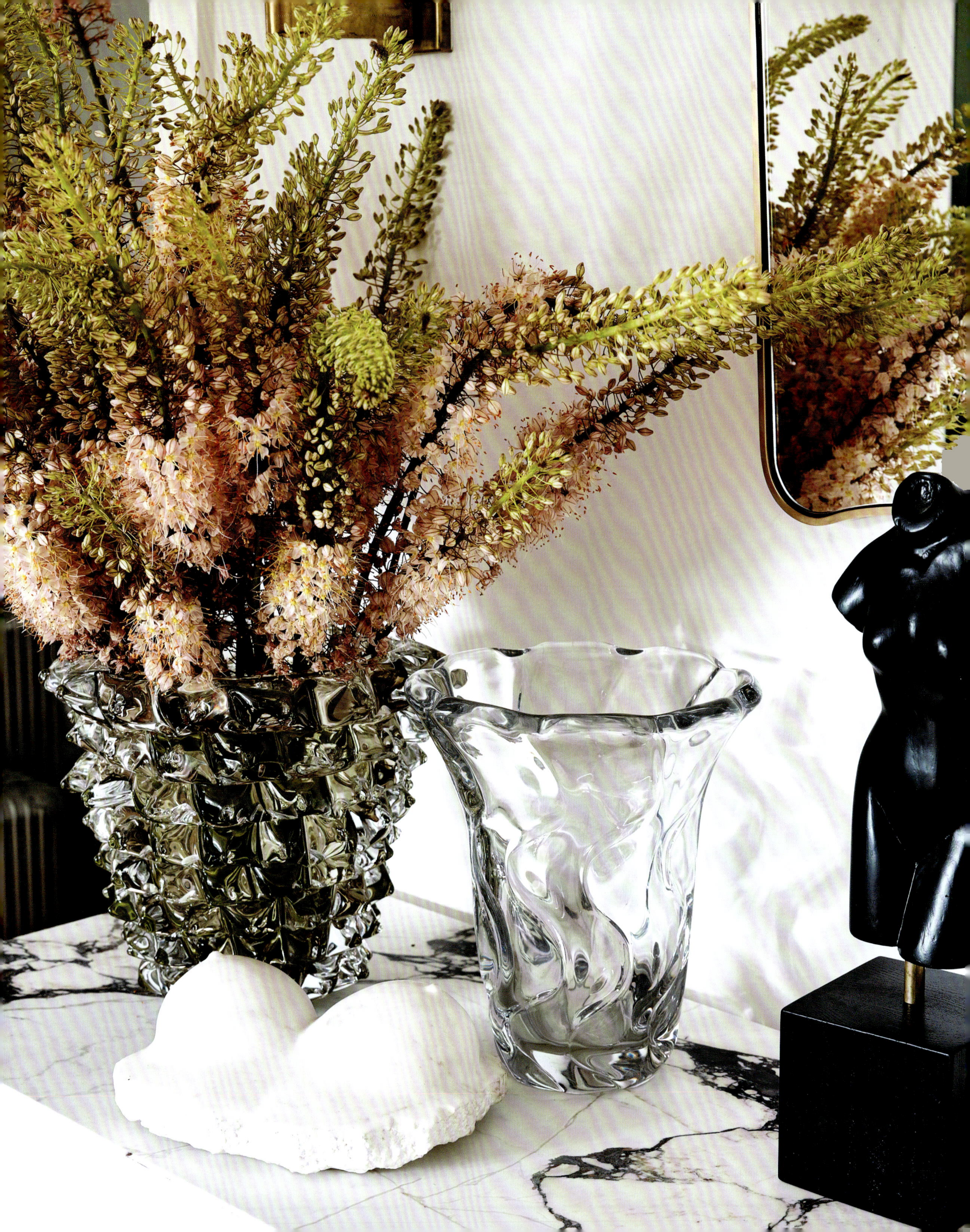

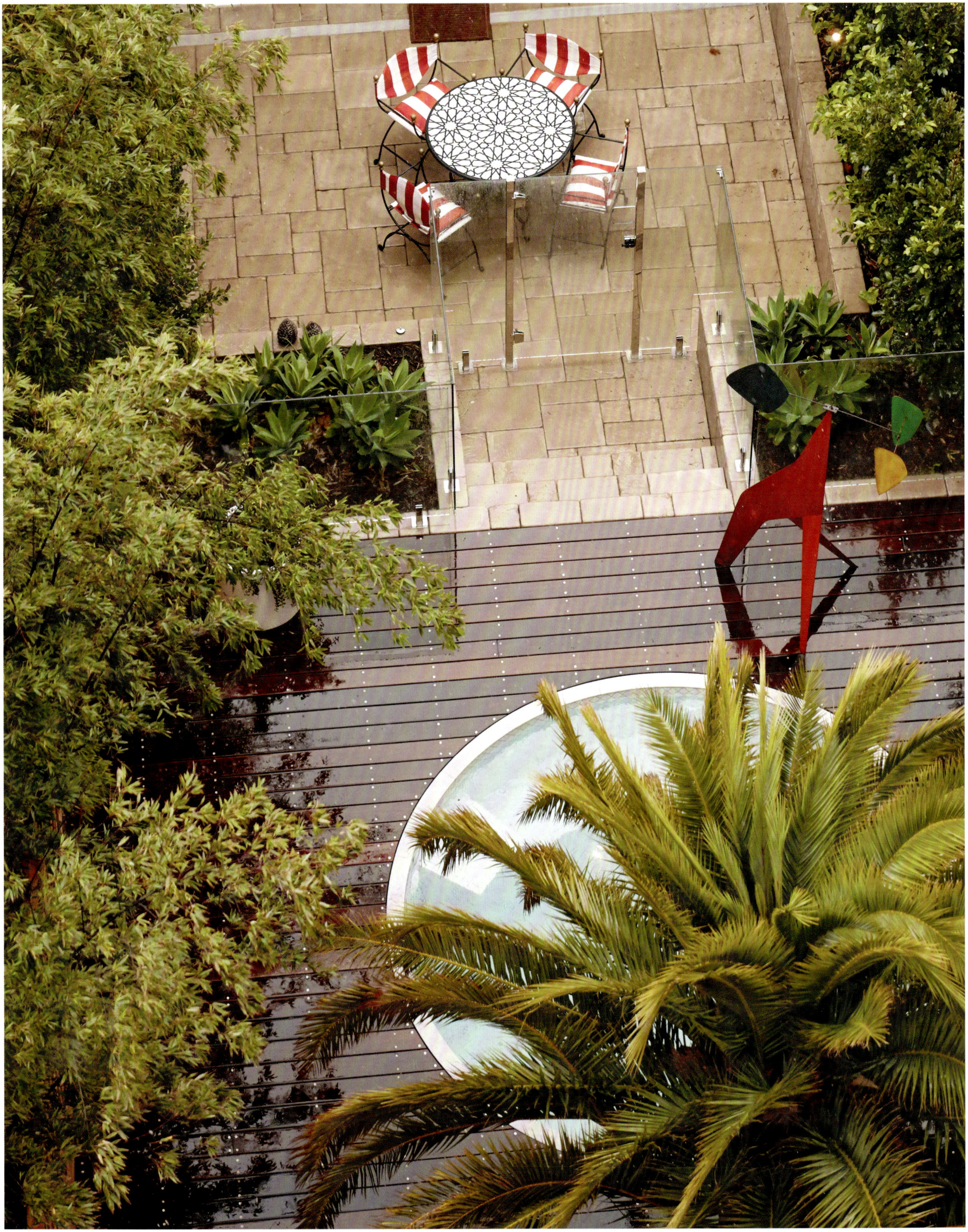

SANCTUARY

Tivoli Road,
South Yarra, Melbourne

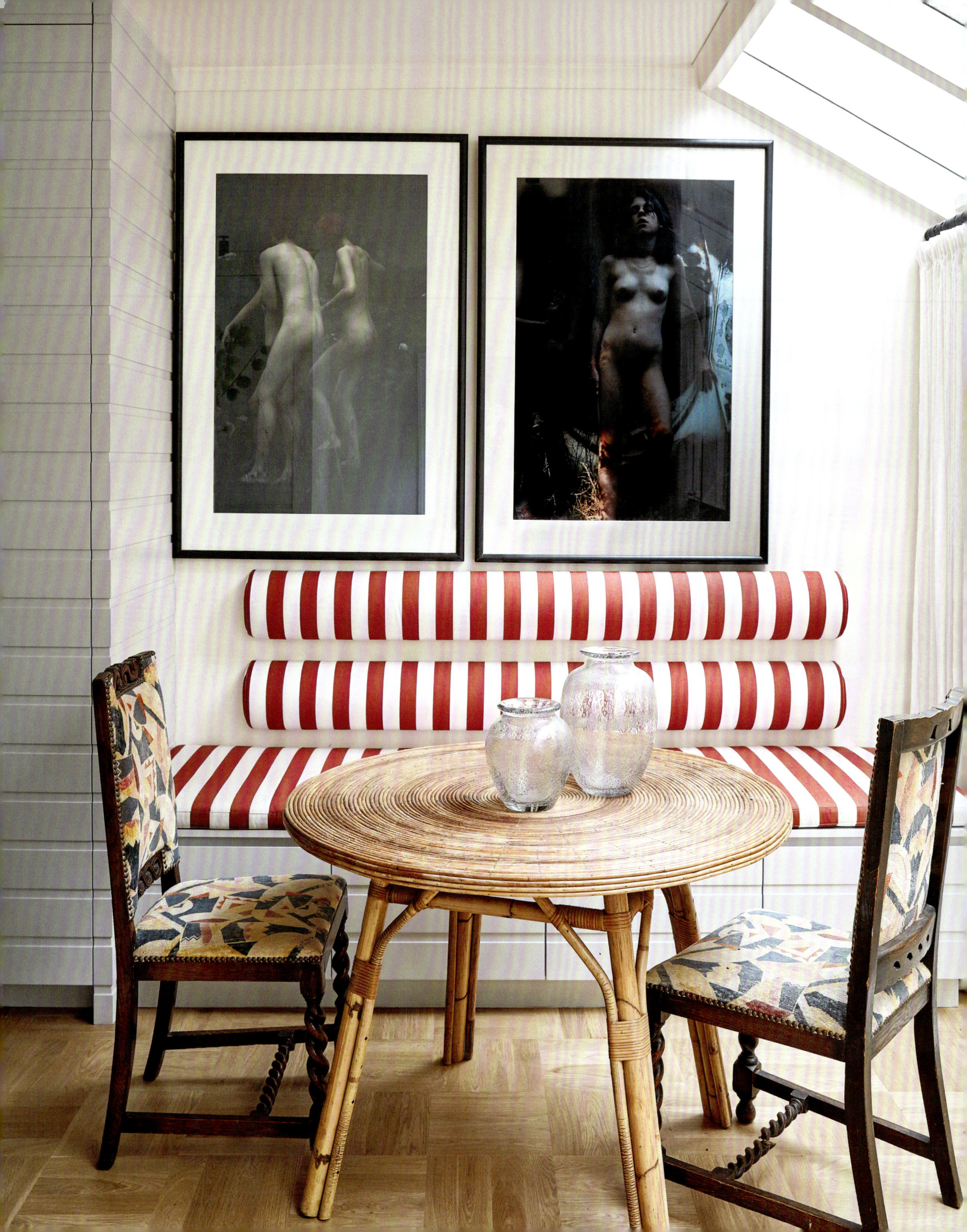

Every Christmas, my sister and I receive a Daum vase from our parents. During their long careers in antiques dealing, they built up a sizeable collection of these vessels from the famous French art glassworks, and this wonderful tradition has evolved from their love and generosity. It extends to other special occasions, when they make gifts to us of pieces from various collections they have assembled. When Tess and I each moved out, they gave us identical nineteenth-century Spanish walnut tables. We don't always receive the same object, but their generosity is always an incredible treat, no matter the gift. And the gifts feel even more meaningful because these pieces are dearly familiar to us from our childhood—we grew up with them and became as passionate about them as our parents. For me, that passion shaped my own career.

When my sister asked me to design a new house for her, it was like designing for myself, not only because I was intimately acquainted with so many of the pieces here, but also because we are very close, so it felt as if I were creating a second home. Tess and her family live in a mid-twentieth-century, two-story house with four bedrooms in the leafy Melbourne suburb of South Yarra. She and her husband wanted a new look for the place that would reflect the lifestyle they enjoy with their two young daughters—a vibrant household full of color and motion, a little irreverent at times, and with plenty of space for the flow and bustle of people and activity. The original house was quite dark, despite the presence of a rather odd internal courtyard, with a nondescript garden outside and an unsightly U-shaped kitchen inside, courtesy of a dreary 1990s update. The redesign included introducing new finishes throughout and reconfiguring the upper level for a better arrangement of rooms, but central to the architectural changes was the fashioning of a cohesive new ground-floor layout. For Tess's family, this is where all the action happens. With the courtyard filled in, a series of tiered, open living spaces now spill beautifully into one another and onto a large outdoor courtyard in the rear with a round, marble-tiled pool. Huge steel-framed windows around the lower rooms and a skylight upstairs deliver far more light than there was before, enhancing the fluid connection that takes place from courtyard to breakfast nook to kitchen, then down to the dining area, and, further on, to a sunken living room. These well-defined zones are generous enough to allow everyone to enjoy their own space yet sufficiently linked for them to be aware of what's going on elsewhere—there is no chance of FOMO here!

p. 128 - Vintage French foldable chairs and a Calder-style sculpture provide colorful moments in the courtyard.

Opposite - A playful bench upholstered in Ralph Lauren fabric (also pictured overleaf) continues the red-and-white pairing from outside. The unexpected mix of pieces, including dramatic Bill Henson photographs and vintage dining furniture, gives this breakfast nook its energy.

Above - A Pierre Jeanneret Kangaroo Chair picks up the warm tones of the raw oak parquet floor. Above an Art Nouveau marble and wrought-iron table from my father, a photograph by Tom Ramsay adds vivid layers of color.

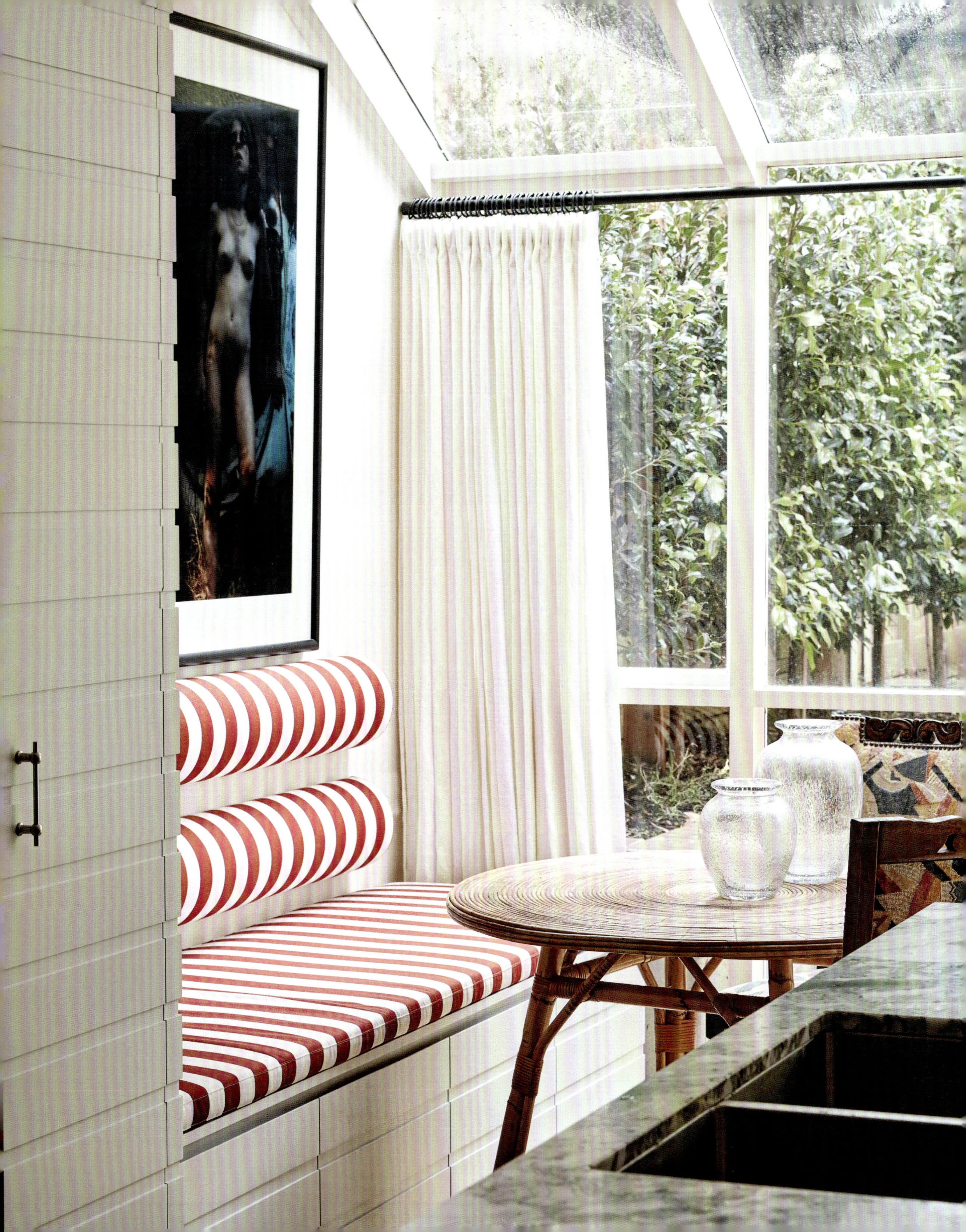

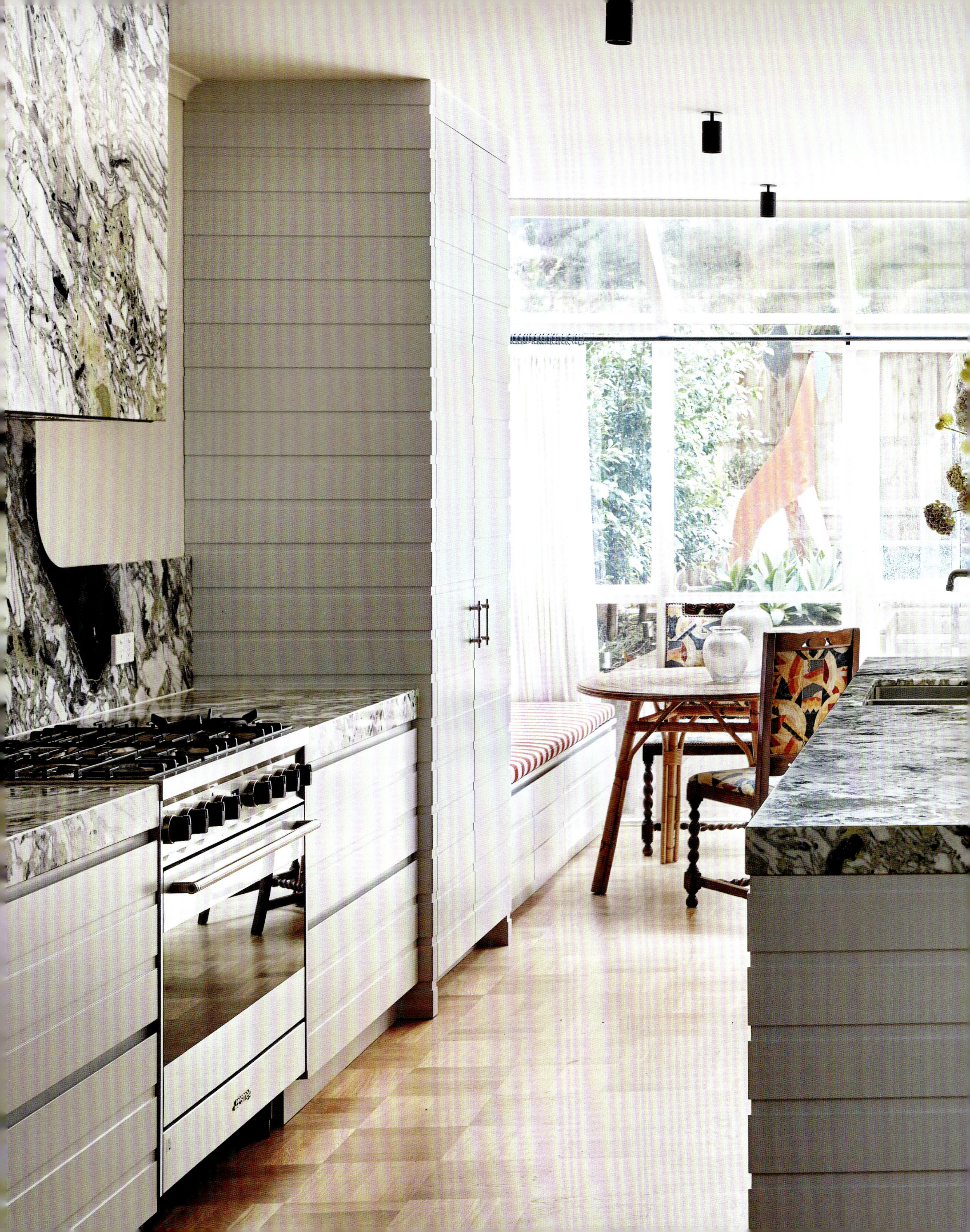

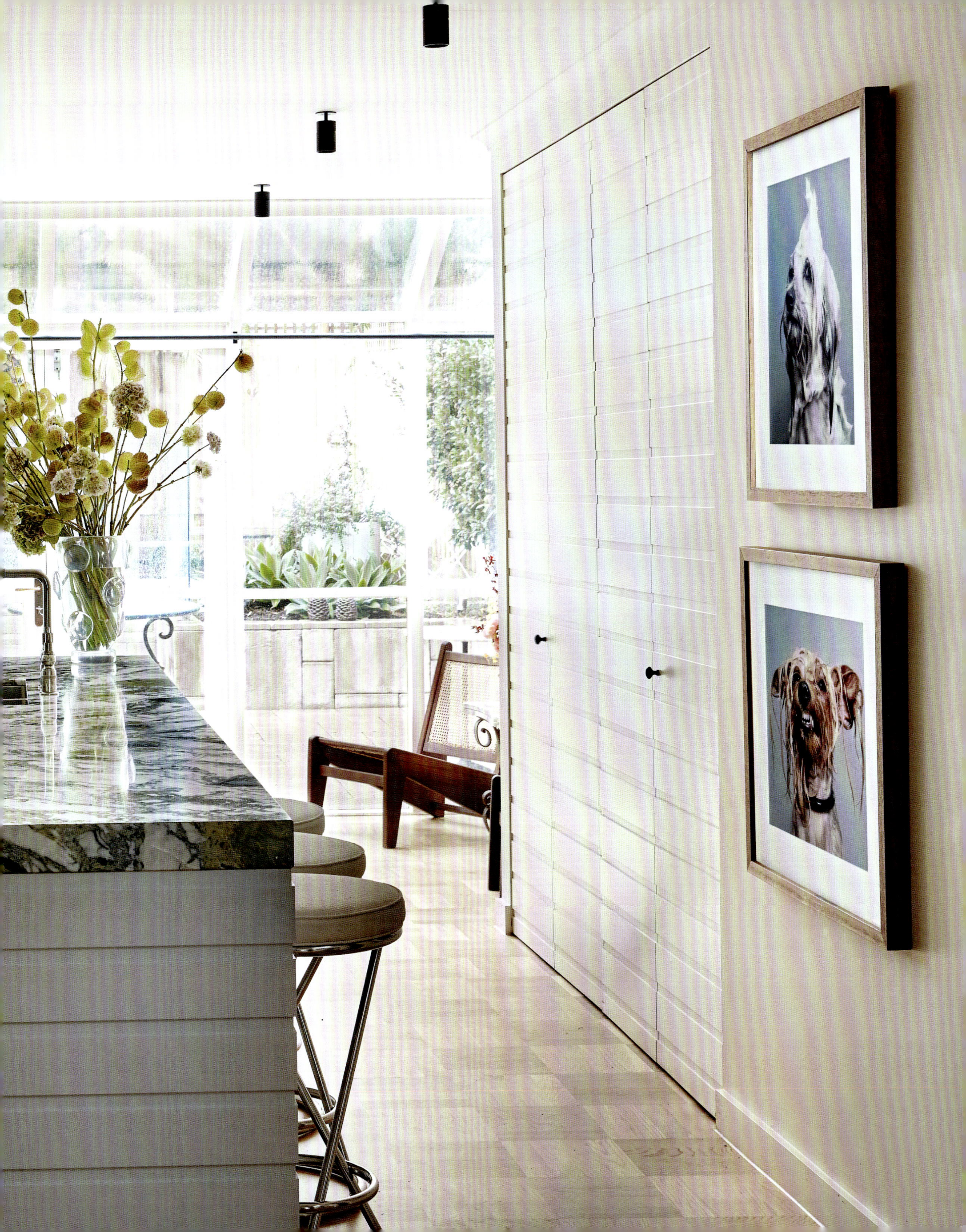

While I felt at home with the interior design, I was also compelled to amp things up a little more in order to suit this family's taste and sense of fun. Color was one aspect where this was easily achievable, through both furniture and artworks. A custom bench, upholstered in red-and-white striped Ralph Lauren fabric, is a lively focal point in the breakfast nook. The stripes provide a playful link to the courtyard outside, which features 1940s French red and white dining chairs and a red sculpture in the style of Alexander Calder. The bench sits beneath a pair of moody, intense photographs by Bill Henson and opposite two 1950s Italian dining chairs in an offbeat, slightly faded print. Nothing about this scene is predictable, yet with a simple 1940s French cane table as its anchor, the grouping works.

A few steps into the kitchen and green catches the eye, in the Fantasia marble used for the countertop, rangehood, and backsplash. The shade is an unexpected choice but it has a soothing quality that works well with the pale gray timber-paneled joinery and raw oak parquet floor. Combined with the symmetry of the backsplash wall, I think the marble creates a center point for the different levels, linking courtyard and breakfast nook on one side to dining and living areas on the other. Opposite, two cheeky photographs of wet dogs by American artist Sophie Garnand deliver a fresh shot of energy to the space. Aesthetically, I wanted to build up a rhythm where unexpected moments are balanced by more muted elements, creating their own dynamic pulse within the house. The two mid-twentieth-century wall lights above the backsplash, for example, would have been too prominent here in their original cherry color, but painted white they take on a subtly sculptural look. Lighting plays a major part in continuing that rhythm through the dining and living rooms of the next tiers down. Like some curious plant, an Italian mid-twentieth-century brass floor lamp reaches into the living room, hovering over a cane living room set that Tess and I have known from childhood. Its spherical shapes are echoed in the striking lines of a Jacques Adnet brass hat rack, a piece as functional and robust as it is attractive, rather like the house itself. On the fireplace, the gray speckle of two Murano glass lights softens the almost brutalist pattern of custom gray terrazzo and white marble Palladiana tiles. A Curtis Jere pendant light brings a bold metallic presence to this space, while its twin hangs in the dining room, above my sister's Spanish walnut table.

In this way, meaningful pieces bring their heritage to the house's layers. The girls' rooms feature pieces from our childhood, such as an antique rocking horse and an old seagull mobile. In the master bedroom, a little mid-twentieth-century red lamp that my mother loved but my father never warmed to is a fun family conversation piece. And the cane table in the vibrant breakfast nook is home to two Daum vases, there to be enjoyed by current and future generations.

Previous spread and opposite - In soft gray timber and green Fantasia marble, the kitchen is the serene center of a series of tiered spaces on the new ground floor, linking the breakfast nook and courtyard on one side with the dining area and sunken living room on the other.

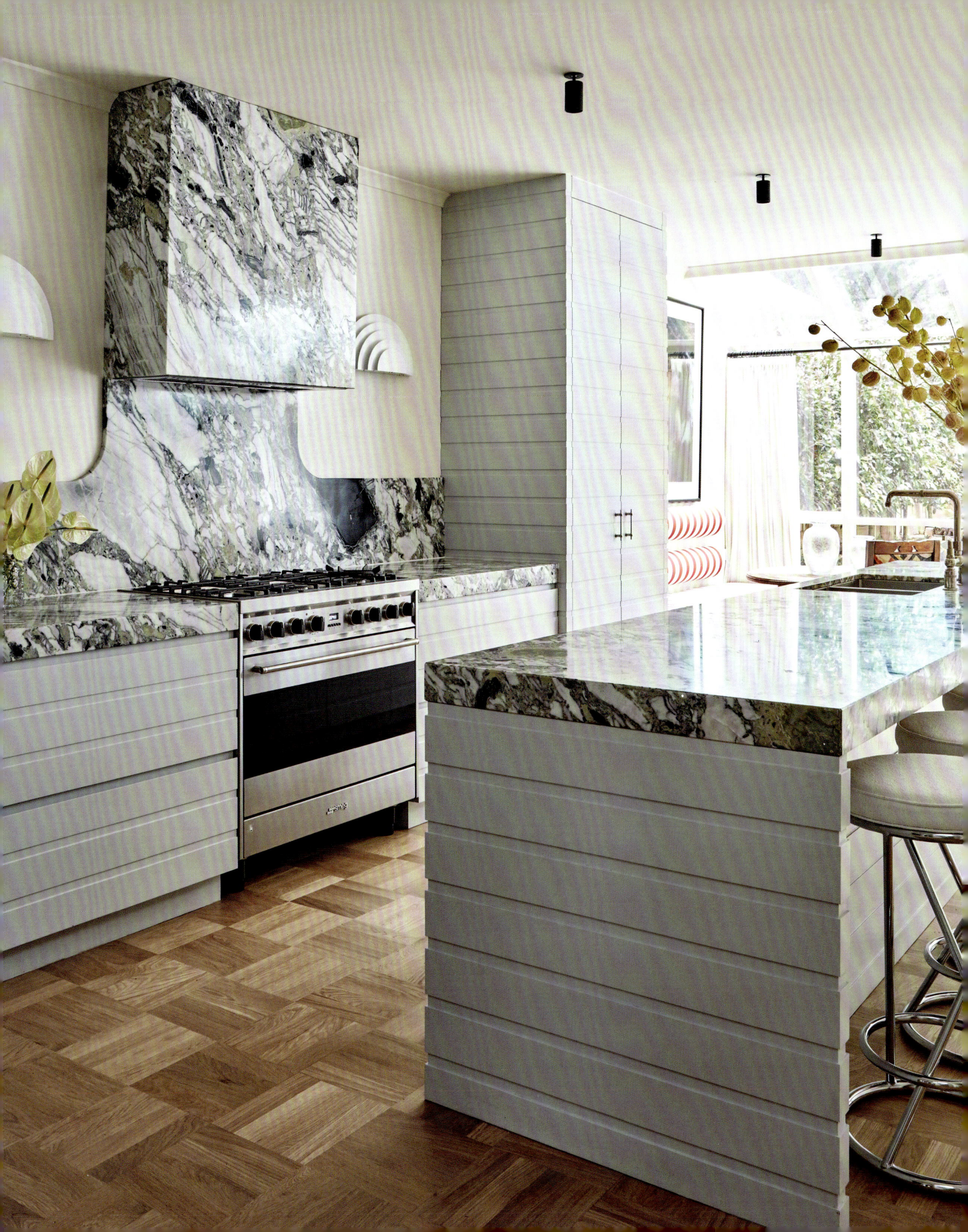

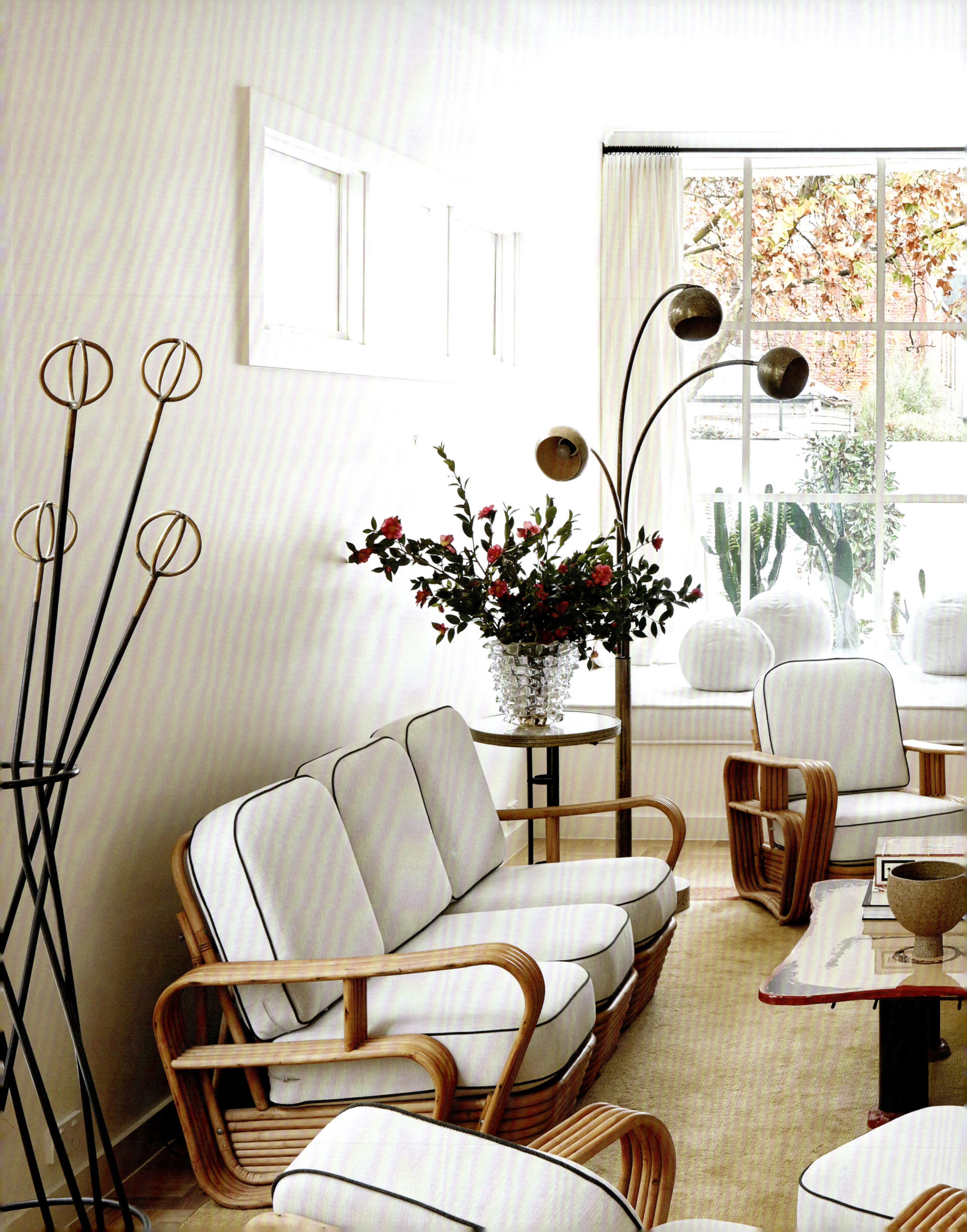

'MORTADELLA'
John Berger
Edition Patrick Frey
JEAN-MICHEL BASQUIAT DRAWING

Previous spread - The eye-catching spheres of a brass floor lamp are echoed in a Jacques Adnet hat rack and a playful set of beach-ball-style cushions on the window banquette. This spot (also pictured above) is a favorite with the children.

Opposite - Mid-twentieth-century French cane chairs bring their unusual shapes to the dining area. The nineteenth-century Spanish walnut table and the Venetian glass mirror on the wall were both gifted to my sister by my parents, while I also received an identical one of each.

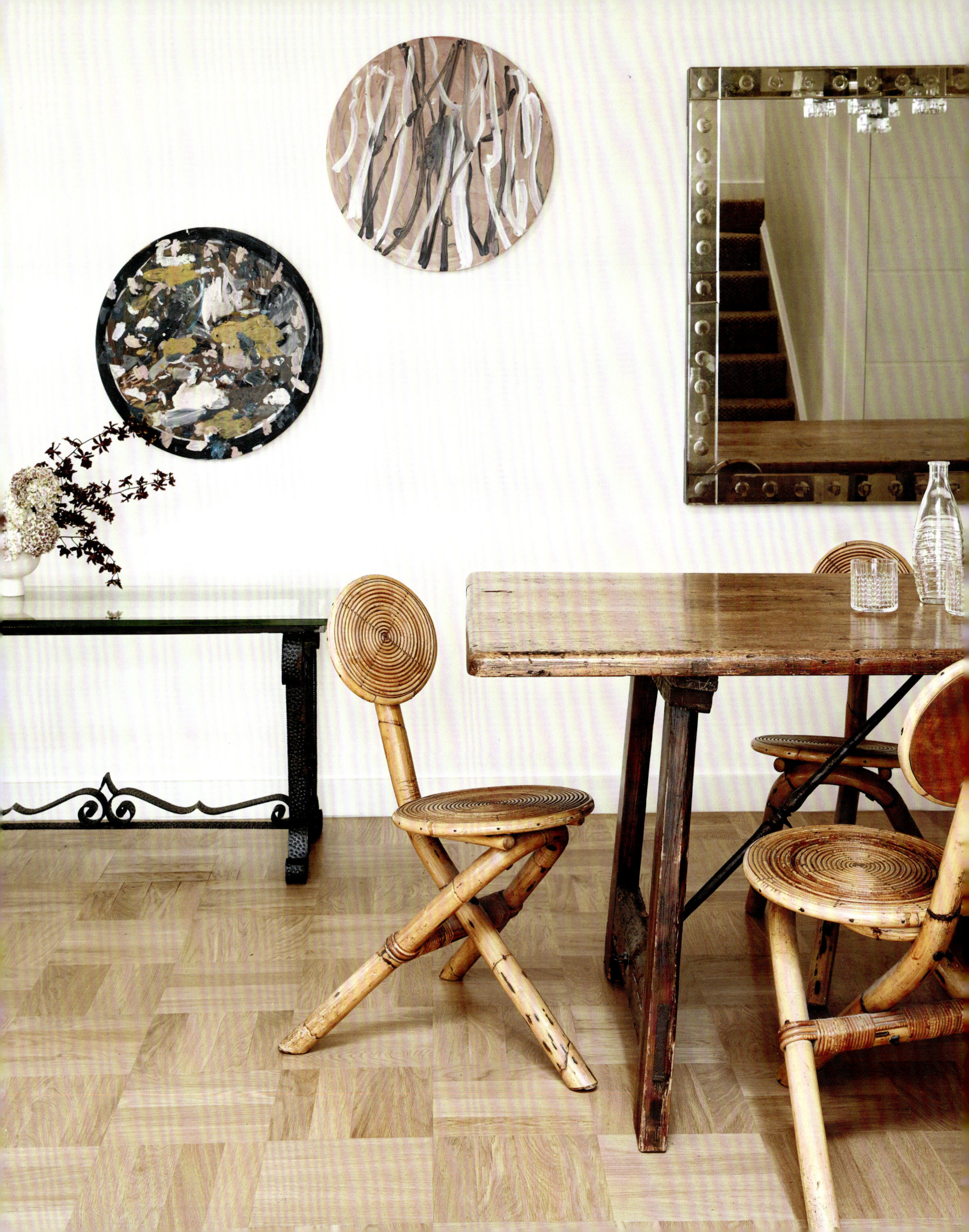

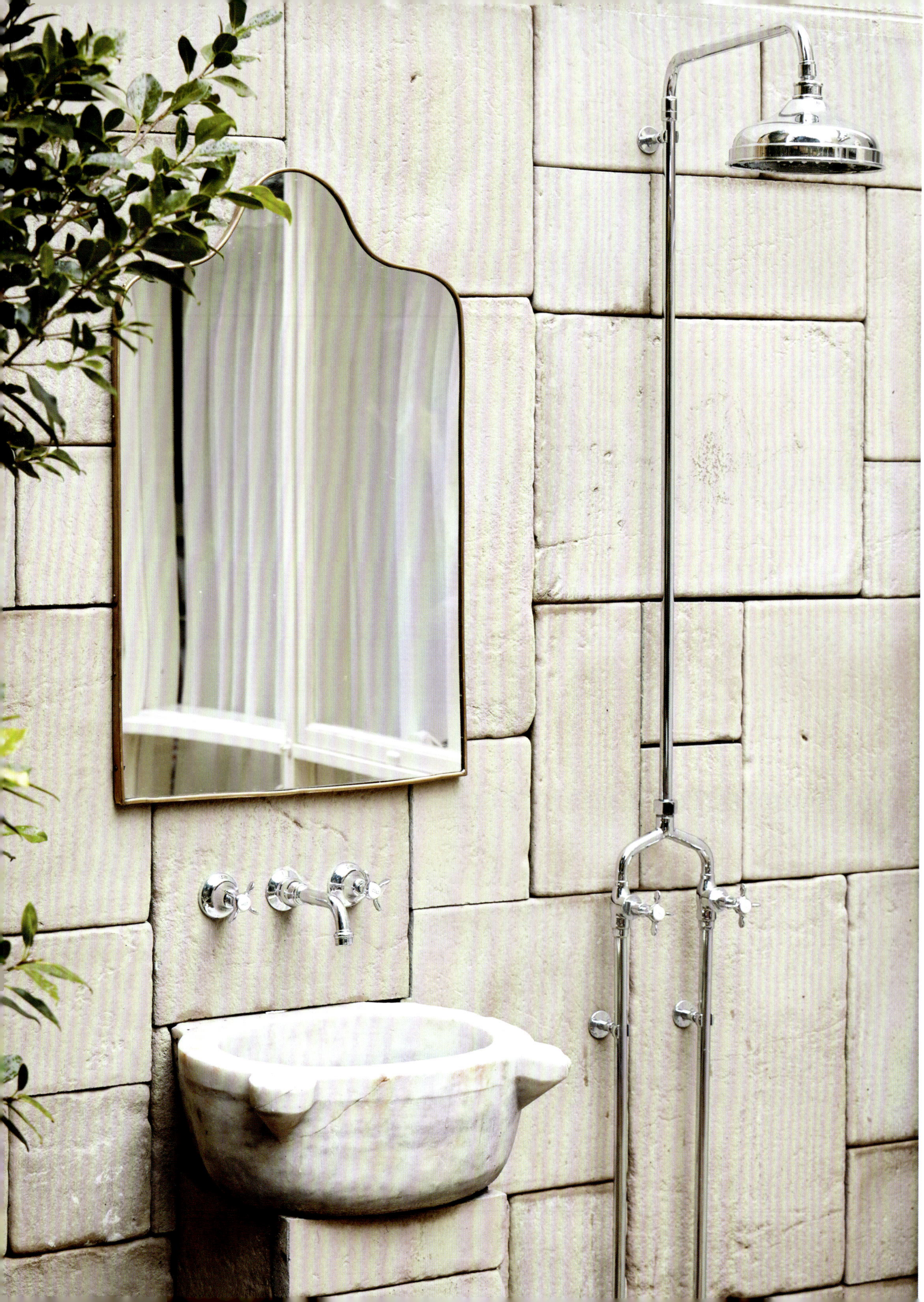

Opposite - The outdoor shower and powder room (above) both feature antique Turkish basins.

Above - In the master bedroom, a mid-twentieth-century lamp, an old family piece, sits under an artwork by Ken Done.
Opposite - The steel-framed window was one of the new additions intended to enhance light flow.

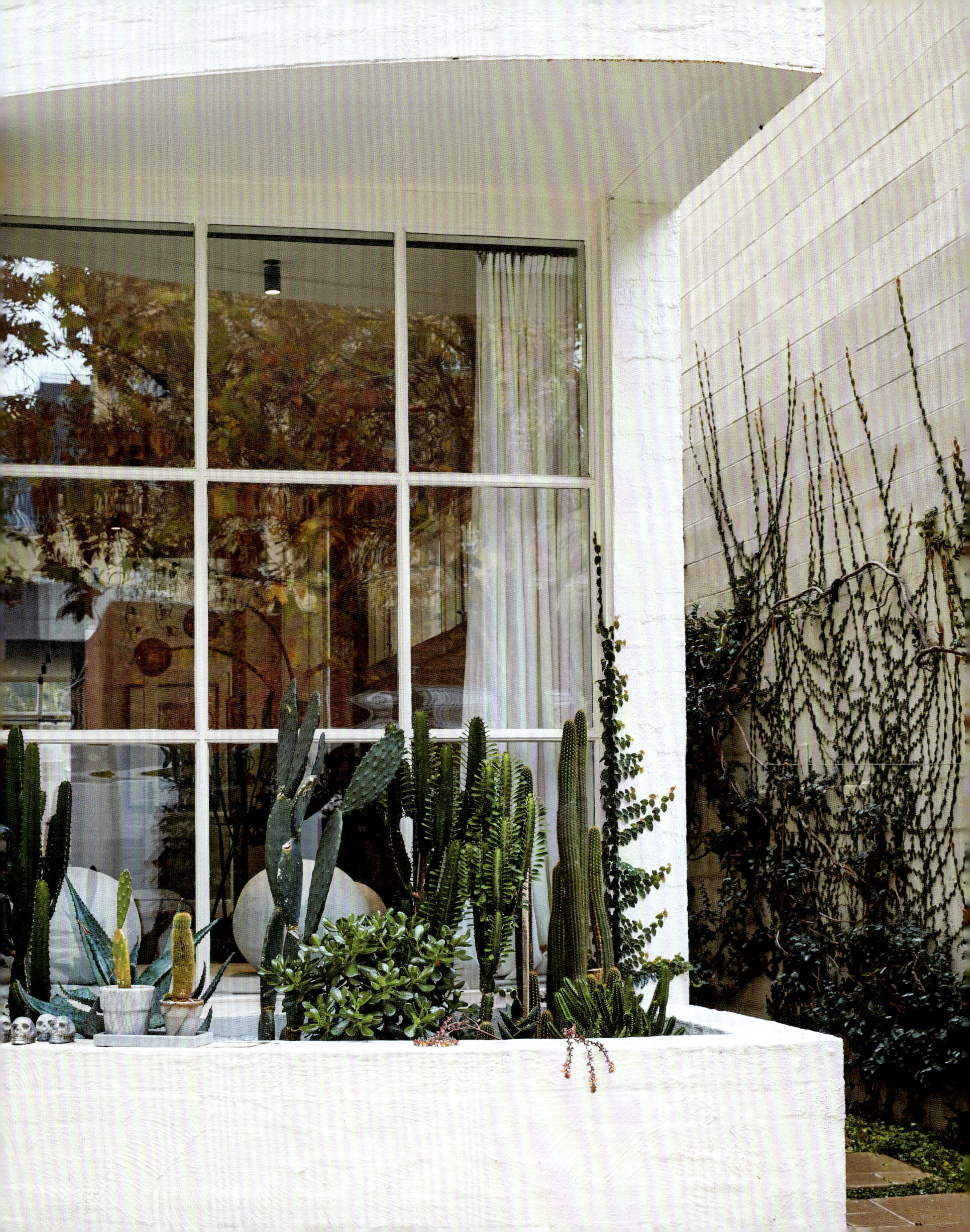

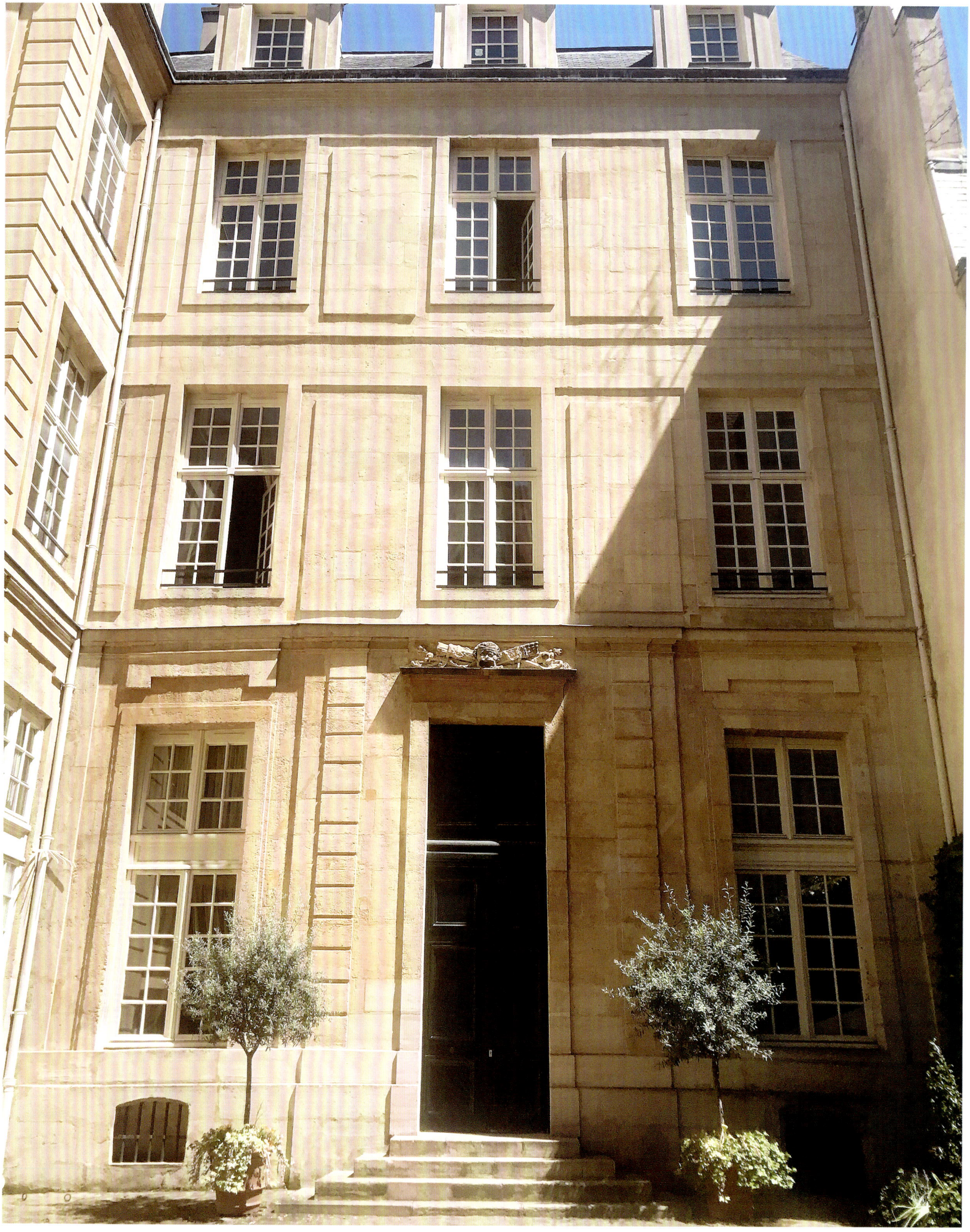

PIED À TERRE

Rue des Tournelles,
Le Marais, Paris

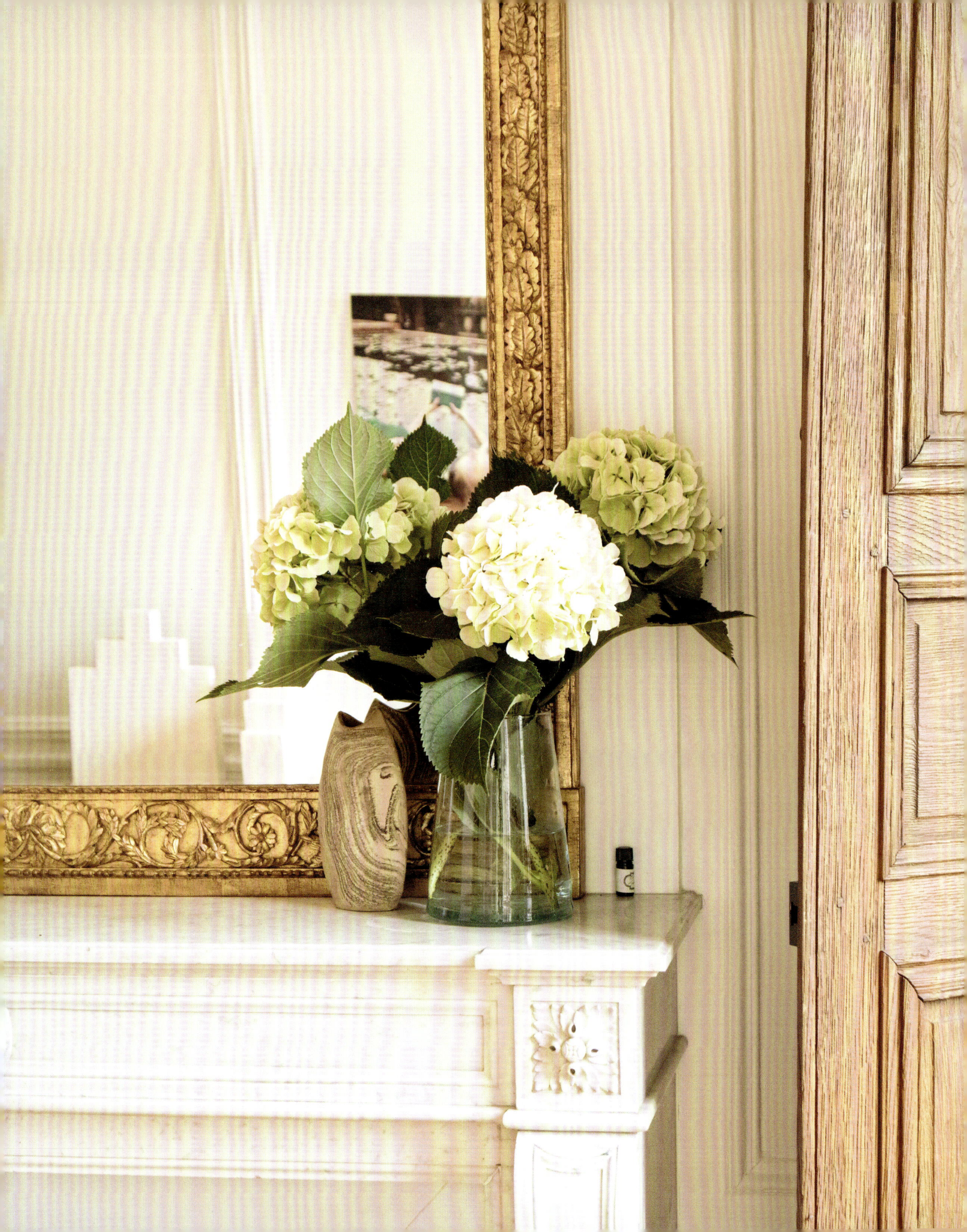

p. 146 - The beautiful internal courtyard shows the seventeenth-century building's architectural details.

Opposite - A nineteenth-century gilt mirror sits above the marble fireplace.
Above - The apartment's impressive entrance, with doors painted in eau de Nil.

150   *Above - The grand stone staircase presents a striking view inside, while pretty views await outside (opposite).*

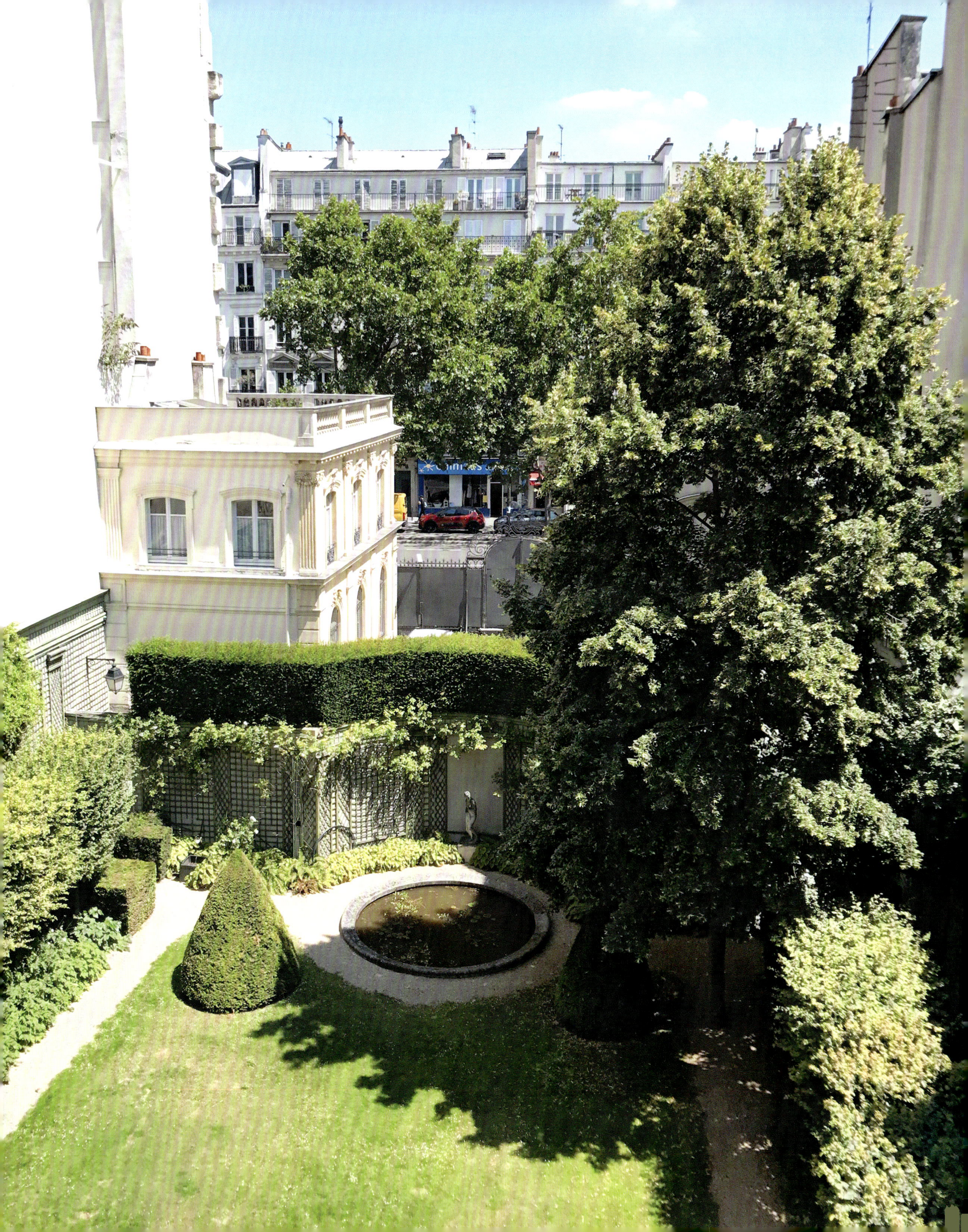

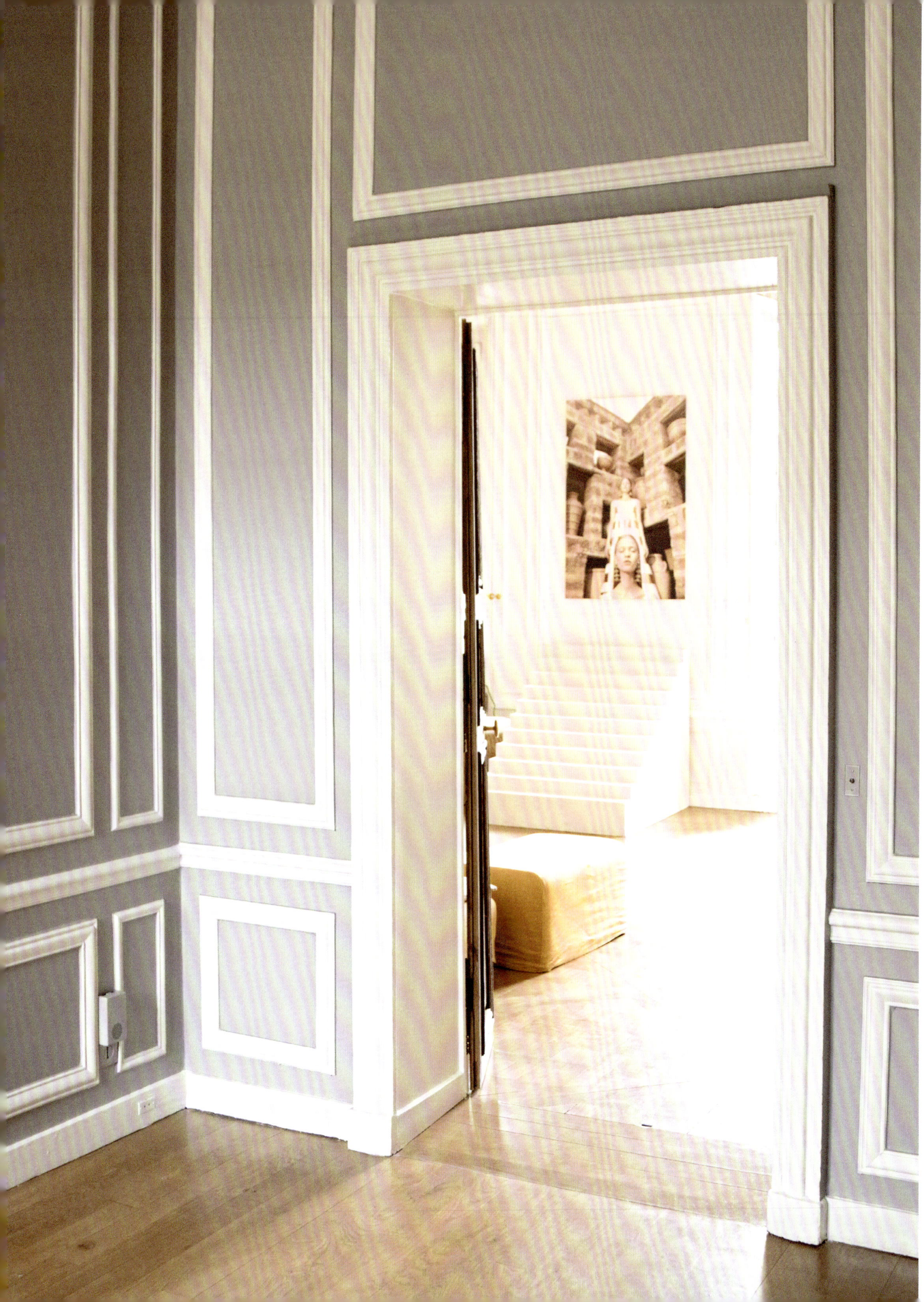

Looking at an ordinary set of dark green doors on a street in the fashionable Paris district of Le Marais, you would never imagine what lies beyond. Step through, and a series of discoveries greet you, each more fabulous than the last. First, a breathtaking internal courtyard, where a pair of olive trees frame the façade of a seventeenth-century building rich in architectural detail. Then inside, a spectacular staircase built on the grand scale, its stone treads over six feet wide! On the third floor, beneath a striking marble pediment, a set of double doors painted in eau de Nil open into an exquisite apartment featuring lofty ceilings, marble fireplaces, and hand-painted murals.

It is here that my friend Lucy Folk, jewelry, accessories, and fashion designer, was based for a few years, drawing on the inspiration of her setting while she shaped her own wearable works of art. The building was designed by Jules Hardouin-Mansart, who became chief architect to Louis XIV and created such icons as the Place Vendôme and the Grand Trianon at the Palace of Versailles. Originally Mansart's house, it was restored and transformed into apartments but retains most of its original features as well as such nineteenth-century additions as the murals. Layered with history and abounding in beauty, it seems a fitting place to nurture creative pursuits. Lucy's style is one of relaxed luxury, with a passion for the hand-crafted, the unconventional, the fun and colorful. When she asked me to help her decorate the apartment, I wanted to honor her aesthetic with a range of pieces that were full of personality yet minimalist enough to work in such an ornate setting. The furnishings comprised finds from local artisans, markets, and stores, treasures acquired on travels, and one-of-a-kind investment items. This was not a "forever" home, but rather one chapter in an ongoing story, and so the intention was to build up an amazing collection that Australian-born Lucy could take with her wherever she lives.

Rather than attempting to blur the line between the old and the new, I opted for twentieth-century pieces, embracing the contrast they bring and the way they give a fresh burst of energy to the apartment.

Opposite - Paneled walls in soft gray and white contribute to the apartment's elegant look. The stepped plinth in the background is one of several we commissioned to display Lucy's designs during showings. Even bare of accessories, its Venetian plaster finish and sculptural beauty work with the apartment's décor.

Above and opposite - A mustard-colored sofa and pink cushion make a vibrant welcoming statement in the living area, with an iconic Vignelli coffee table and little vintage side table adding their own bold blend of line and form.

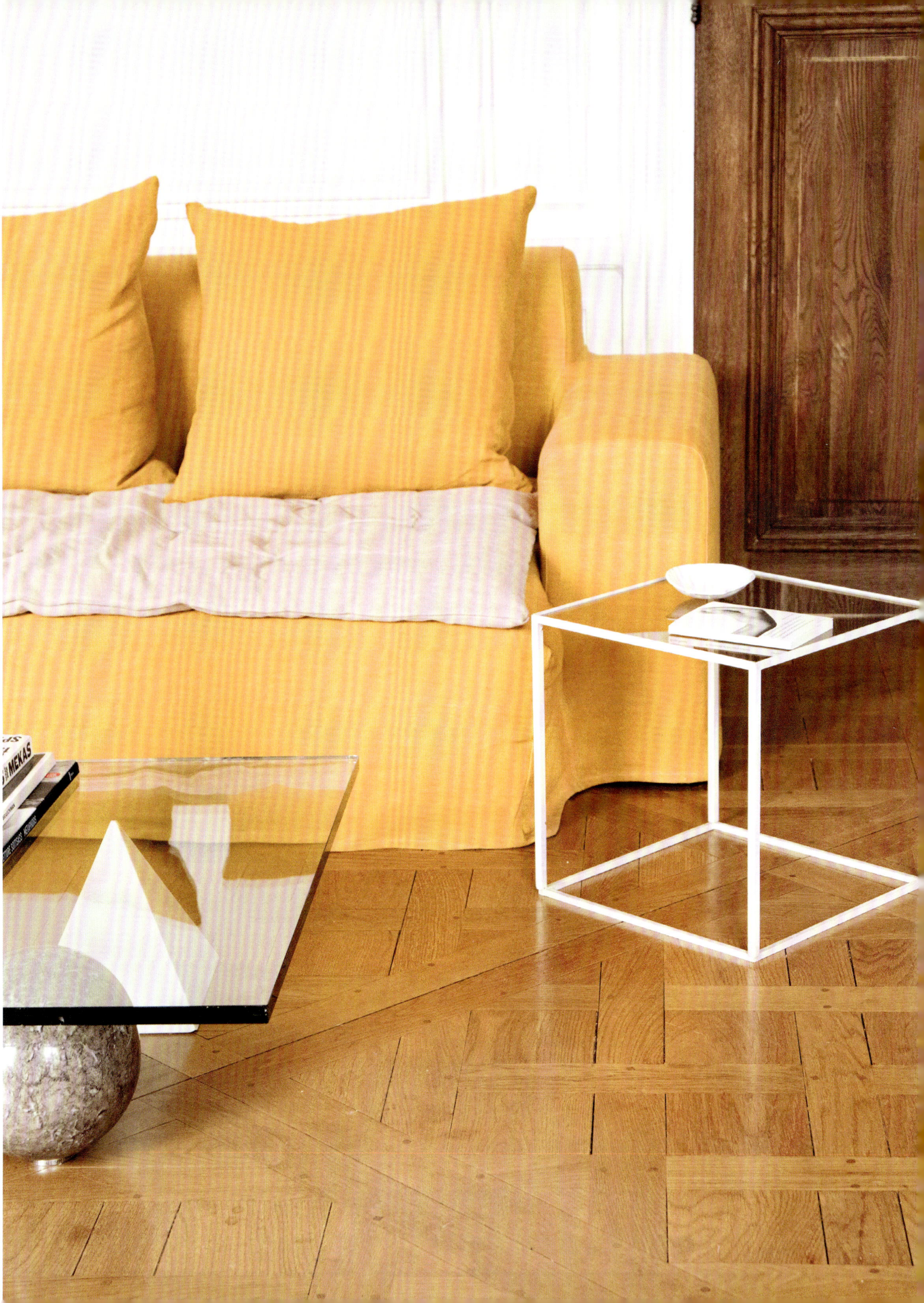
MEKAS

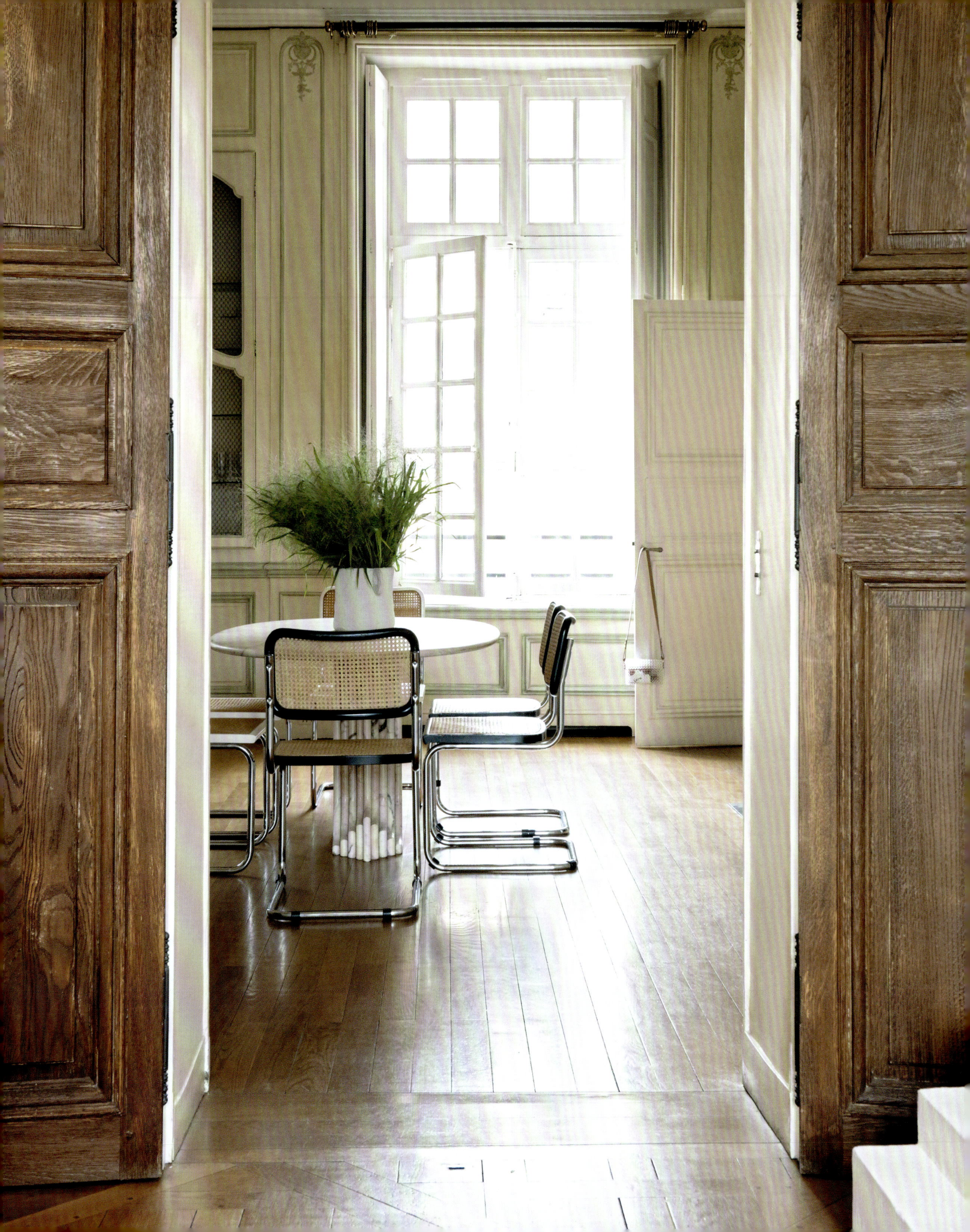

There's an almost deceptive simplicity to the furniture in the living area, with its defined shapes and bold lines. The generous form of a mustard-hued sofa, which caught our eye in the window of a nearby store, brings a sunny block of color to the space. A custom-made muddy pink cushion on top breaks up the expanse of yellow, with the two forming a heavenly color combination that is often used in Lucy's designs. In front of this, a 1979 glass-topped coffee table by legendary Italian designers Lella and Massimo Vignelli is a study in form and geometry, with each solid marble leg in a different shape. A small vintage metal and glass side table delivers its own light touch and completes this contemporary vignette in the classic space. Surrounded by the beautiful hand-painted walls of the dining room, more furniture takes pride of place, with the sculptural beauty of a Carlo Scarpa marble dining table offset by Marcel Breuer rattan cane chairs—three with black frames, three with white frames. The cantilevered chrome legs of the chairs present a fluid line against the table's more substantial base, with the setting bringing an edgy, modern vigor to the space. It's crucial to me that interior designs are as sympathetic to the lifestyle and individuality of the client as they are to the surroundings. These iconic pieces of furniture showcase their creators' dedication to their craft, yet they're also loved and livable objects that are a functional part of Lucy's everyday world. In this way, life and art have been intertwined throughout the apartment.

As well as home, the place served as a creative studio and sometime showroom, with buyers from key stores visiting during every fashion week to view Lucy's designs. In response to this, I wanted to ensure the layout conveyed a sense of openness and ease, where all are welcome and everything is on show and appealingly accessible. We commissioned a local set maker to construct a series of lightweight plinths in order to display jewelry, sunglasses, and other accessories during showings. Inspired by the sculptures of Constantin Brâncuși, these stepped pyramidal forms have been hand-layered in Venetian plaster for a luxurious finish. Even unadorned, they seem to both contrast with and complement the parquet floor and paneled walls, becoming beautifully integrated into the apartment's interior décor. Similarly, a set of built-in oak shelves in the guest bedroom provides a handy neutral backdrop for showcasing fashion pieces as well as personal objets d'art.

A mélange of pieces throughout the apartment pay tribute to Lucy's nomadic spirit and passion for hand-crafted designs. Like the pink cushion on the sofa in the living room, the floor-to-ceiling curtains that frame some windows were custom-made by the same Marrakech atelier who dyes and weaves her clothing designs. Other treasured items were acquired on forays closer to home, such as a stout vintage rattan ottoman (one of a pair) and an old oil painting, both from the local Paul Bert Serpette antiques market. The very first pieces to grace the apartment were a pair of classic bistro chairs from a nearby store, which Lucy and I carried back on foot for several blocks in the middle of a steamy Parisian summer. They join the happy mix of décor that celebrates the life of this apartment, joyfully proclaiming that here is a place for discovery, inspiration, and boundless creativity.

Opposite and overleaf - Marcel Breuer chairs and a Carlo Scarpa dining table present a striking setting of contemporary minimalism against the elaborate hand-painted walls of the dining room.

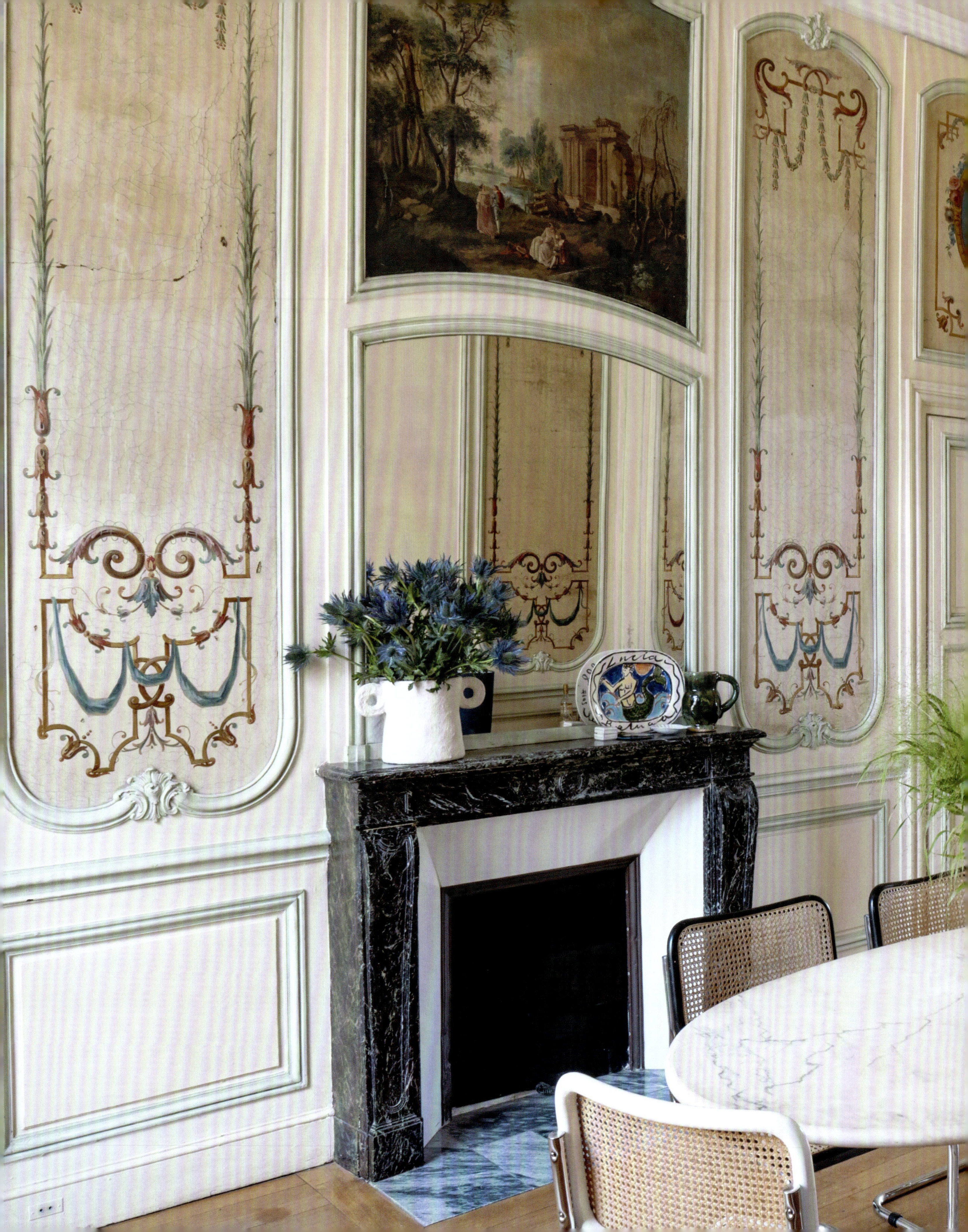

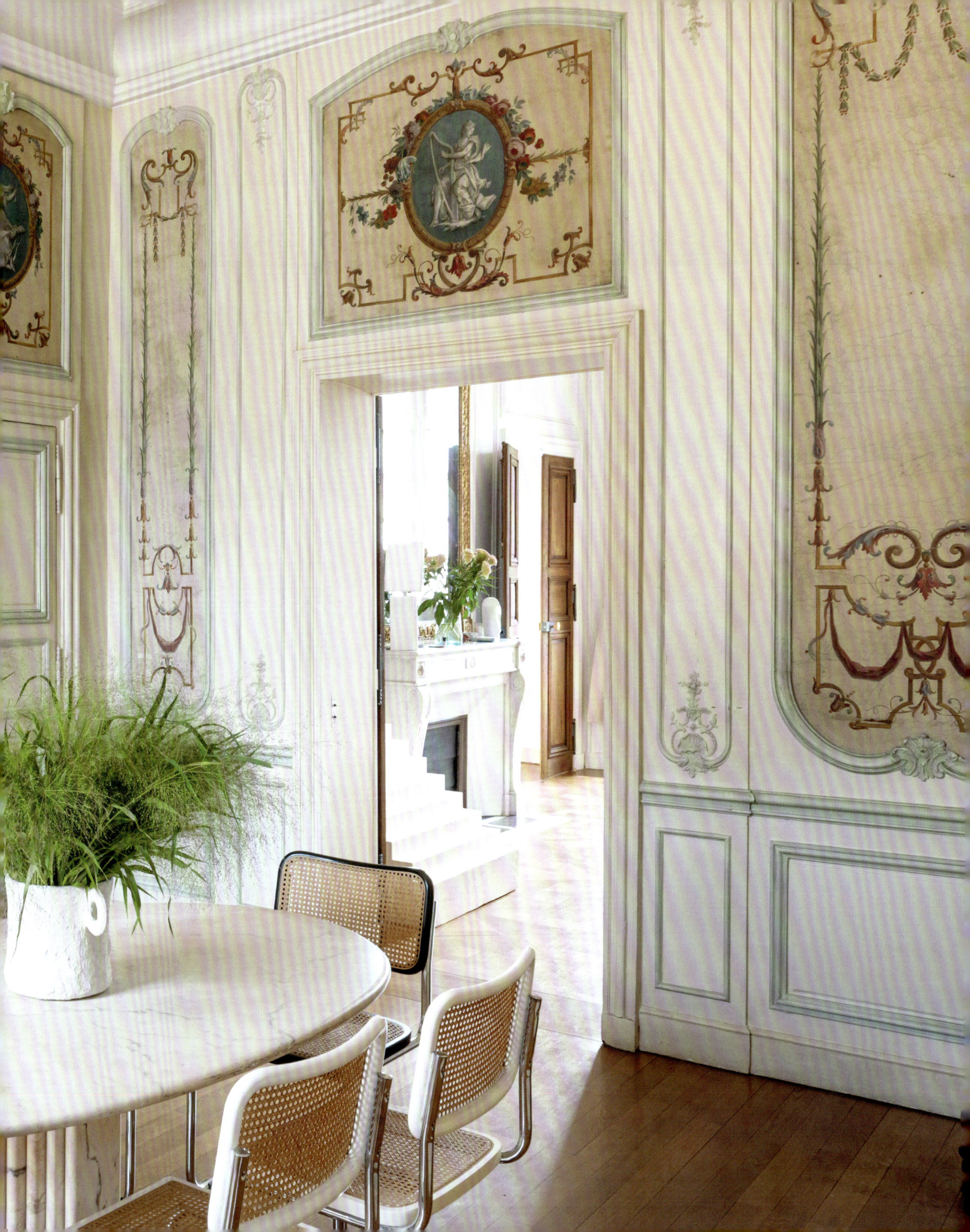

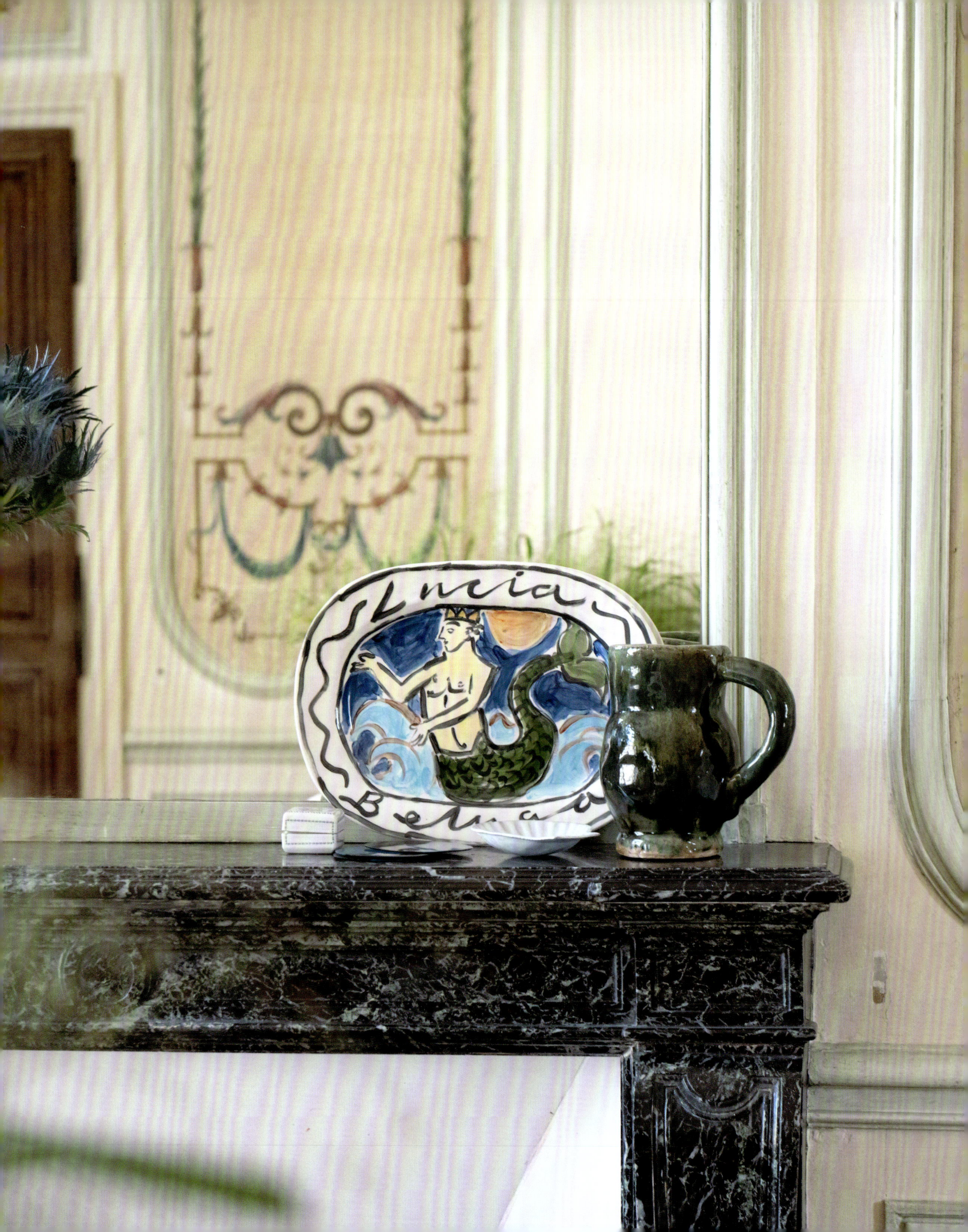
Lucia

Opposite - Ceramics from a local vendor adorn the marble fireplace.
Above - The bistro chairs, which Lucy and I hauled through the streets of Le Marais, were the first pieces in the apartment.

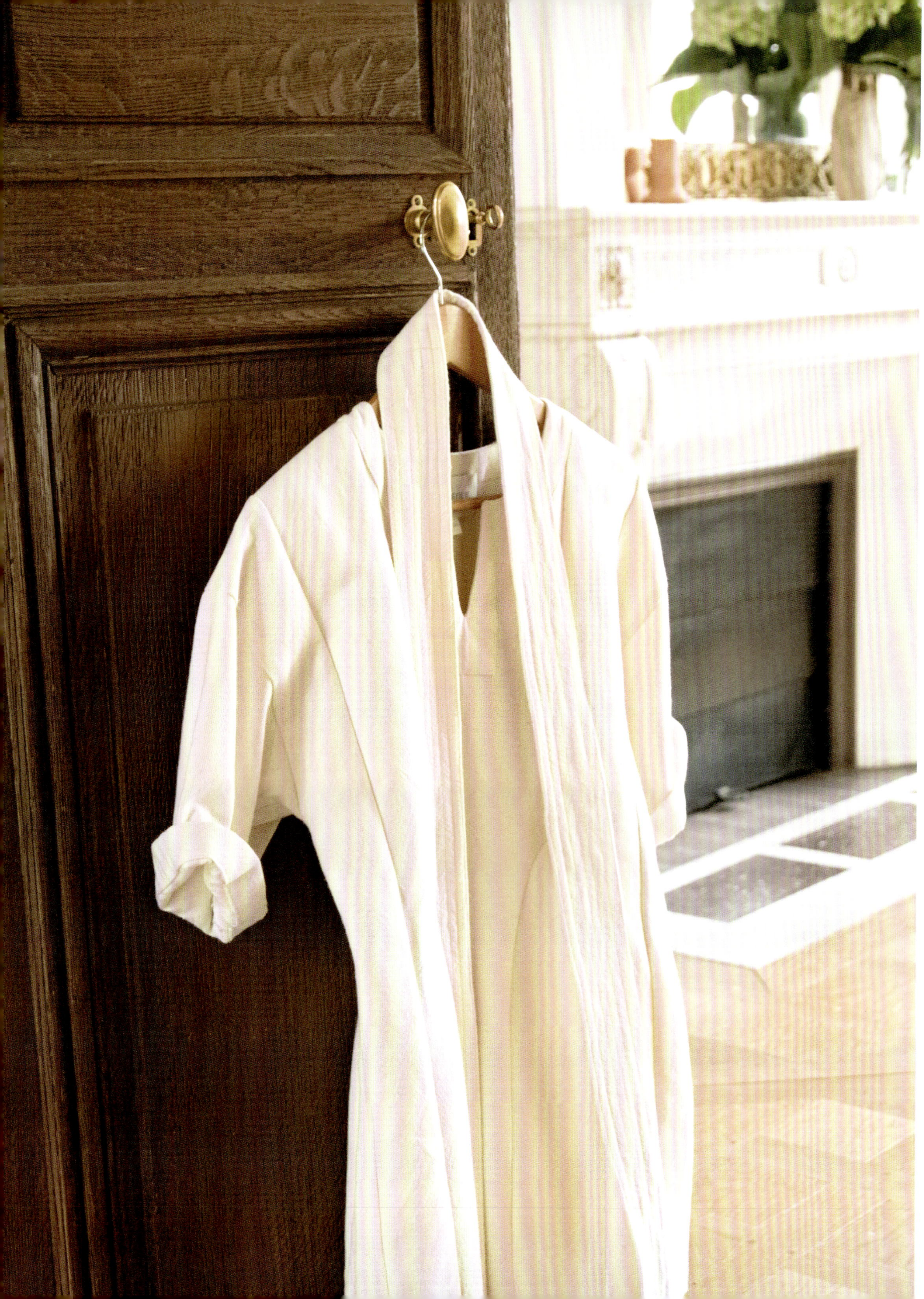

Opposite - One of Lucy's designs hangs invitingly on the door of the guest bedroom (my bedroom, as I came to think of it).
Above - More market finds in the living area: the rattan ottoman and oil painting, with a retro-style speaker.

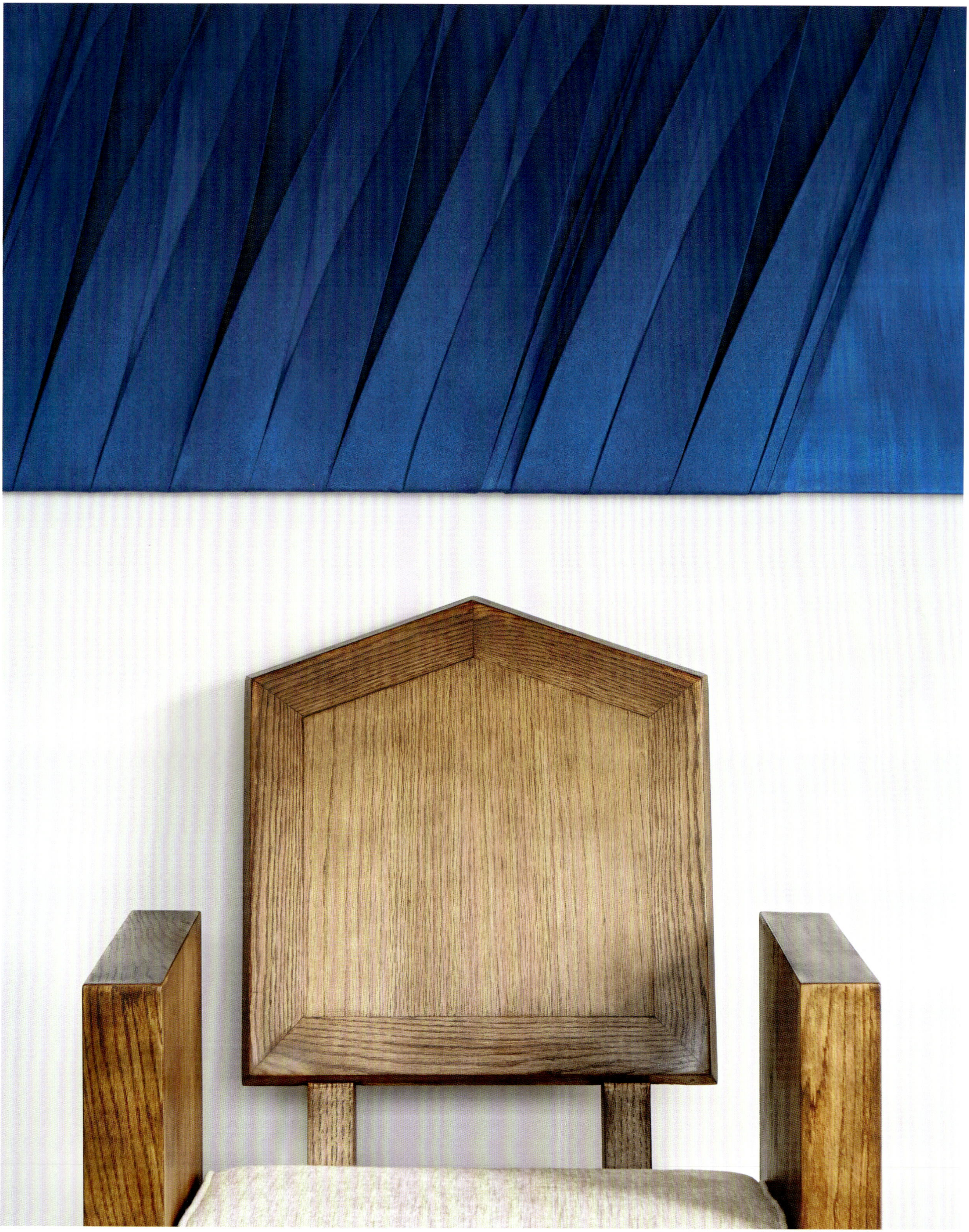

CAPSULE

Irving Place,
Gramercy Park, New York

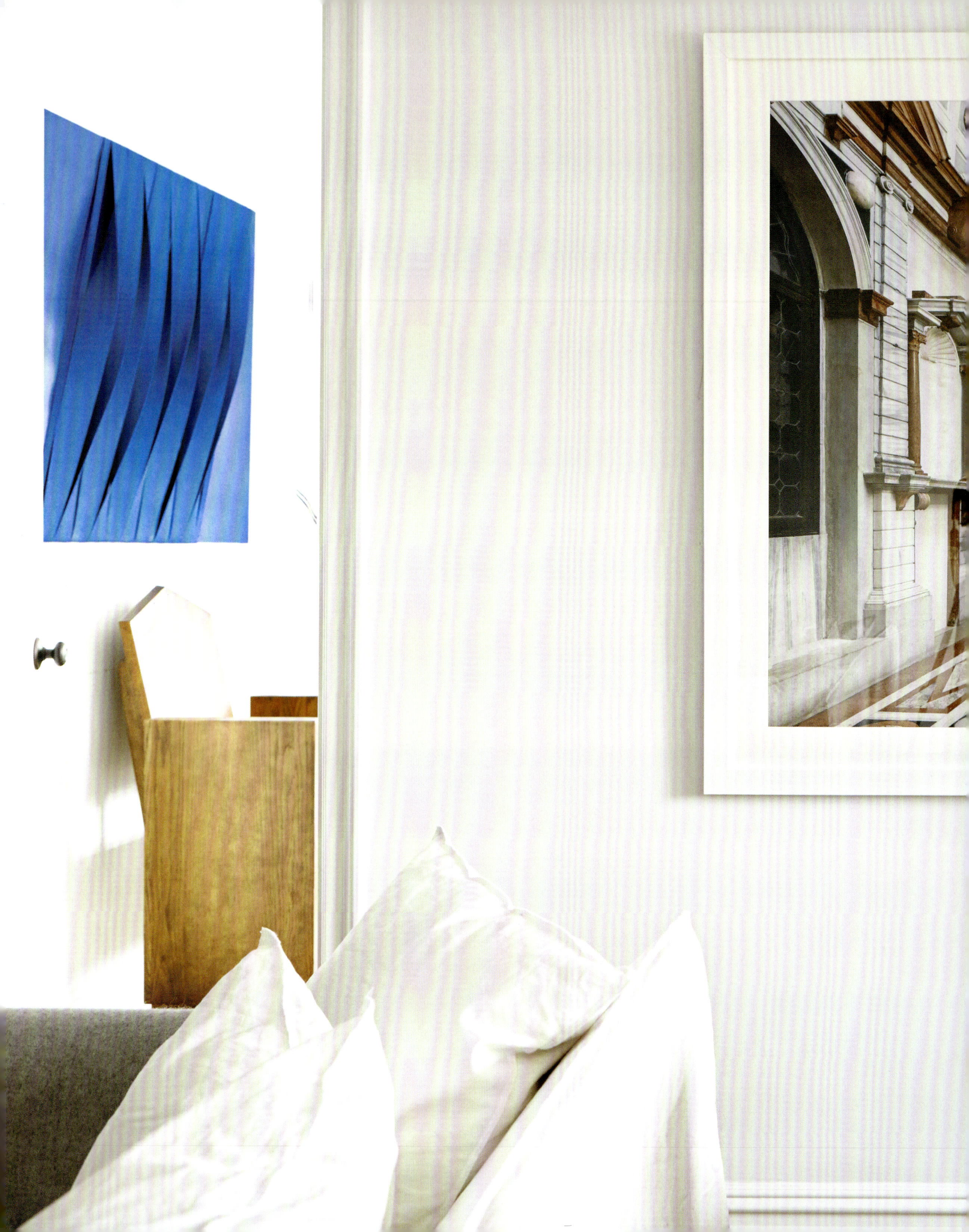

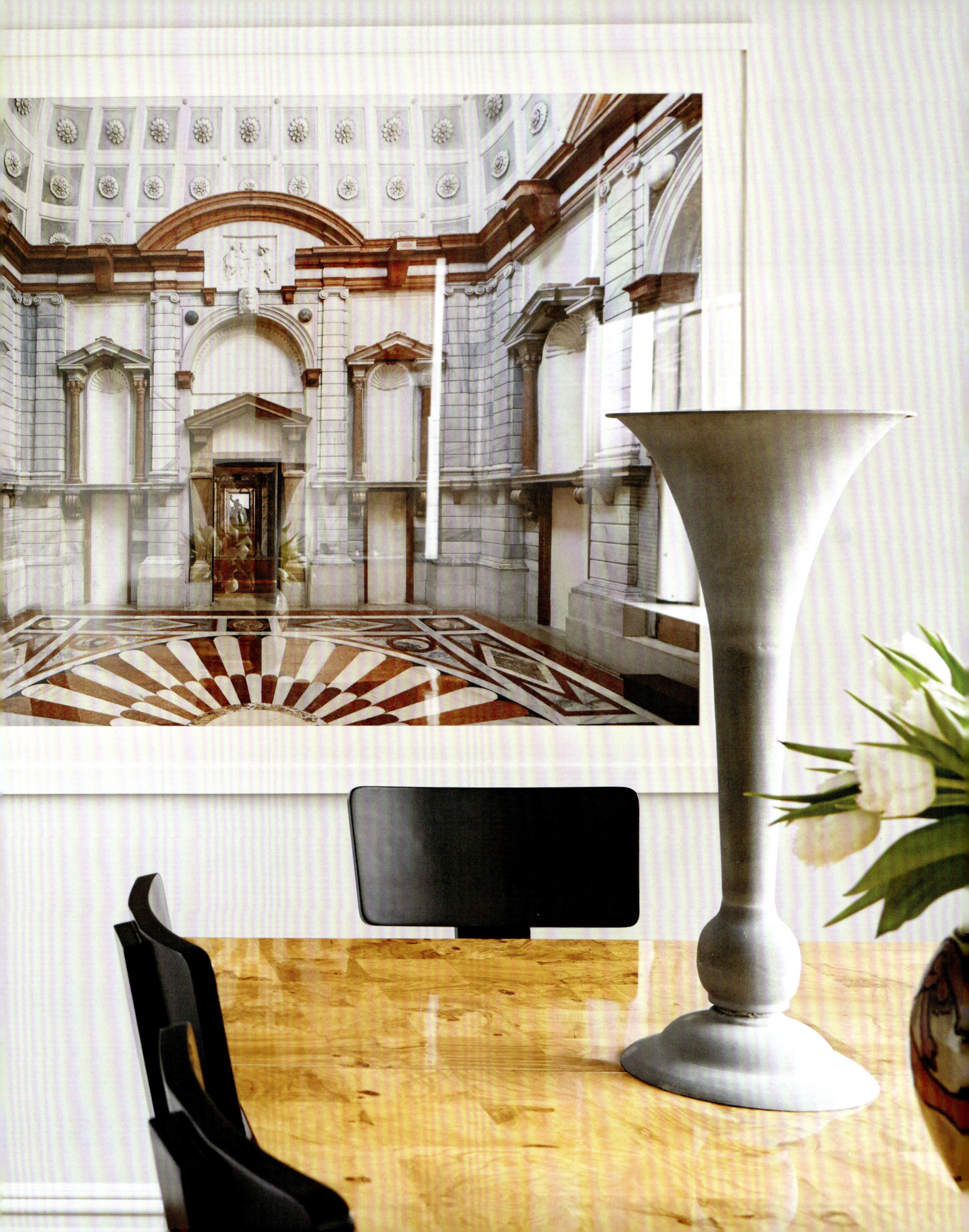

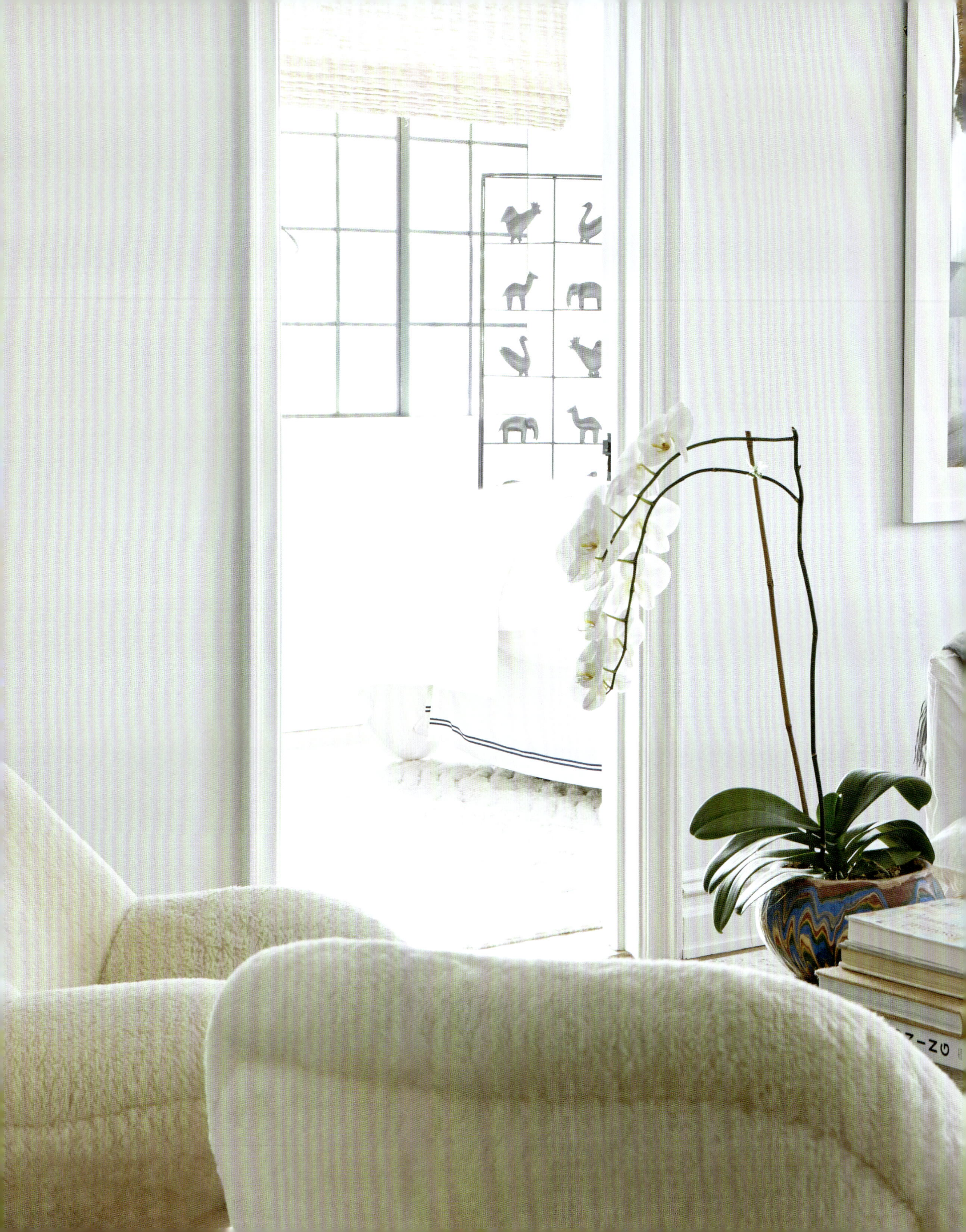

The Essential Cy Twombly
PETER BEARD
RUDOLF STINGEL
AXEL VERVOORDT

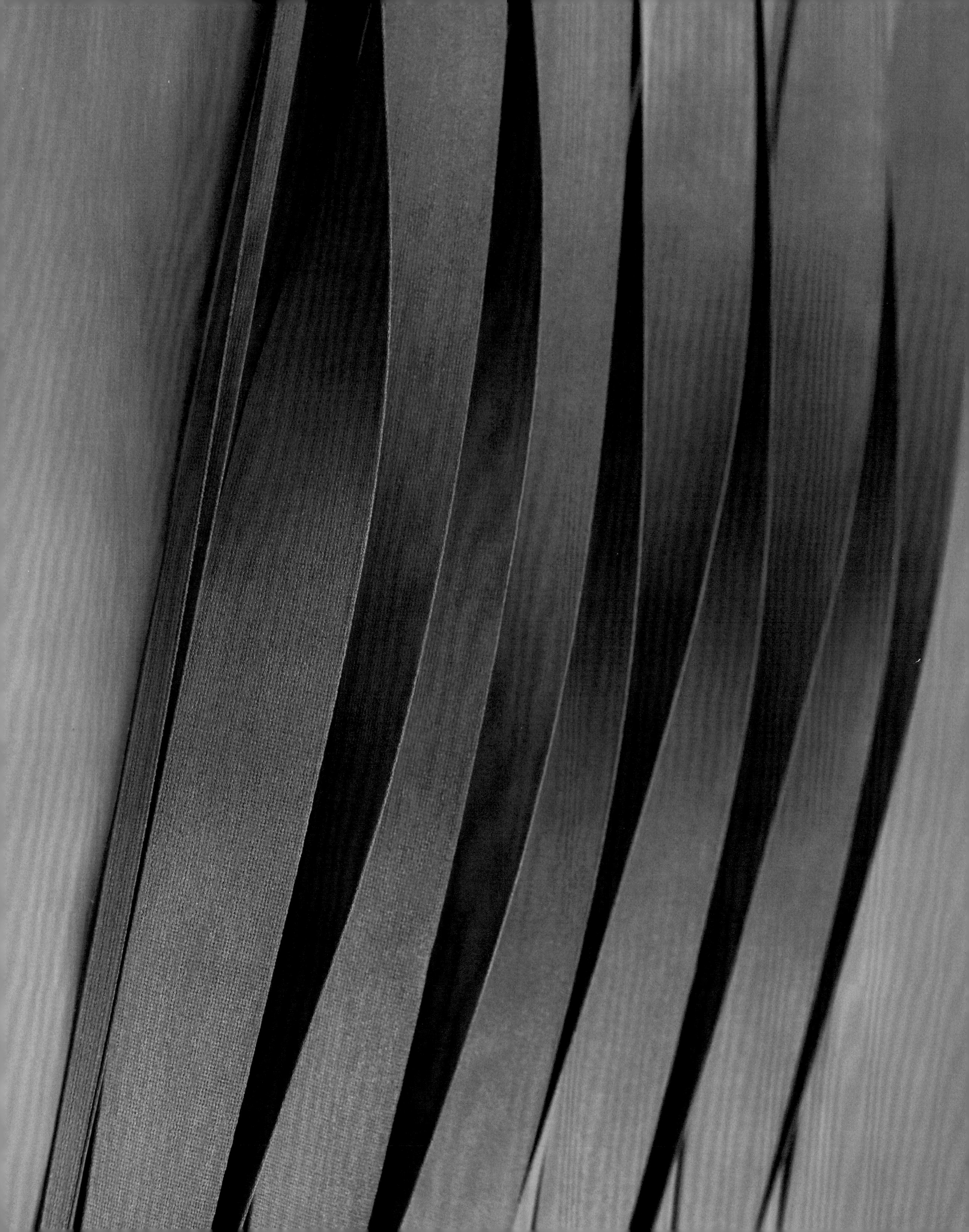

When your passion and profession involve the sourcing of beautiful pieces to create memorable interiors, there is something incredibly liberating about having the opportunity to start from scratch in your own place. At the beginning of our year's sojourn in New York, Patrick and I arrived with just a suitcase full of clothes and total freedom to furnish our apartment however we chose—once we found an apartment. We were there to set up a showroom for Patrick's tailoring business, which at the time had locations in Sydney and Melbourne, and was ready to grow in order to meet overseas demand. We'd signed the lease on a space in SoHo for the showroom and, after an uninspiring stint of short stays and rental viewings, we found a one-bedroom apartment in peaceful Gramercy Park that suited us perfectly. The place was small but full of light, with freshly painted white walls, oak floors, great city views, and gargoyles perched on the building's exterior.

Early purchases were obviously practical yet still considered. First was a bed, which we dressed in an Egyptian cotton set by Olatz Schnabel—its swathe of white with a thin black trim presents a crisp, calming picture in the tiny bedroom. Then a white cotton Gervasoni sofa-bed for the living area—we knew that during our time there we'd have a procession of friends and family coming to stay, so a fold-out was a must. After that, some comforts to prepare for the New York winter such as cashmere throws and a Moroccan Berber-style wool rug. And to complete the backdrop, some sets of rattan blinds, which we commissioned to be made for the windows, an unusual request for a New York interior, we were told. We were also having blinds made for the showroom, which was being furnished at the same time. In contrast to the plethora in New York of club-style men's tailors that feature antique leather sofas and mahogany tables, we wanted the interior of Patrick's showroom to reflect the brand's relaxed approach to tailoring and to evoke a certain Australian lightness of spirit. The idea was for the place to feel like an escape from the intensity and bustle of the city, offering a serene, almost Zen-like atmosphere, and that concept carried over to our home as well.

p. 164 - A timber chair in the style of Frank Lloyd Wright, one of a pair, provides an appealing austerity of line.
pp. 166–67 - The view of a Venetian palazzo, by photographer Reinhard Görner, presides over the contemporary dining setting. The zinc plinth was one of a pair we discovered in an antiques store upstate and would later find a new home with a client of mine back in Australia.
Previous spread - White tones in the living area suit the apartment's tranquil Zen vibe.

Opposite - A detail of a blue twisted canvas by Pino Manos.

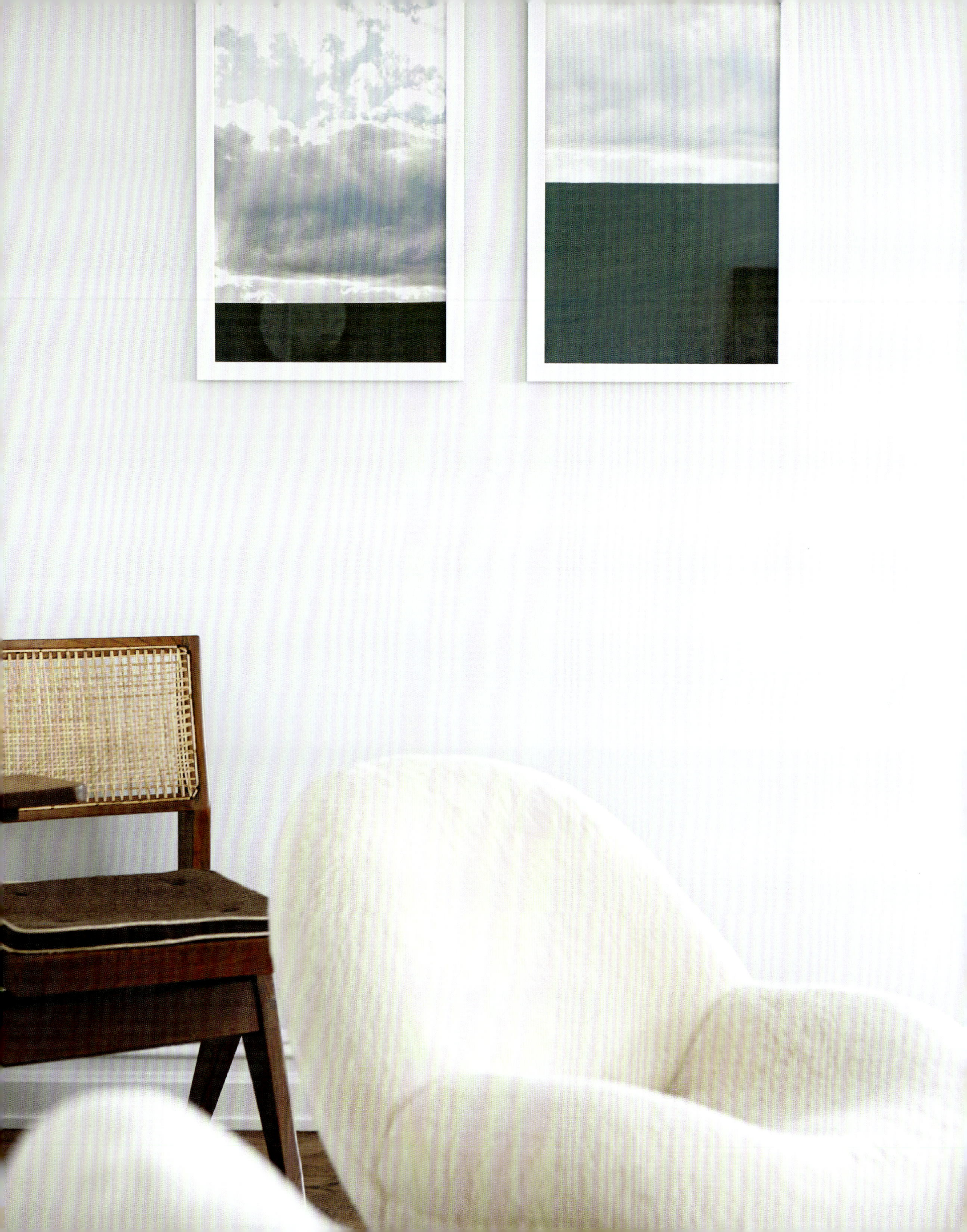

So we set out to create our own little New York story, imbuing the apartment with a fresh, clean aesthetic that packs a punch through the character and quality of its pieces. Our aim was to acquire a core collection of furniture and art that we could bring home with us afterwards. To source some pieces, we pursued avenues established through our professional lives, contacting dealers with whom I was working in Los Angeles to have furniture shipped to New York, and buying art from auction houses. For others, we pounded the actual avenues of our adopted city, browsing stores, museums, and galleries as well as scouring local vintage shops, a rewarding activity at any time. Some of our antiques were bought on trips we took upstate to Hudson, known for its amazing antiques stores. A pair of tall, sculptural zinc plinths accompanied us on the two-hour-long train trip back to Gramercy Park, together with a stack of fabulous glassware and cutlery. An antiques center in the Flatiron district introduced us to an eye-catching wrought-iron screen that, to me, recalls the playful style of Jean Royère. It is at once childish and sophisticated, and I love the drama of its negative space as much as its witty black silhouettes. These pair well with the black steel-framed windows of our bedroom, offering a striking contrast in the predominantly white space. Mid-twentieth-century furniture contributes much to the layout, with its minimalist lines and natural materials. Among the pieces sourced from Los Angeles are a teak and rattan cane Pierre Jeanneret writing chair and a Milo Baughman dining table with a warm veneer, which I teamed with Nickey Kehoe chairs custom-made in ebonized timber with tan leather seats. The various wood tones give a warmth to the interior that is further enhanced by a pair of rather clunky 1930s wooden chairs I discovered in New York. They're designed in the style of Frank Lloyd Wright and while you couldn't call them beautiful, there is something almost monastic about their plain, unusual shape that harmonizes with the contemplative mood of the apartment. The array of artworks, a mix of abstract art and photography, enhances that mood. While I will always love the romantic layers of heavily brushed oil paintings, they wouldn't have been appropriate for the pared-back contemporary aesthetic we were trying to achieve here. In the same way that those chairs produce a special moment out of simplicity, a pair of landscape photographs by American artist Danelle Manthey takes an everyday subject and transforms it. The pictures are of fields and clouds, but with their intense tonality and shifting viewpoint, they both make you feel as if you are almost lost in a Rothko painting.

We changed the pace on the walls with a couple of vividly hued artworks: a red sculpture by Lucio Fontana and a work of blue twisted canvas by Italian artist Pino Manos. Their bold primary colors deliver a strong visual effect in an otherwise subdued palette. Just as impactful for its scale and subject is a picture of the Palazzo Grimani in Venice by German architectural photographer Reinhard Görner, which hangs in the dining area. Its generosity of scale and captivating perspective somehow make the small space feel a lot grander, while its palette of terracotta, pale gray, and white brings vibrancy without dominating. Sitting at the dining table, with the New York cityscape on one side and a Venetian palazzo on the other, it was a powerful reminder that a meaningful interior can merge the wonders of travel with the comforts of home.

Opposite - Our time in New York was spent building a collection of art and furniture that would accompany us home. Here, two deceptively simple landscape photographs by Danelle Manthey present a mesmerizing display.

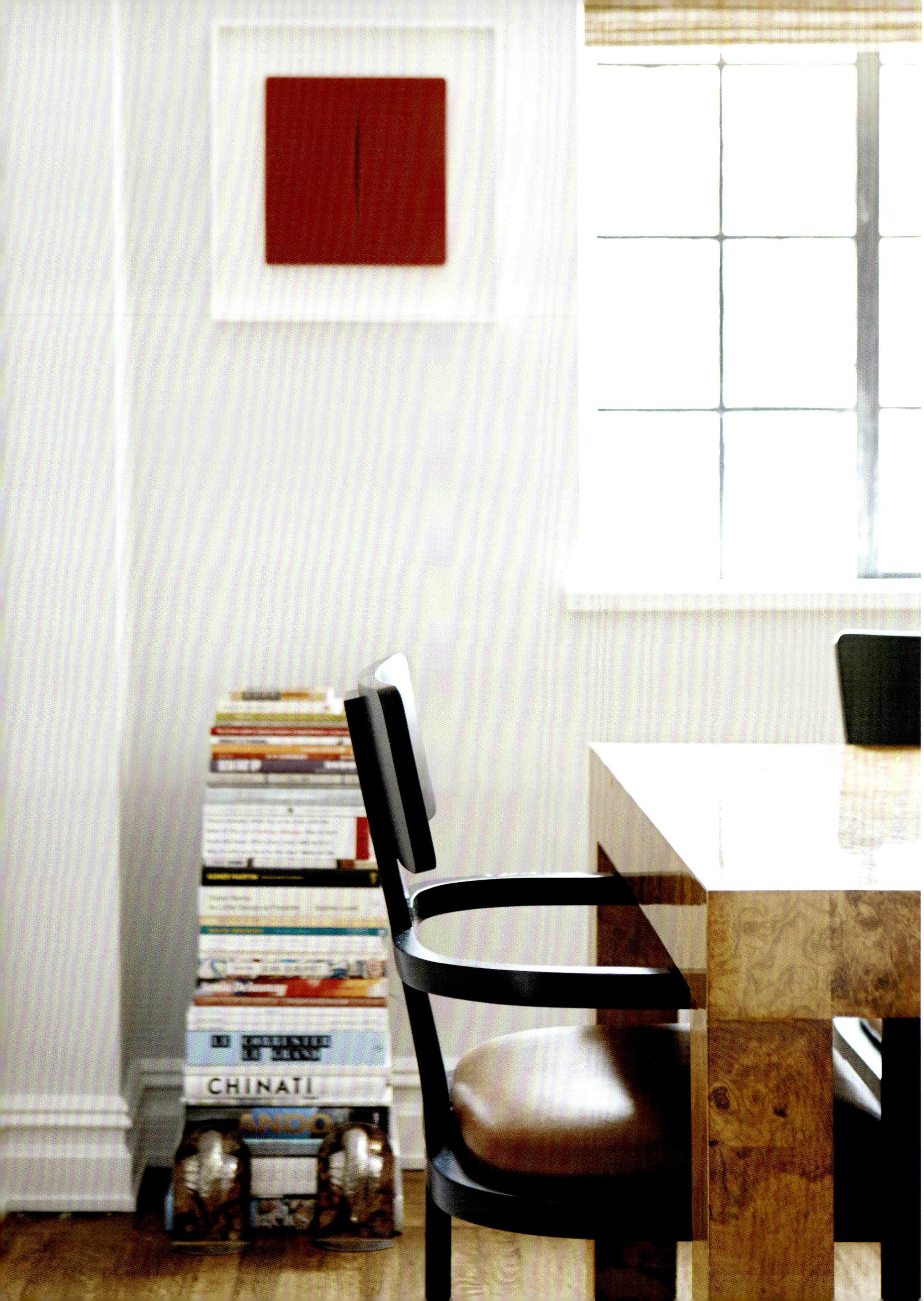

Opposite - Bathed in natural light, the furniture, art and books offer an appealing study in clean lines.
Above - The silhouettes of a black wrought-iron screen bring a playful touch to the bedroom.

175

Above - Black steel-framed windows capture the cityscape outside.

Opposite - In the small bedroom, the slimline lamp base echoes the trim of the bed and the window frames.

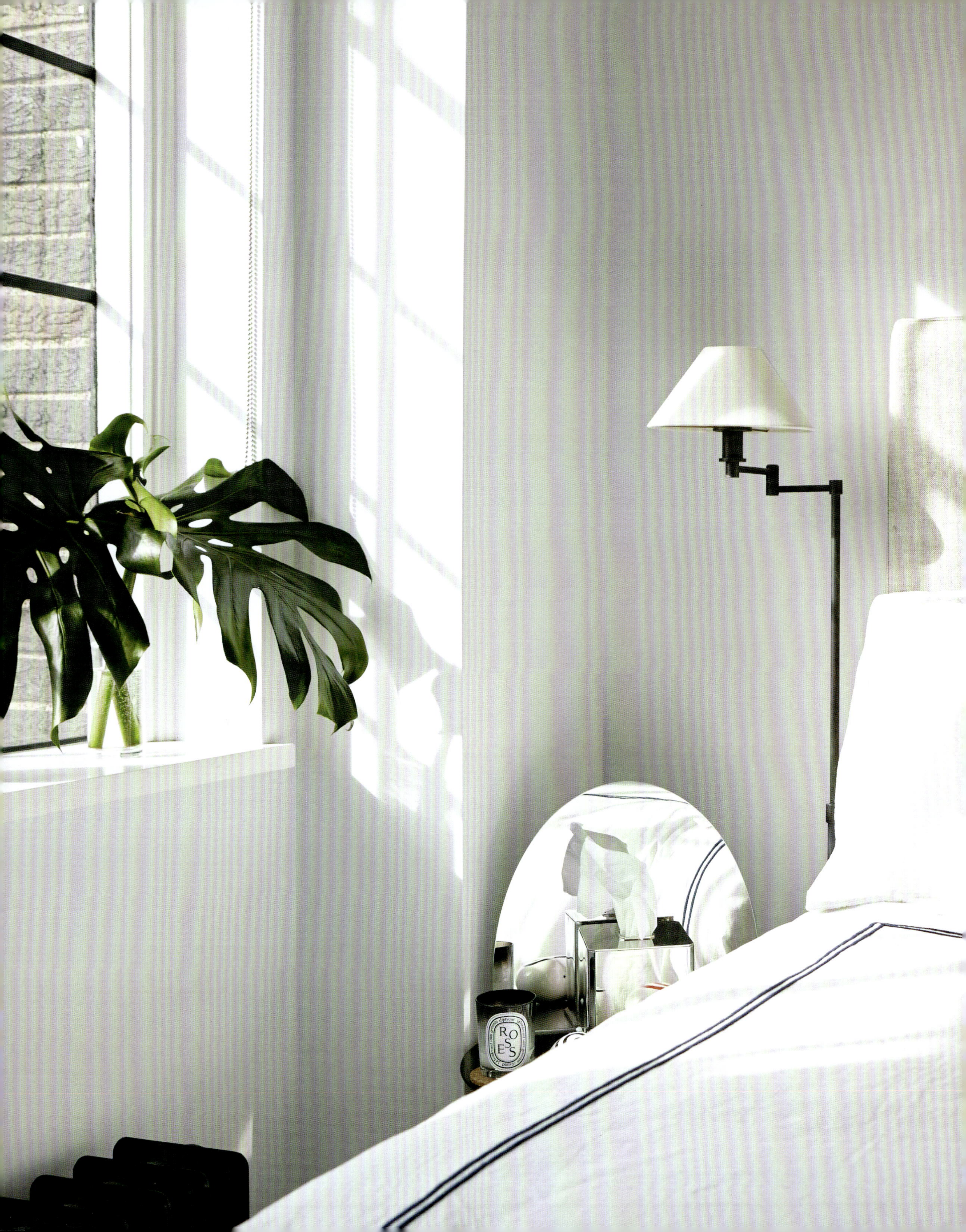
ROSES

TOWN HOUSE

Edgecliff Road,
Woollahra, Sydney

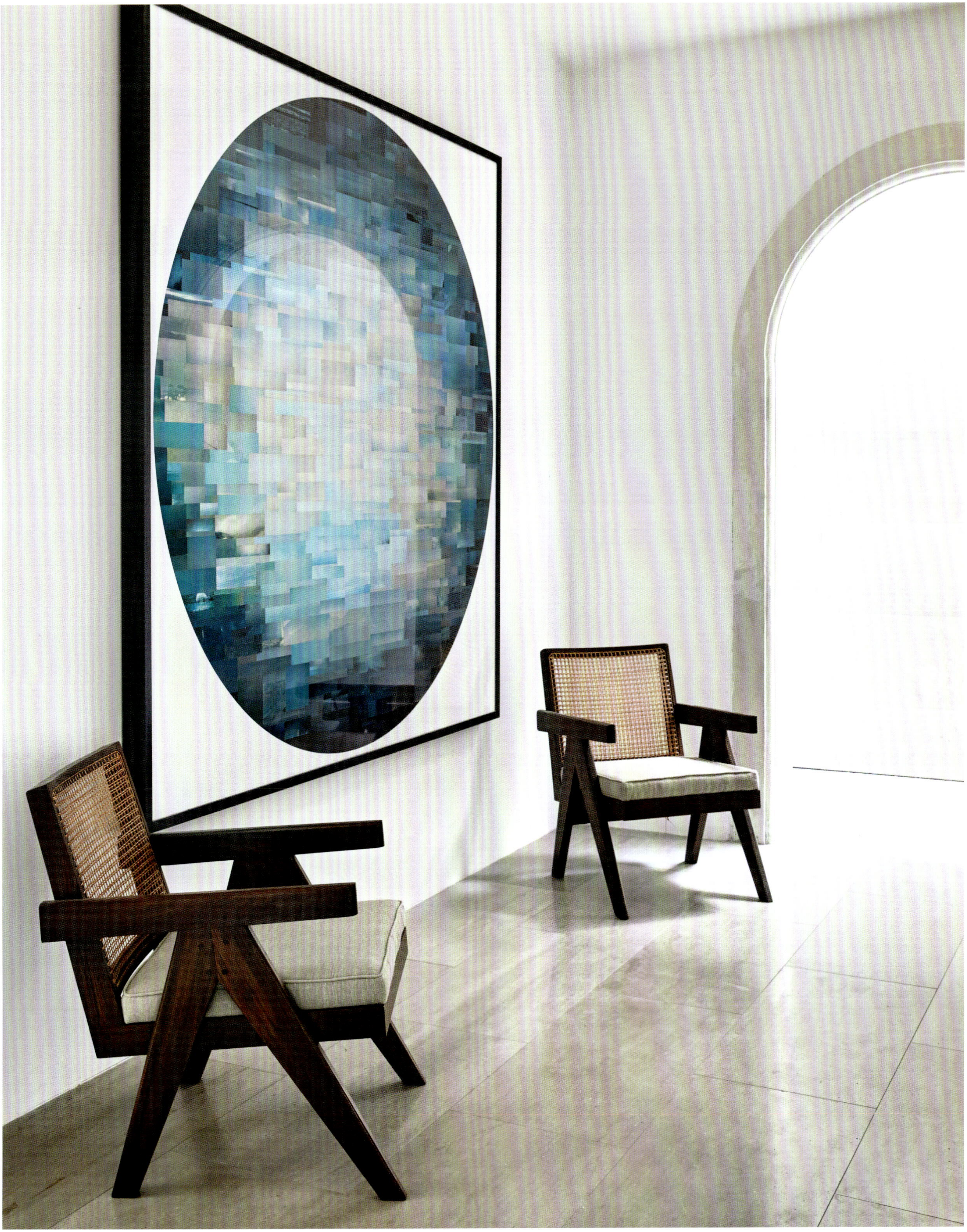

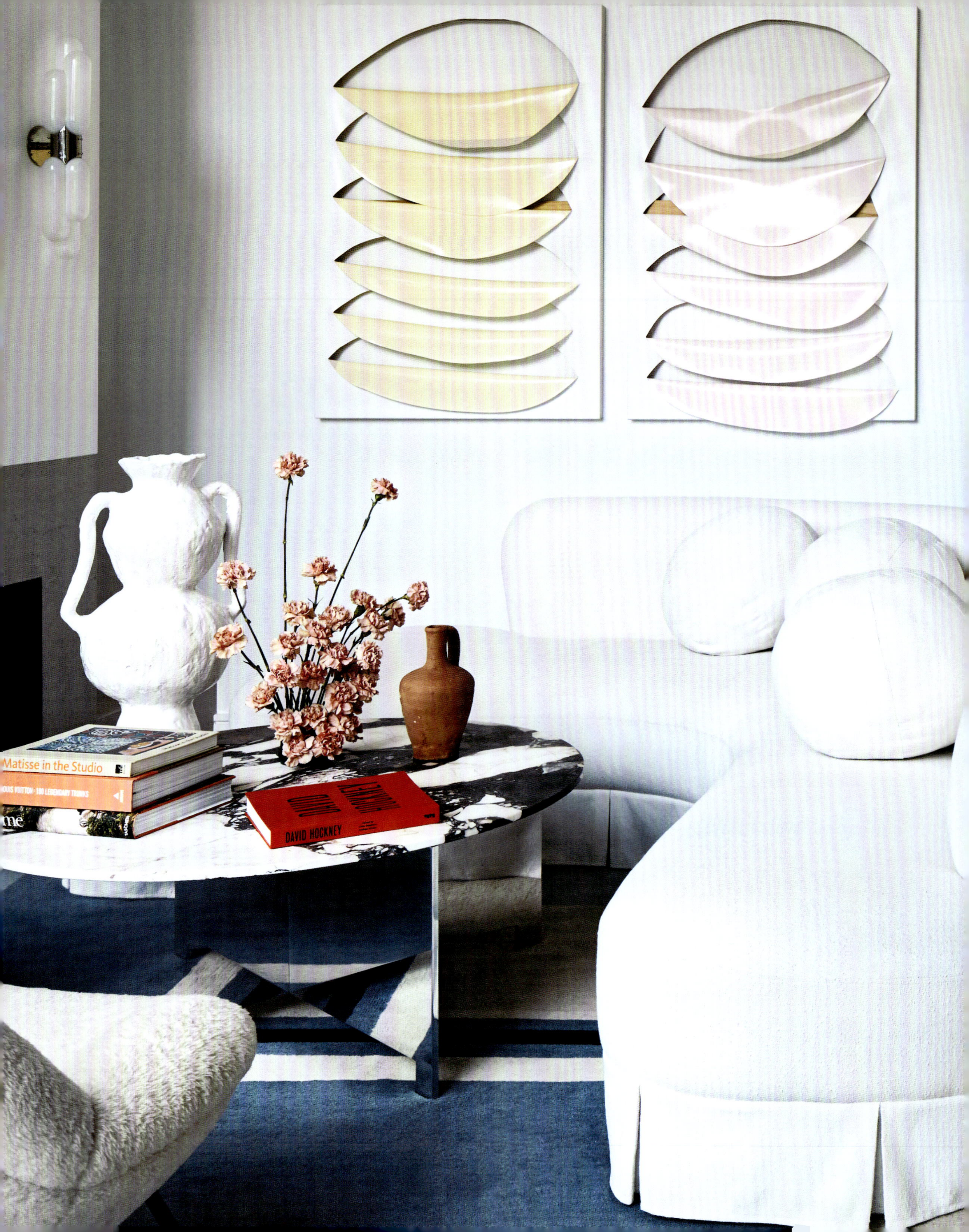
Matisse in the Studio
DAVID HOCKNEY

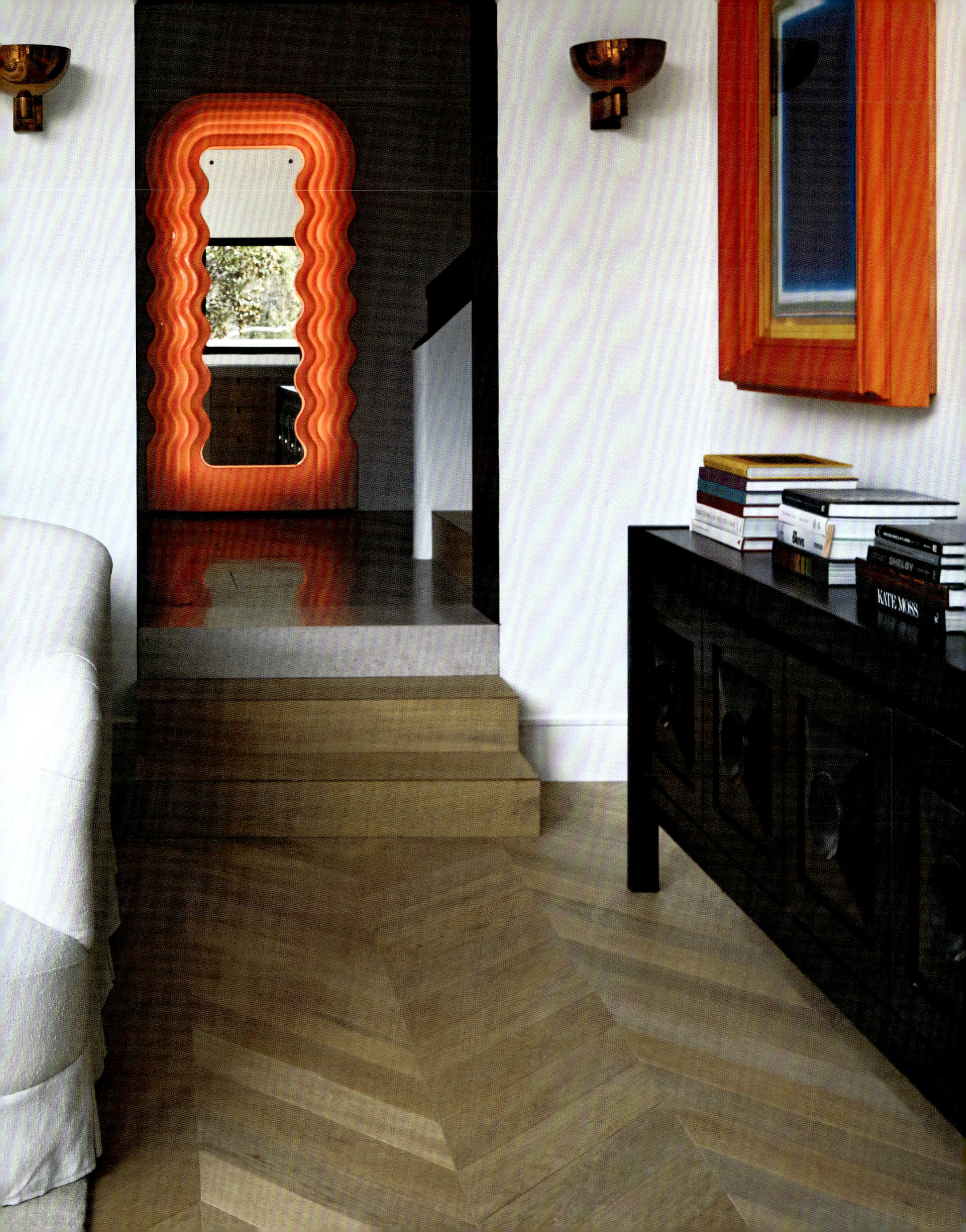
KATE MOSS

Bohemian Residence
LIVING IN STYLE LONDON
DUTCH INTERIOR DESIGN
LIVING IN STYLE PARIS
VOGUE LIVING COUNTRY, CITY, COAST
MENZIES
MENZIES
MENZIES
THE DRIVE
THE CALENDAR · 50 YEARS AND MORE
SHELBY
DAVID HOCKNEY
LOUIS VUITTON · 100 LEGENDARY TRUNKS
KATE MOSS

NUDE
Camera
PORSCHE BOOK
MERCEDES-BENZ 300 SL BOOK
THE STYLISH LIFE YACHTING

A vibrant artwork sits between the living room and kitchen of this family home, its clash of colors at once calm yet also exuding a hypnotic energy. "Unruly behavior" is how the artist's work with form and color has been described, to the point where "one wonders how each of the aspects will ever get along ... but they do, settling into a wondrous logic of their own." The words are those of gallery owner Andrew Jensen, speaking about the creations of Tomislav Nikolic, one of my favorite artists. I love this quotation, not only because it captures the essence of Nikolic's powerful chromatic works, but also because I think it could just as easily be speaking about this four-bedroom house in Sydney's stylish eastern suburbs. In a space that spans Victorian-era rooms built on grand proportions and renovated additions, I wanted to create unexpected combinations: the collected and the custom, the contemporary and the antique, balancing edgy elements with softer ones, and punctuating moments of serenity with elements of surprise. Nowhere is this mix more eloquent than in the entrance, a luminous space of cool gray travertine floor and matte white walls. On one wall, a huge blue collage by Melbourne artist Lillian O'Neil is flanked by the robust timber frames of a pair of mid-twentieth-century chairs by Pierre Jeanneret. Opposite, an ornate eighteenth-century Italian gilt console with a marble top sits below a pair of peach-hued 1960s Cristal Arte wall sconces and a Gio Ponti mirror, which fuses the two with its perfect simplicity. Old and new come together here, in an area that acts as the anchor of the house, both stylistically and spatially.

The owners wanted a relaxed environment that could serve as home to their impressive art collection as much as their active young family. With four children, they're delightfully realistic about their lifestyle, yet happy to have their beautiful things on display. I felt it was important to create the feeling of coziness and warmth that comes not with clutter but with a refined sense of comfort and a certain minimalism that allows the place to be filled with personality, color, and motion. The artworks, the light fixtures, the pieces, the books—these provide the movement in a dynamic, open design where one space invites you into the next. The living area is another pivotal part of the house, looking onto the kitchen and dining spaces, garden, and entrance, so I created an inclusive design here that didn't block off the room. A white custom sofa looks good from every angle, its curves continued in a pair of Fritz Neth sheepskin-covered chairs and two stunning cut canvases by Sydney-based artist Huseyin Sami. The blue rug, which I designed in the style of Agnes Martin, echoes the hue of the O'Neil collage in the entrance, while its lines are reflected beautifully in the mirrored stainless steel base of the marble-top coffee table.

p. 179 - In the entrance, a blue collage by Lillian O'Neil and two robust Pierre Jeanneret chairs form a striking group.
pp. 180–81 - Pastel cut canvases by Huseyin Sami continue a play on curves in the formal living room, which is echoed in the arresting Ettore Sottsass mirror beyond.
Previous spread - The boldly hued artwork by Tomislav Nikolic is an integral piece in the house, its lines working powerfully with those of the kitchen behind.

Opposite - The casual dining room features a vintage Italian chandelier and mid-twentieth-century dining setting.

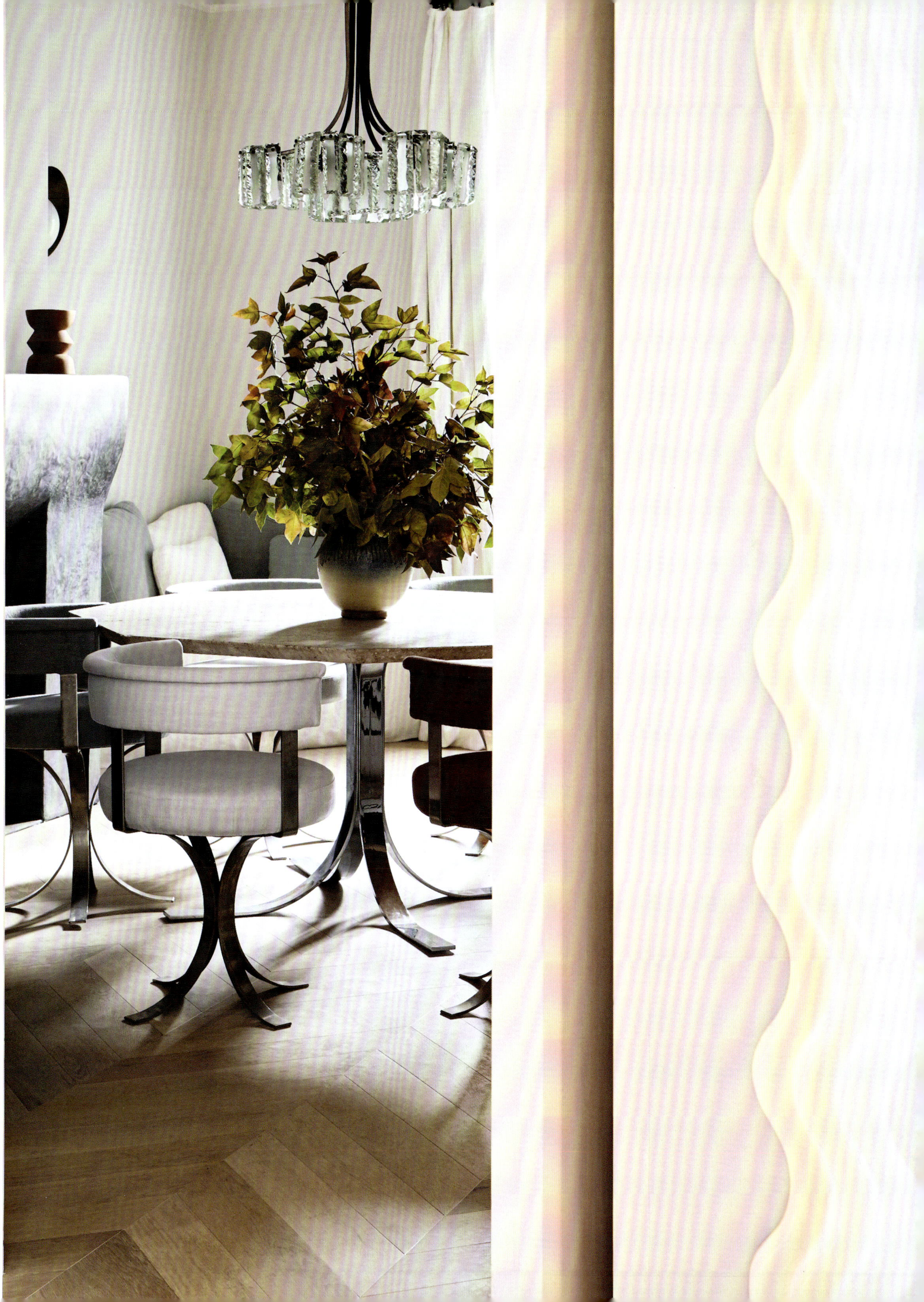

Opposite the living area, a 1940s French ebonized oak cabinet provides a strong contrast to the pastel arcs of Sami's works, with another, more contemporary, glossy black USM cabinet sitting in the dining area beyond. Here, the defined shapes of a white Saarinen Tulip table and Nickey Kehoe black dining chairs with tan leather seats are offset by the bold brushstrokes of a painting by award-winning Australian artist Ben Quilty. The subject—a skull with a cigarette in its mouth—is an unexpected choice for the setting but brings a hit of color to the whitewashed oak kitchen adjacent. I like to counter black and white with elements of warmth and something a little surprising just like this, and the bright orange frame of the nearby Nikolic artwork takes things a step further. And then there's the mirror lamp. Ettore Sottsass's show-stopping piece adds its stylized curves to the mix, transforming from the most amazing pinky orange when it is on to a peaceful grayish white when turned off. It's almost a metaphor for the house's own changing looks—this is a place that's resilient yet stylish, adapting around the family's lifestyle.

Upstairs, a mood of subdued comfort prevails, where pieces, just as people, have room to breathe. A fabulous stainless steel and Murano glass wall sconce above a vintage French wrought-iron and brass chair creates a vignette of restrained elegance on the landing. The family bathroom is tiled in simple gray travertine with detail courtesy of a green Fantasia marble vanity and backsplash. The bedrooms are cozy and welcoming, although nothing is furnished merely for the sake of it, and each room features its own subtle color scheme. Moving from room to room, I wanted the experience to be one of transition rather than contrast, with a tonal shift between each space reflecting its inhabitant's personality. These areas are about serenity rather than surprise—there's sufficient space for that elsewhere. The house's interior layout displays a little of the "unruly behavior" suggested in Nikolic's artwork by turning the conventional renovation floorplan on its head. The original front rooms, usually the formal part of a house, contain a media room and casual living and dining spaces, while the formal living area (with its curved white sofa) and black-and-white formal dining area both sit in the modern extension. This gives the house a unique energy, where old and new entwine, and every space has a role to play in daily family life.

All these spaces converge at the entrance, where another unexpected combination of elements plays out. In the powder room located here, bold graffiti-style wallpaper acts as a dramatic backdrop to a scalloped-edge marble sink, with a mid-twentieth-century French amber-colored Lucite mirror above and a brass kickplate below. To me, the room's warm tones, metallic gleams, and varied finishes encapsulate the scheme for the entire house. With the glowing strawberry tones of the Sottsass mirror to one side of the powder room and the distilled blues of the O'Neil collage to the other, these diverse parts certainly settle into their own "wondrous logic" to create one lively, happy whole.

Opposite - Amid the black-and-white tones of the formal dining room, color comes courtesy of a painting by Ben Quilty.

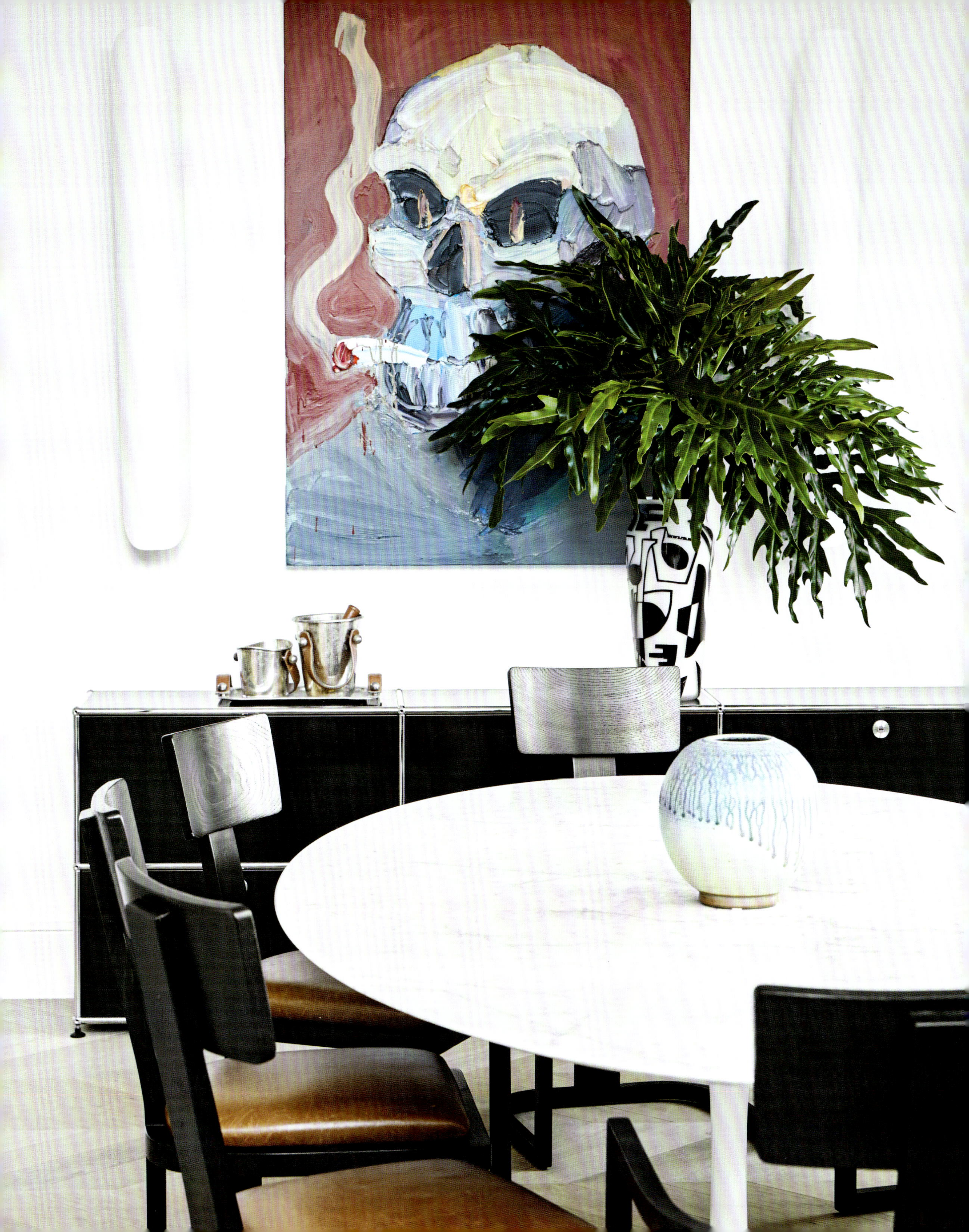

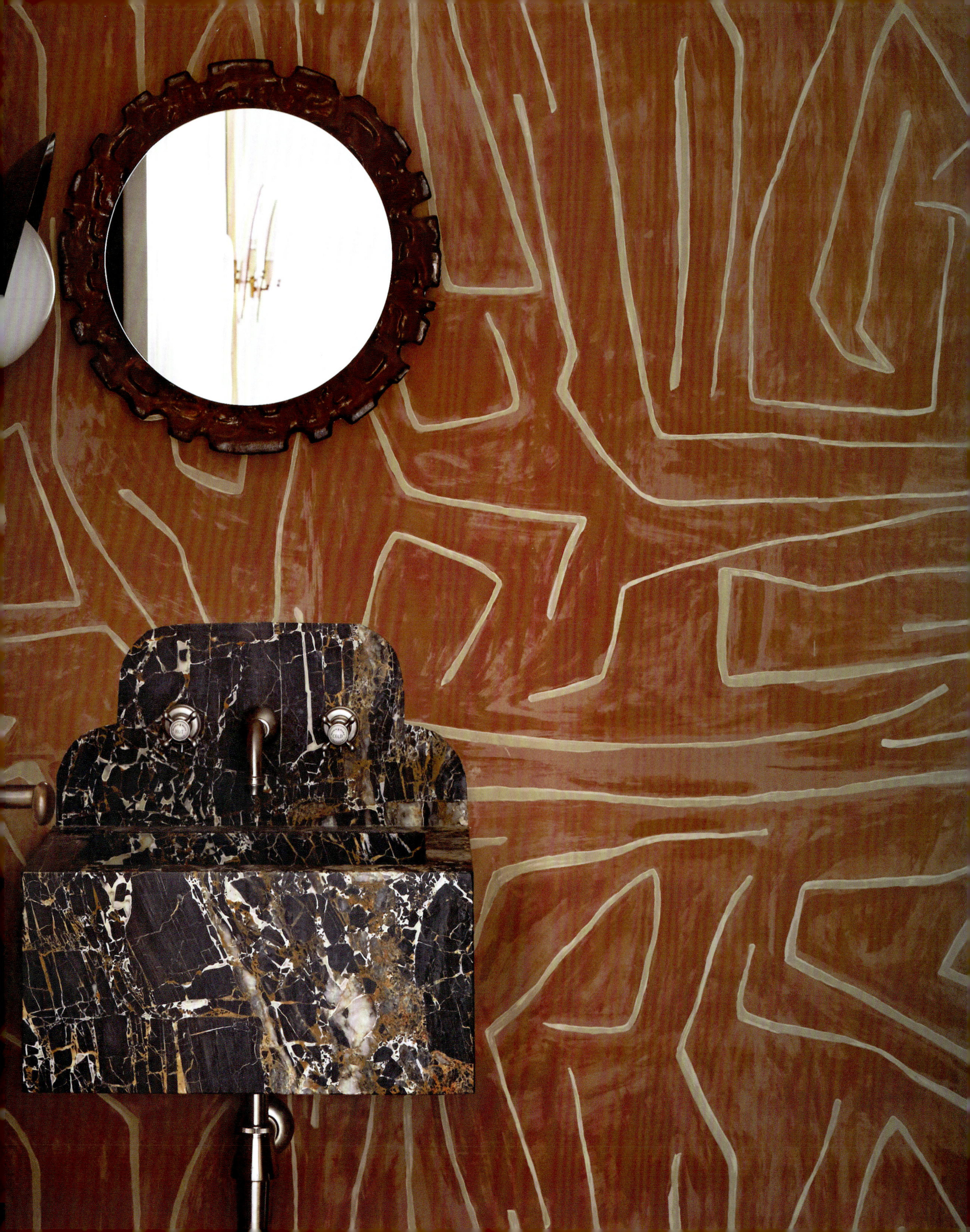

Opposite - From the graffiti-style wallpaper to the Lucite mirror and marble sink, the powder room is a surprising treasure trove of finishes.
Above - A blackened steel handrail follows the curve of the powder room door to lead upstairs.

*Above - The mix of vintage pieces, such as a 1920s French carved timber console, blue
Murano glass vase, and Italian copper wall sconces, brings a variety of color and form to the house.
Opposite - In the entrance, an eighteenth-century Italian marble and gilt console teamed with
1960s Cristal Arte wall sconces and a Gio Ponti mirror encapsulates the house's blend of old and new.*

Bohemian Residence
LIVING IN STYLE LONDON
DUTCH INTERIOR DESIGN
LIVING IN STYLE PARIS

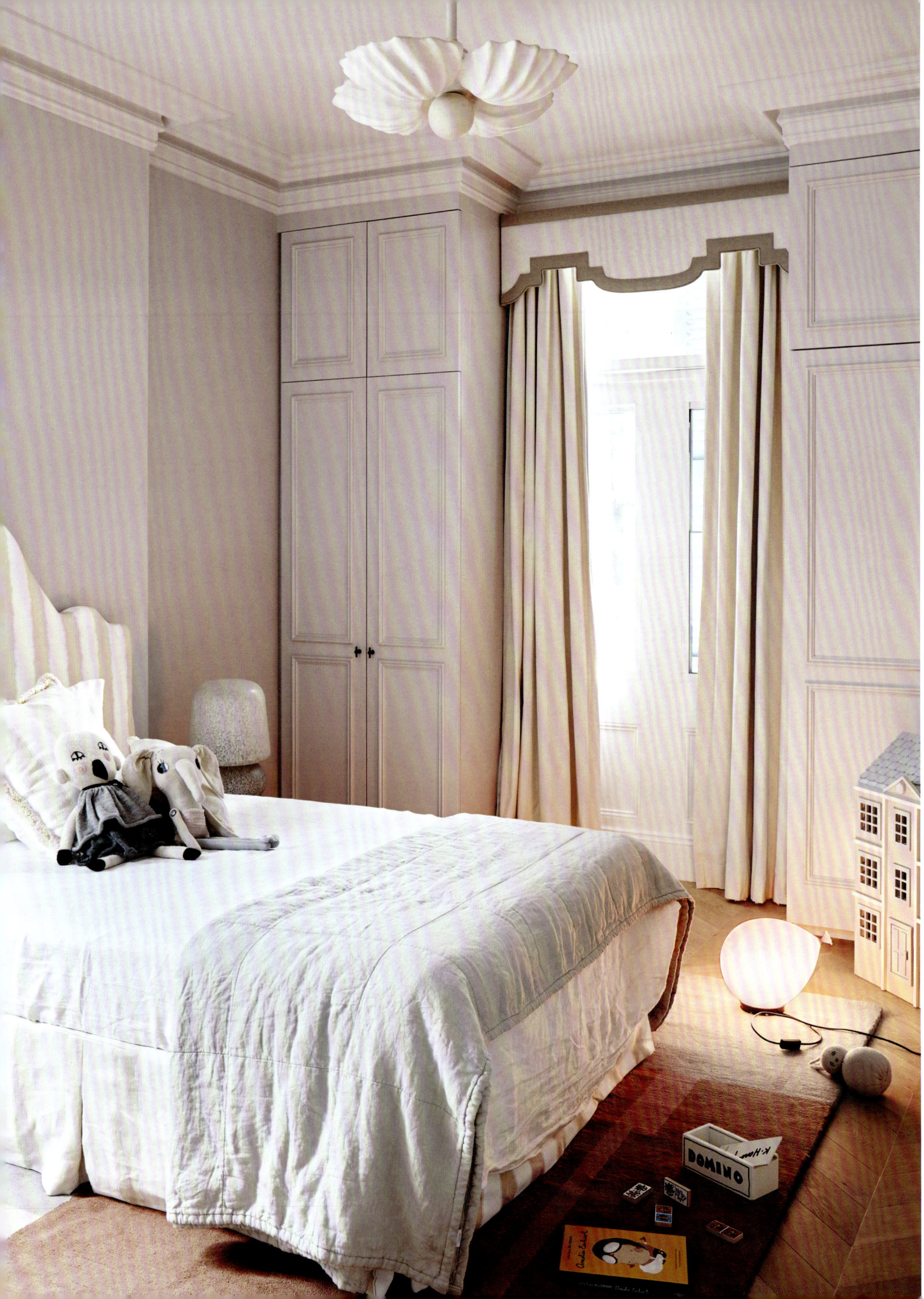
DOMINO

Opposite - Delicate pink sets the tone for this child's bedroom, with whimsical lighting choices such as a vintage French plaster pendant and a pink balloon floor lamp.

Above - A nineteenth-century hand-painted French bookcase provides a deep block of green against the paler shades.

Above - In the family bathroom, swirls of green in the Fantasia marble vanity and backsplash work with travertine walls and floors to create a serene space. Opposite - Picking up the bathroom's gray tones, a vintage French chair and Murano glass wall sconce make a harmonious pairing.

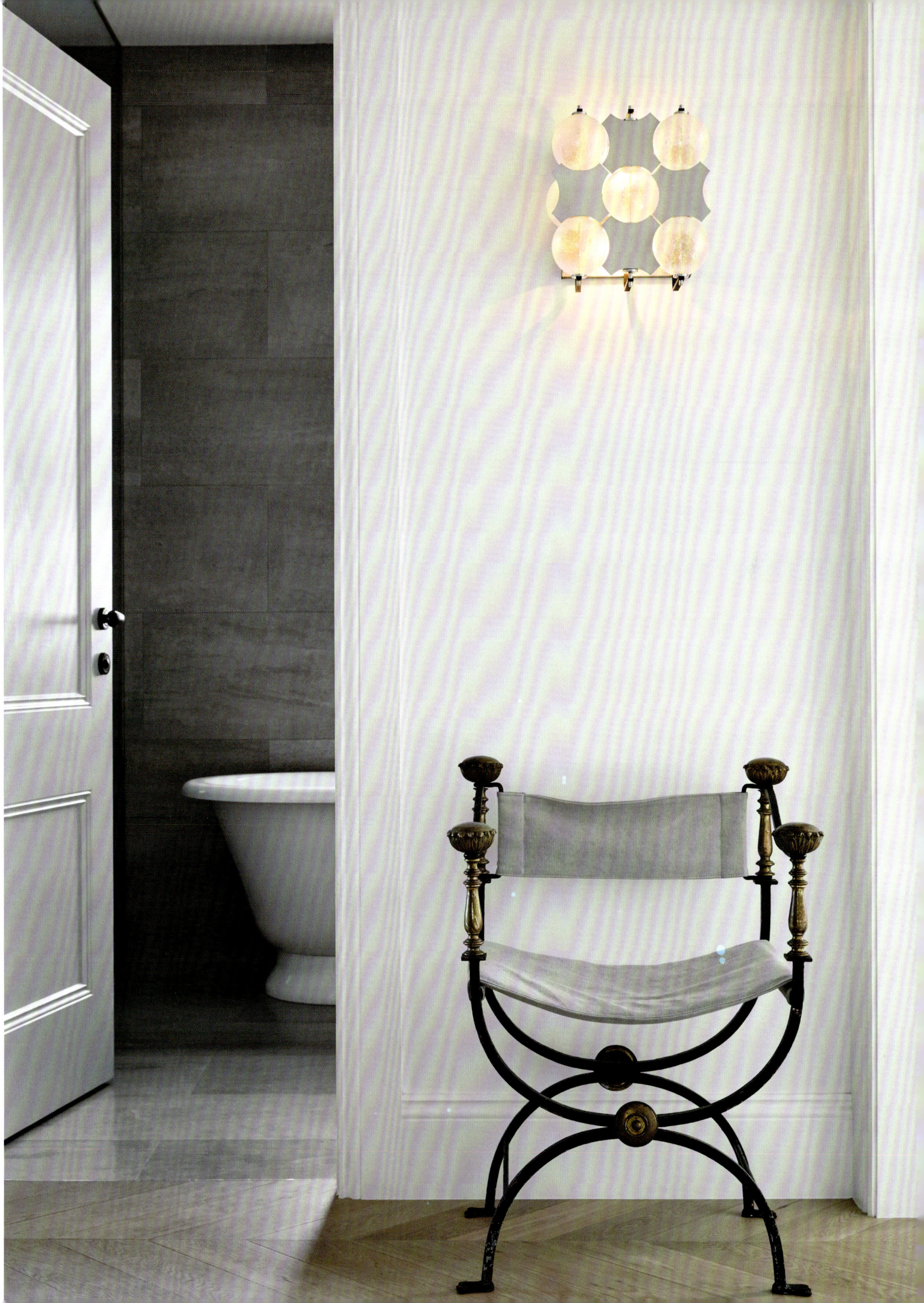

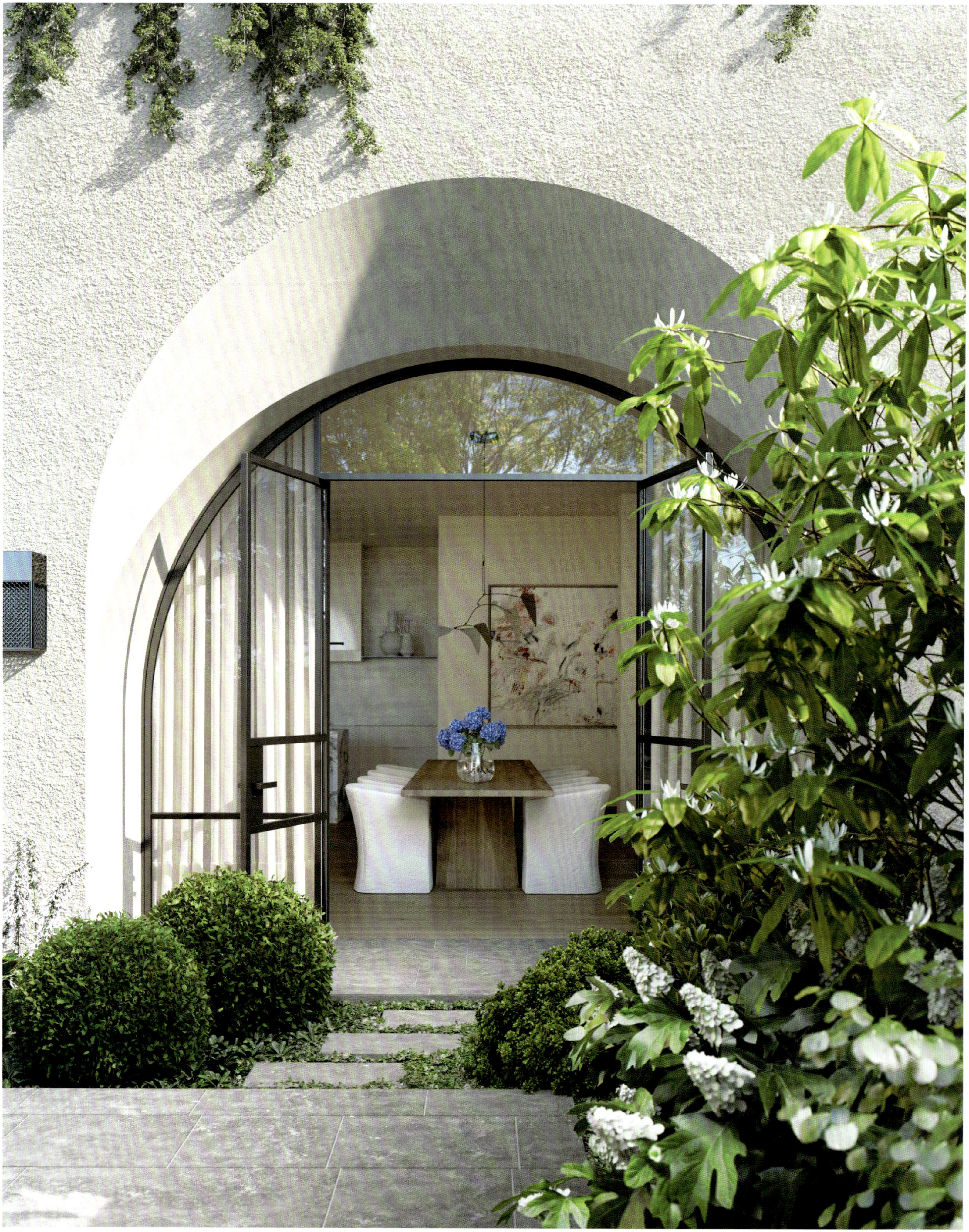

VAULT

Huntingtower Road,
Armadale, Melbourne

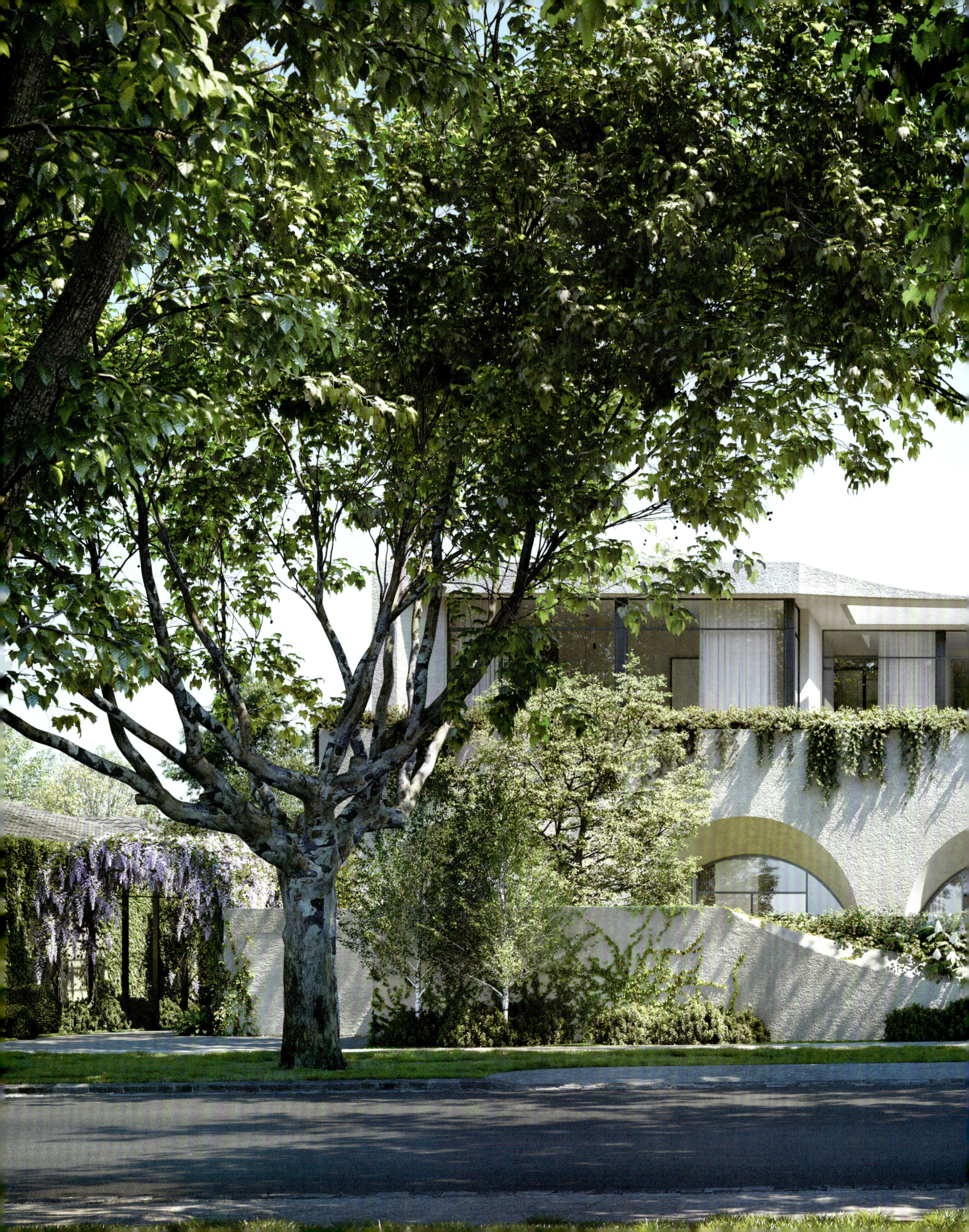

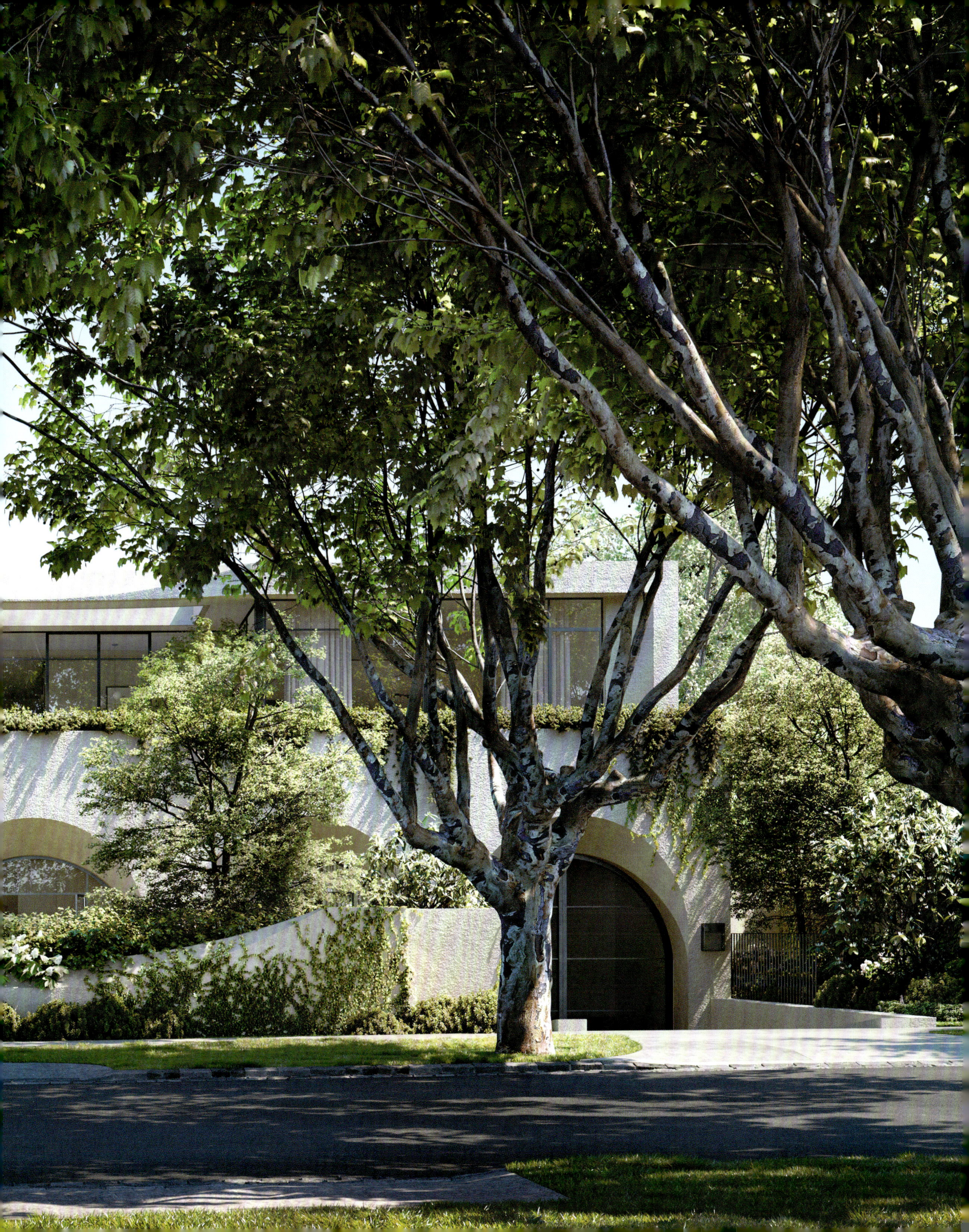

Designing a dream interior presents a different sort of challenge when there is no owner as yet. Here, rather than responding to a particular brief, you are responding solely to the architecture in order to build a story, working with the space to create a layout that showcases its possibilities. In the case of a model apartment, the client is imagined yet your design requires enough depth of vision and breadth of appeal to illustrate how the space could work for different owners with different dreams. I was engaged by a luxury property developer to provide the interior decoration for two such places in the Melbourne suburb of Armadale. The two-story, three-bedroom garden apartments are part of a block of ten large, sophisticated spaces built as a high-end alternative to houses for those looking to downsize a little. Leafy, family-oriented, and fashionable, the area is very familiar to me—I grew up a few streets away, and my mother went to school on this street. But of course these apartments weren't about my experience, but rather creating the imagined experience of living here.

The building is a beautifully conceived piece of architecture, constructed along contemporary lines and with a distinct Mediterranean feel that is partly due to its loggias and its magnificent exterior arches. Another contributing factor is the intertwining of indoor and outdoor spaces, enhanced by floor-to-ceiling glass windows and doors throughout. All is open and flowing here, with the high-ceilinged rooms enjoying generous proportions. I wanted to create an interior design that was contemporary in every aspect and quite minimal, leaving plenty of negative space in which the architecture could be appreciated, inside and out. To work with the black steel window and door frames, white walls and ceilings, and blond oak floors, I introduced a subdued palette and a clean, simple aesthetic that was elegant yet engaging. This meant choosing pieces that could convey the luxury experience but were still comfortable and unpretentious—lots of loosely upholstered seating and natural materials such as linen, stone, timber, and rattan. With the generosity of scale being such a key factor here, it was also important that the furniture was of a size and layout to suit the vast spaces, so I focused on custom-made oversized rugs, sofas, and tables, and different seating options in a series of inviting clusters.

p. 196 - The dining room, with its cozy white linen tub chairs, enjoys the apartment's seamless use of indoors and outdoors. Previous spread - Curves play a big part in the architecture of the apartment block.

Opposite and overleaf - Amid gardens created by landscape designer Myles Baldwin, seating clusters echo the simple aesthetic of the interior.

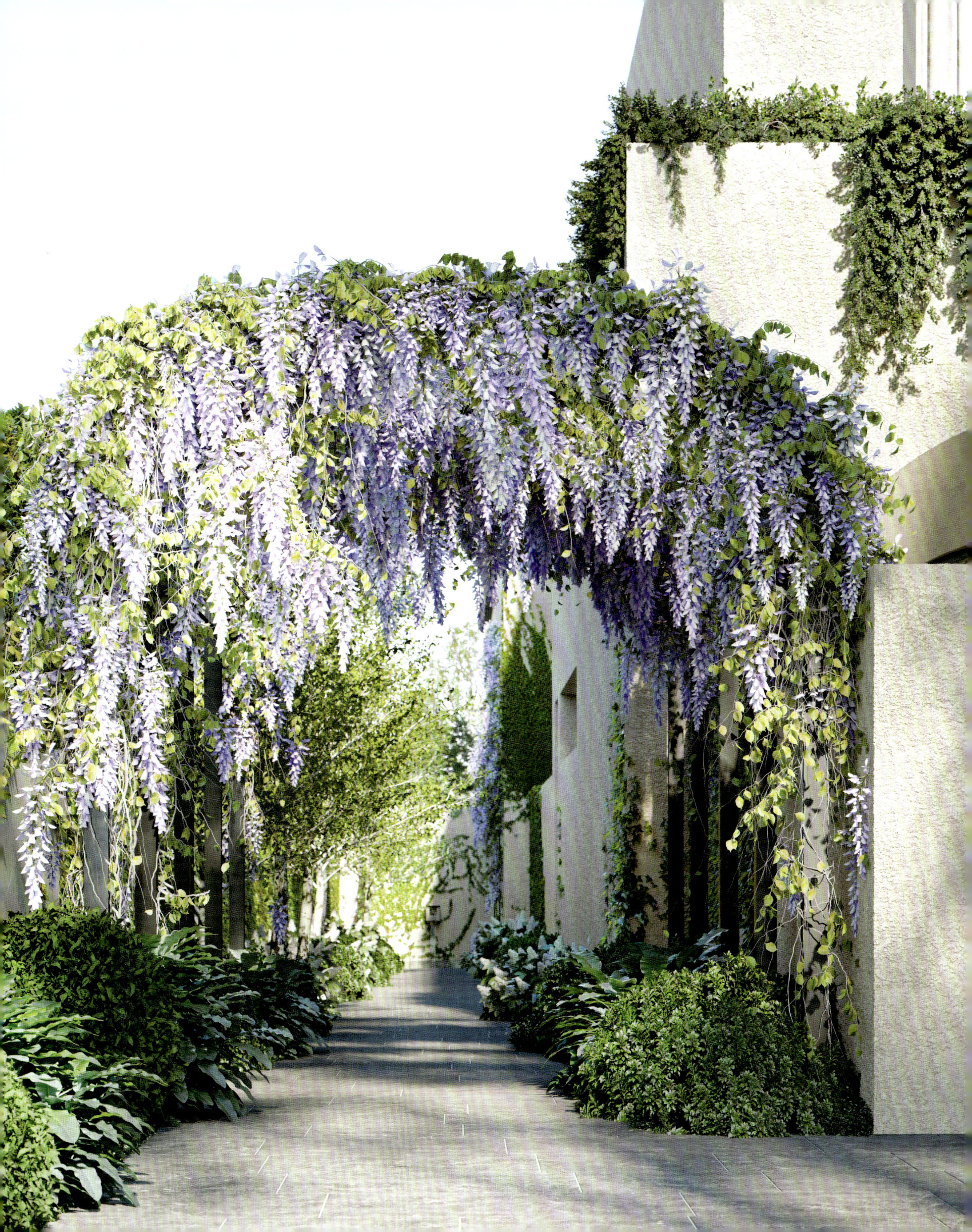

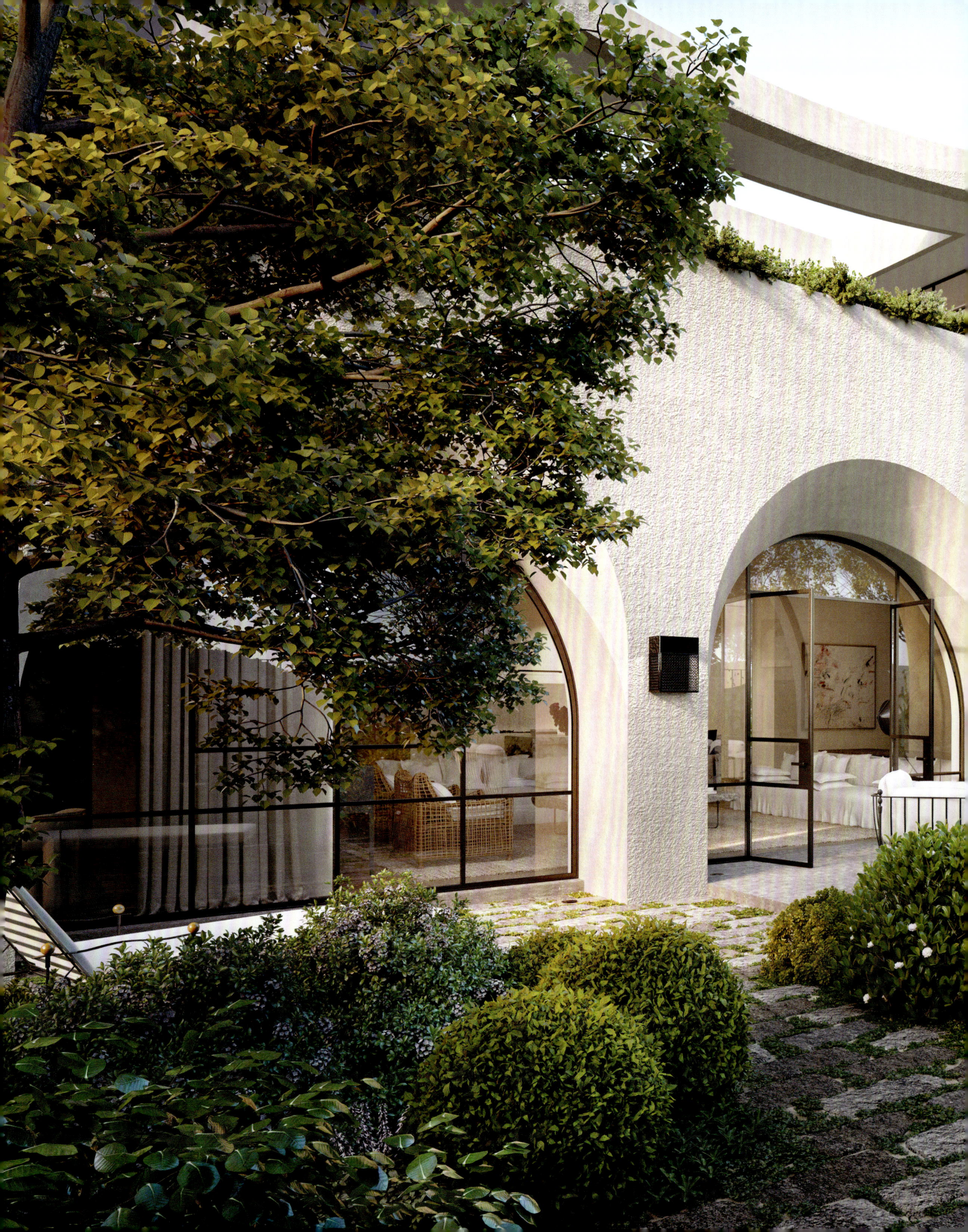

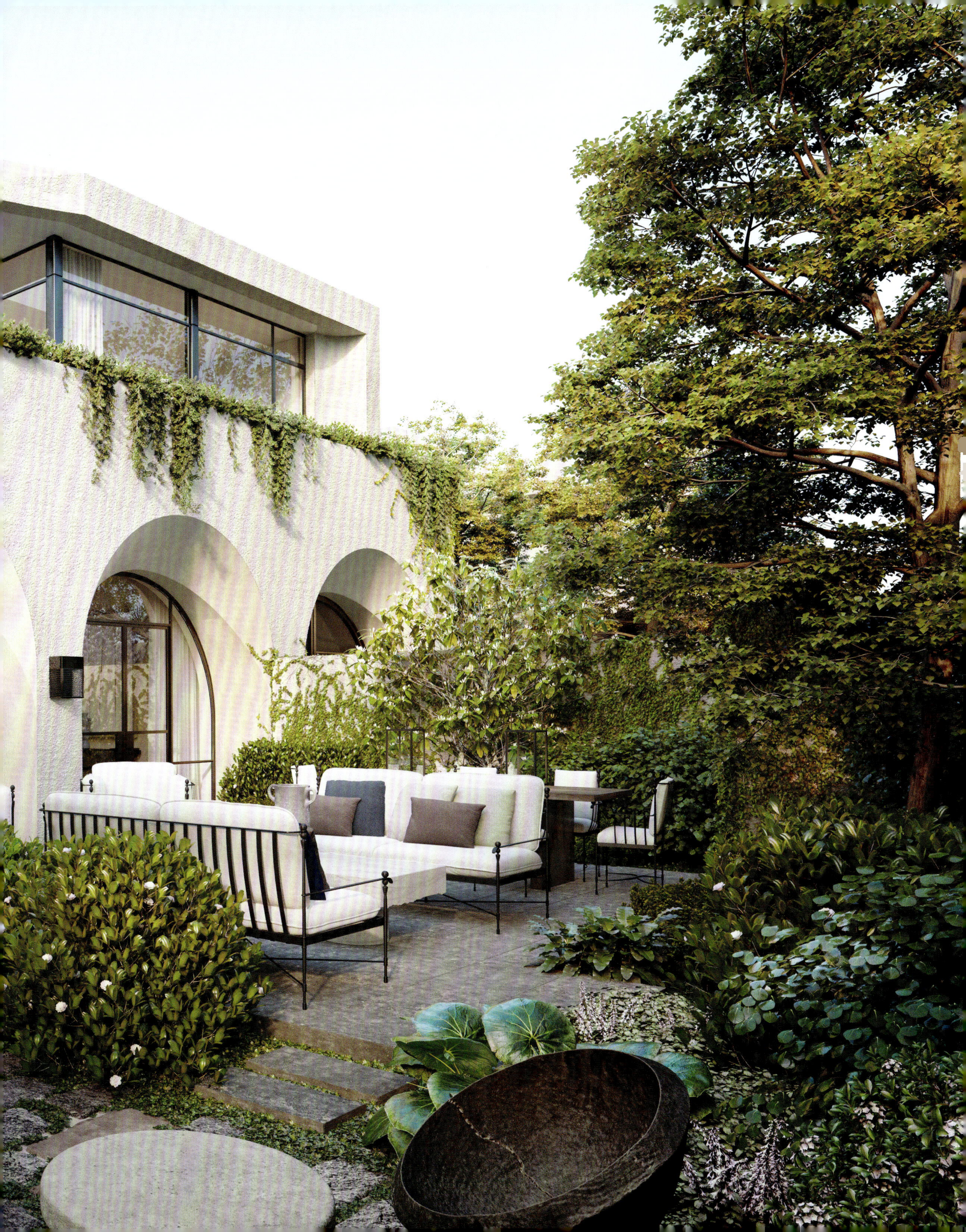

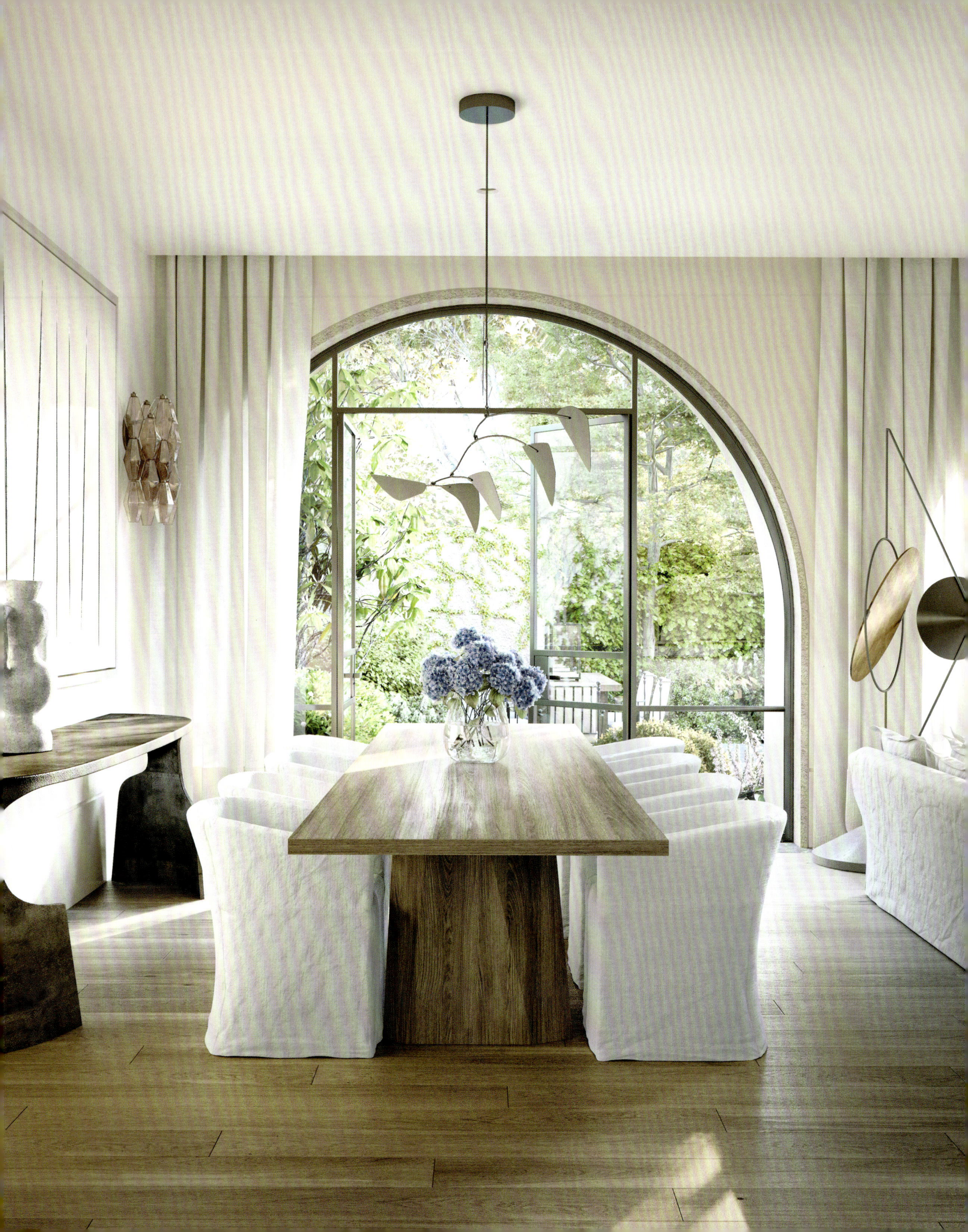

In one living area, a huge modular sofa with its pleasing expanse of white linen creates an enticing comfort zone. I love the little stacks of weighted cushions that subtly divide the sofa to establish individual nooks. A chunky Belgian sisal rug provides a warm textural layer, gently delineating the seating space and continuing the palette of the apartment with its sandy hues. In front of the sofa, a pair of square concrete coffee tables break up the space in a far more appealing way than a single giant piece would have done, while their raw-cut edges bring another welcome tactile element to the area. Rattan armchairs with white velvet upholstery and white concrete drum side tables complete the setting.

The kitchen behind resumes the tonal mix, with a pair of black leather Cassina Cab stools beside the gray marble kitchen countertop, and some white ceramics by a local artisan bringing their own soft curves. The nearby walls play host to a changing display of artworks, including a Cy Twombly painting in vivid blue and another in grey and pink tones, a cut canvas by Lucio Fontana, and a black-and-white collage by Lillian O'Neil. While artworks play a significant part in the impact and ambience of the apartments, I didn't want to crowd the walls with distracting pieces. Rather, I opted for some memorable paintings and freestanding sculptures, which highlight the structural beauty of each space. In the modular living area, a contemporary brass sculpture purchased in New York presents an airy delicacy of line, its reflected light bouncing around the room. Above the dining table, a mid-twentieth-century mobile by Alexander Calder appears to float amid the trees viewed beyond. The metals of these artworks echo the prominent steel frames of the windows and doors, while their abstract shapes temper the frames' strong lines. At the foot of the curved stairs, a plaster and foam sculpture by London artist Annie Morris offers a boldly organic display, with its stack of boulder-like shapes intensified by the shadows they cast on the bare wall behind. Again, it is the abstract nature of the artwork that maintains a contemporary vibe but also provides a certain softness of line in harmony with its surroundings. The art stands out, yet no piece dominates the space.

Different groupings of furniture continue those organic lines, from the curves of linen tub chairs and a timber console in the dining room to a deliciously plush pair of Jean Royère *Polar Bear* armchairs in another living area. Like the artworks, these pieces maximize the appeal of each area without overpowering. Even a living-room setting in darker tones, which features brown mohair and teak Pierre Jeanneret armchairs, follows the architectural arches with its circular timber tables and rounded chair arms. Outside in the gardens, created by award-winning Australian landscape designer Myles Baldwin, more seating clusters beckon, their finishes of marble, metal, and hard-wearing white fabrics echoing the textural mix inside. Sitting in a sunny urban backyard in southeastern Australia, surrounded by Italianate arches and terraces, you could almost imagine yourself to be in the courtyard of a Milanese hotel. And I think that's what these places offer: light, air, openness, and the space to dream.

Opposite - Sculpture and lighting work with the interior architecture to enhance and emphasize its lines.

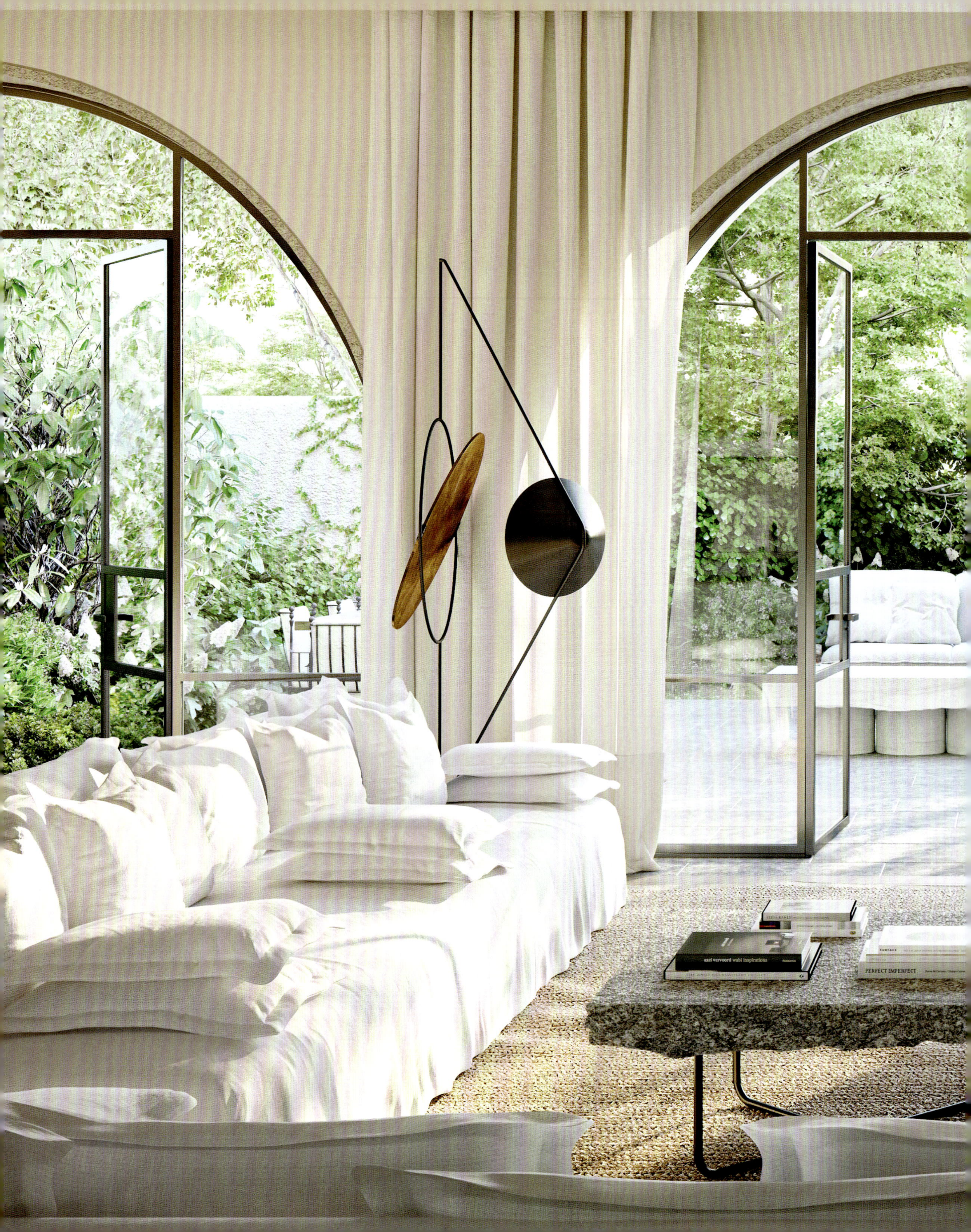

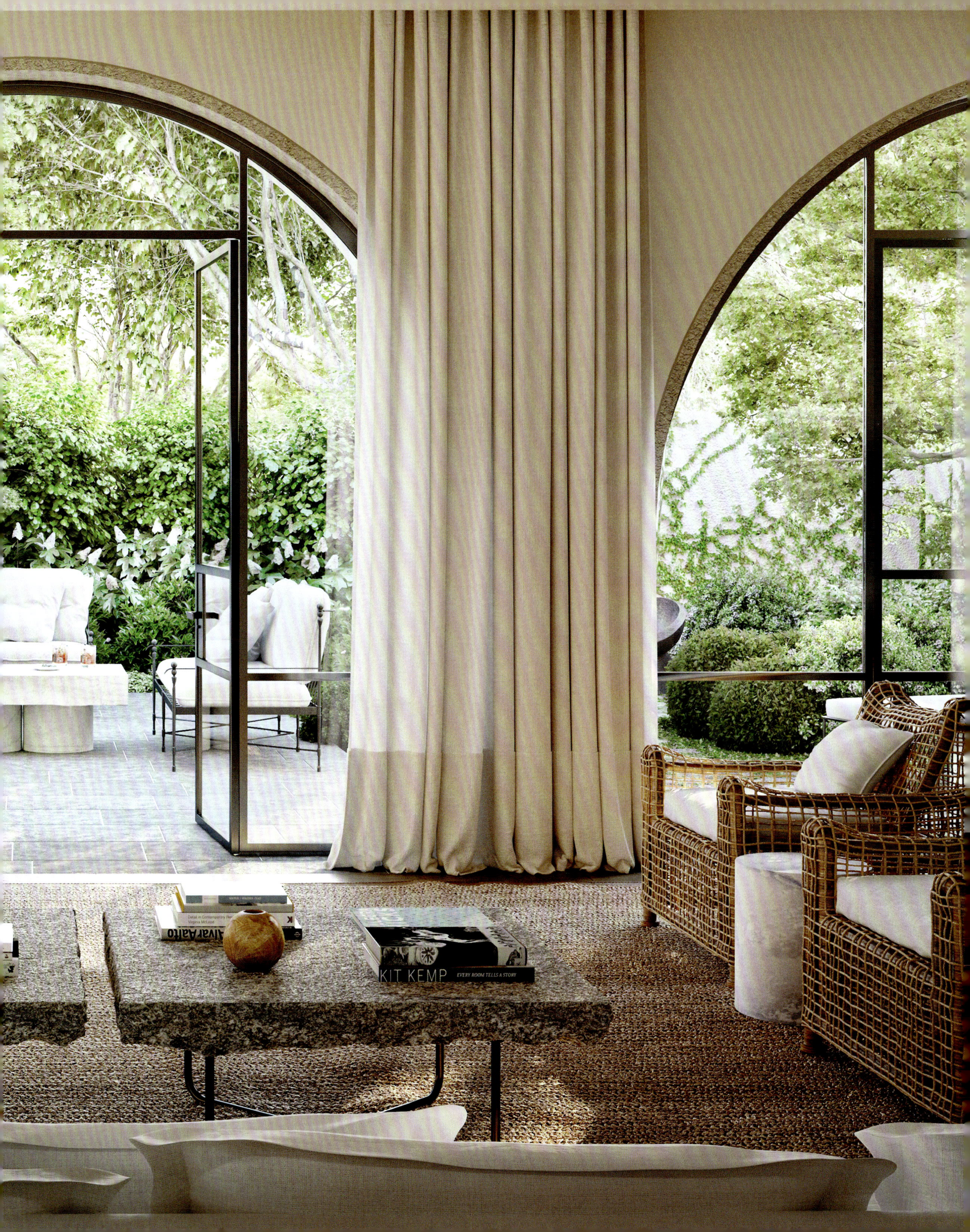
KIT KEMP
EVERY ROOM TELLS A STORY

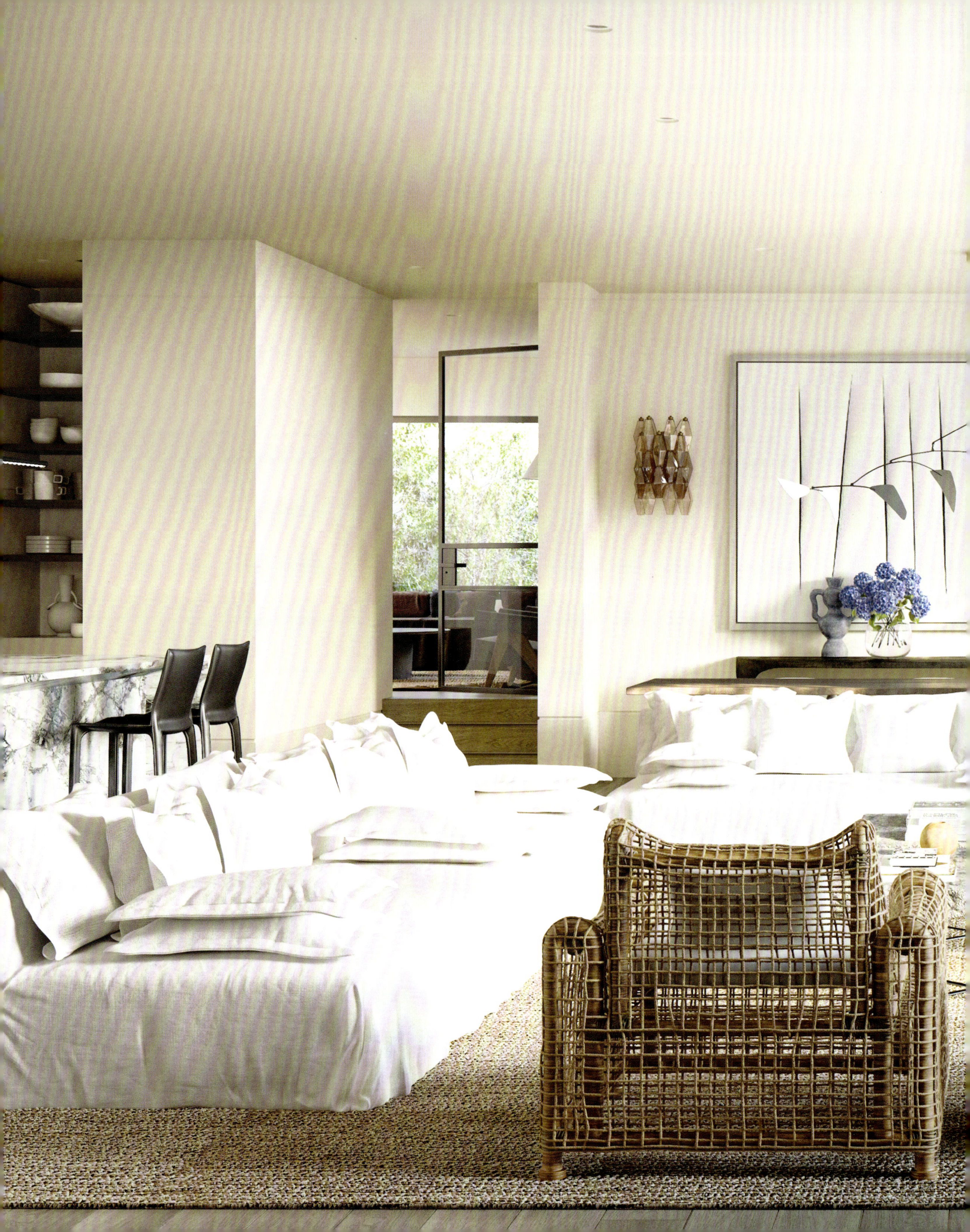

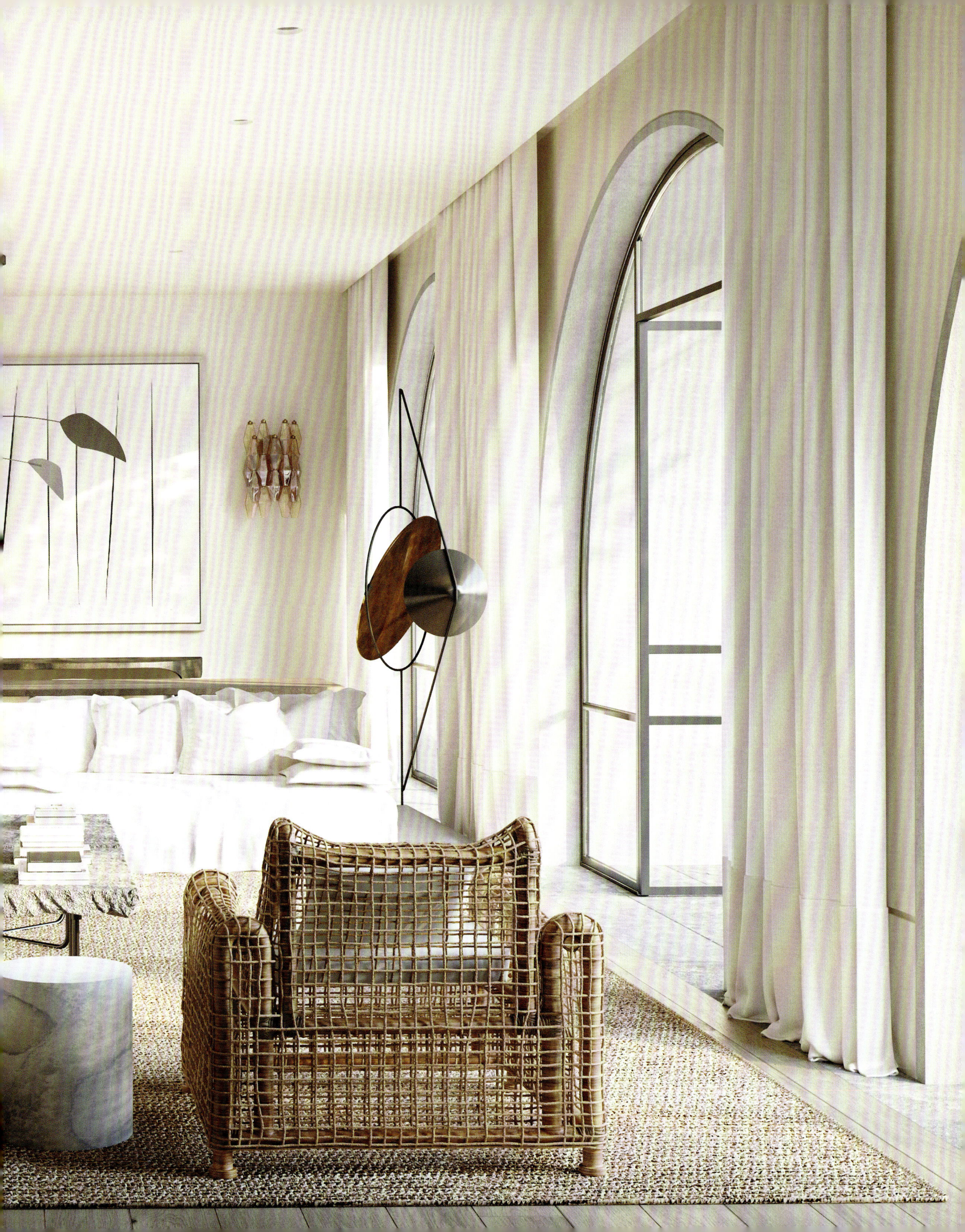

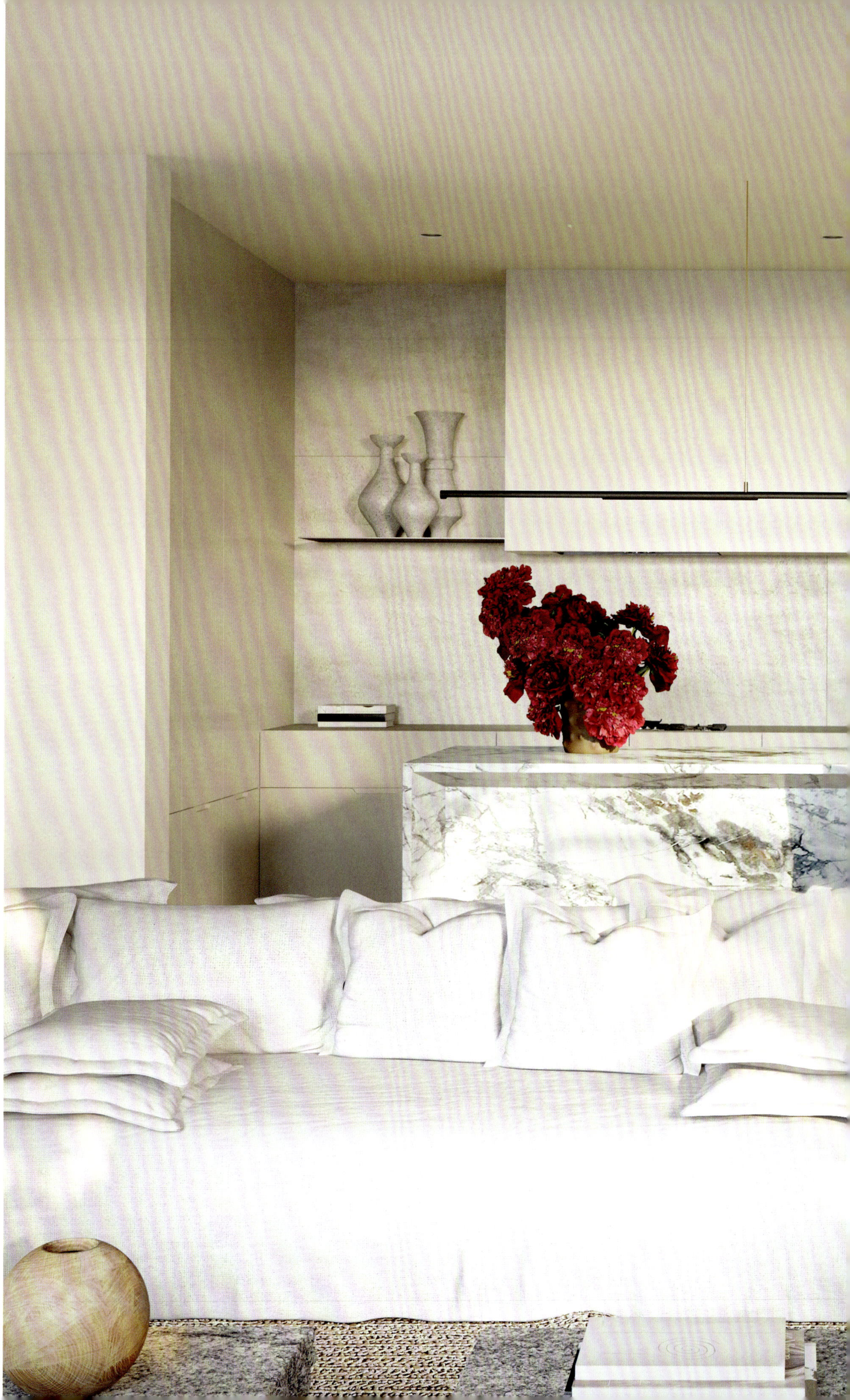

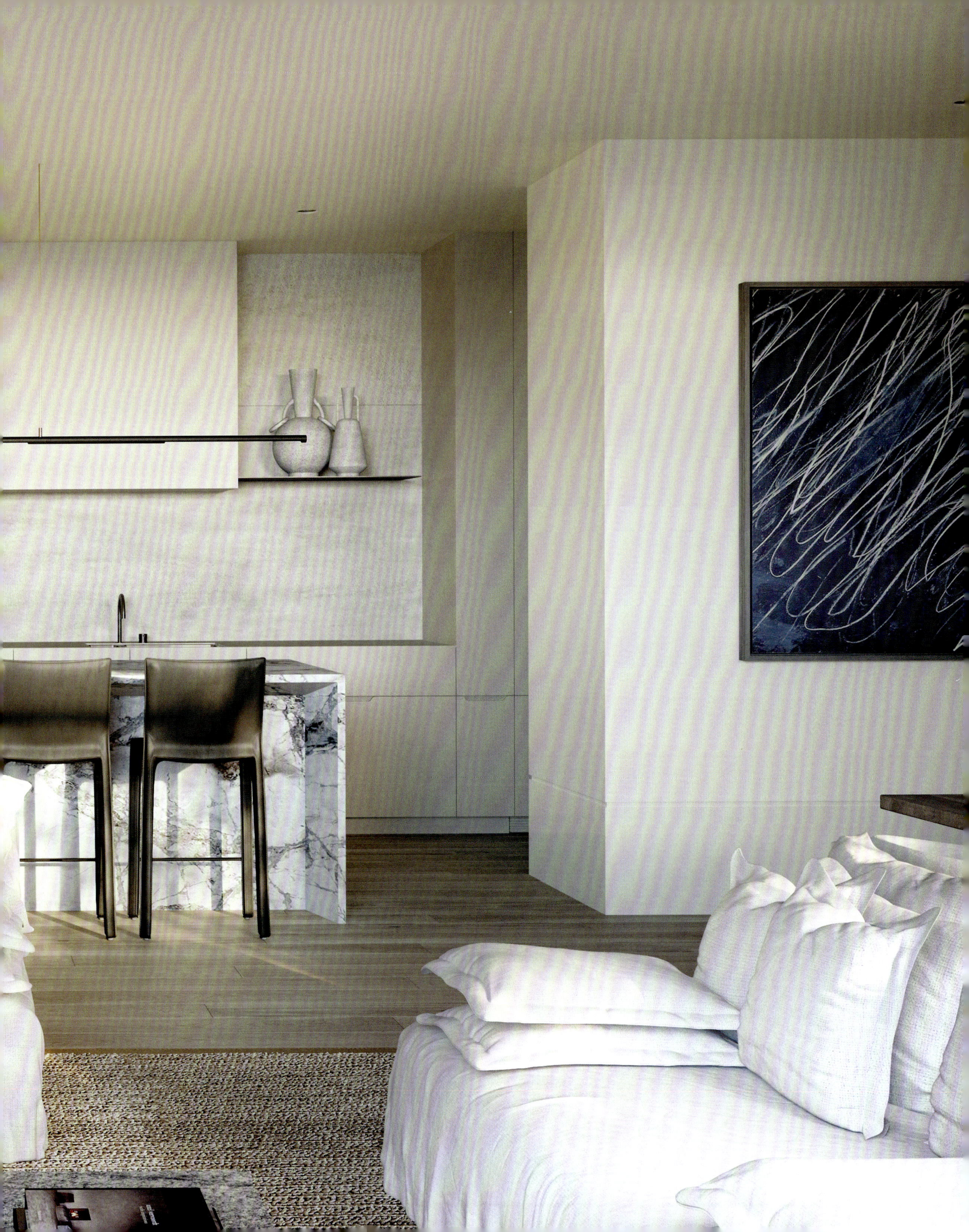

pp. 206–11 - The sizable proportions of the living area and adjacent spaces allow for generous furnishings such as a huge modular sofa, alongside a shifting display of artworks on the walls.

Above - An Annie Morris sculpture and its shadow make twice the impact in the space.
Opposite - Brown Pierre Jeanneret armchairs establish a darker palette in one room, balanced by the abundant light through the steel-framed windows.
Following spread - A Lillian O'Neil collage suits the monochromatic scheme of another apartment.

ALLIED WORKS ARCHITECTURE
BRAD CLOEPFIL
OCCUPATION
History of Art
PORTRAITS
YIRUMA
RICHARD SERRA EARLY WORK

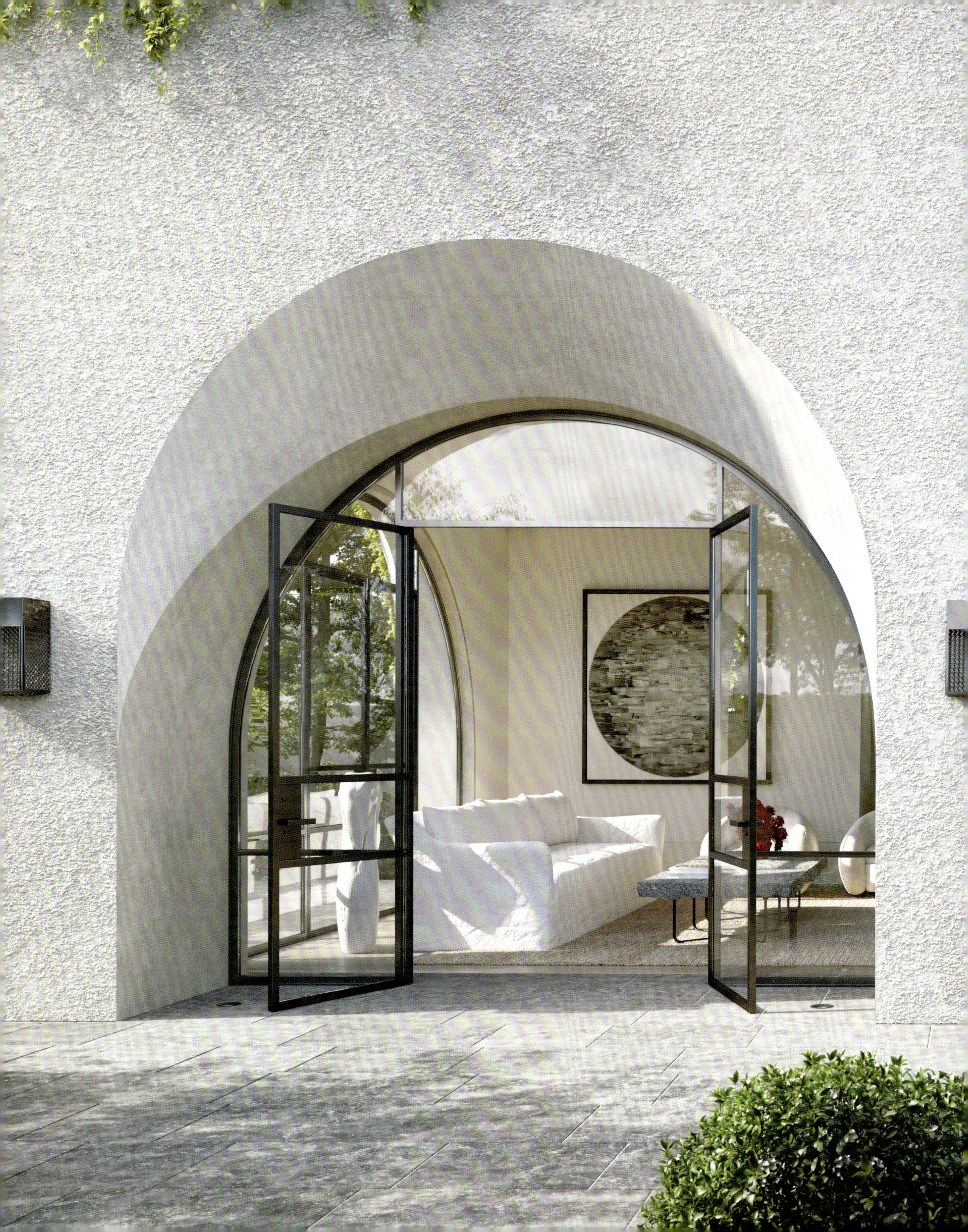

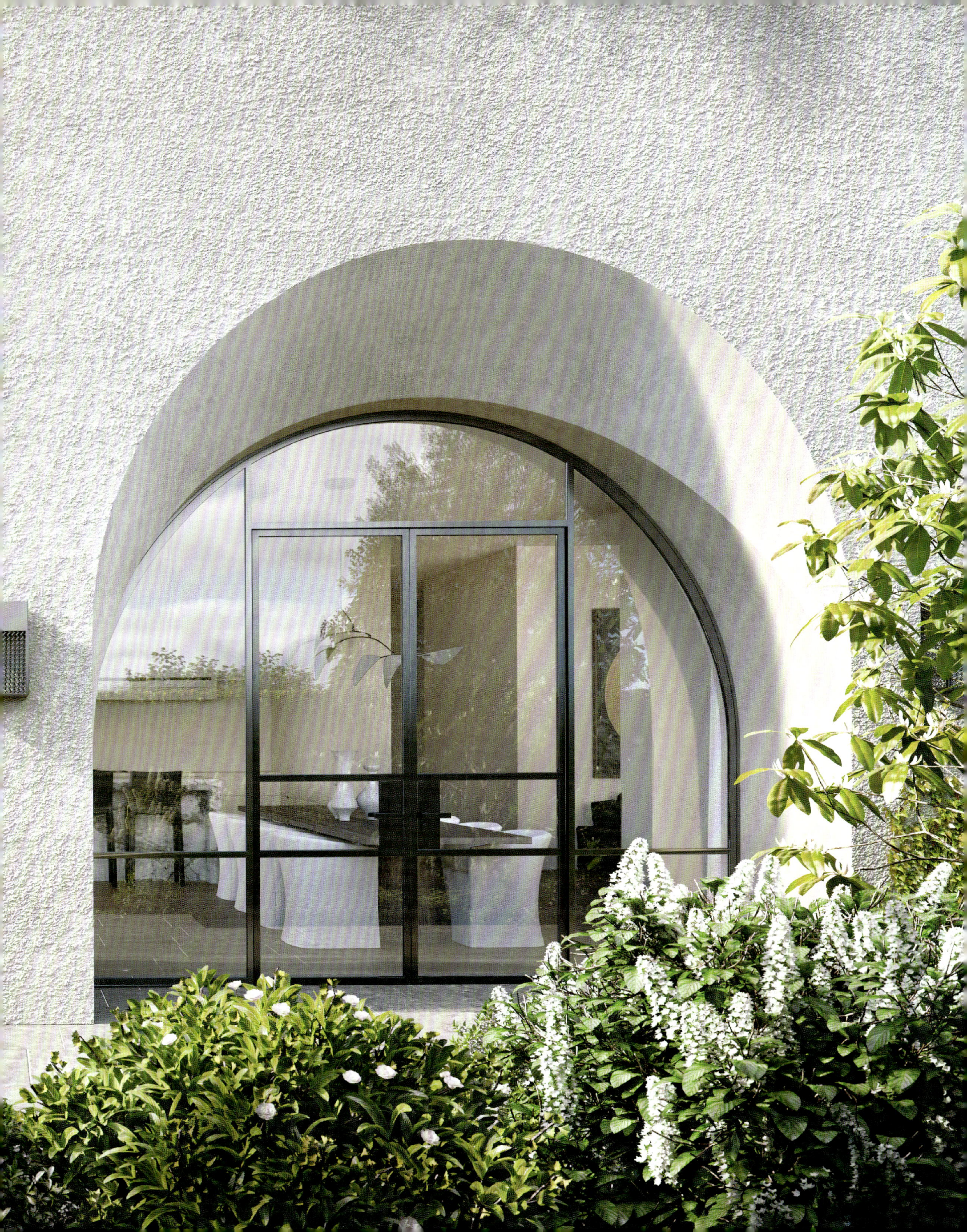

GREEN HOUSE

Wallaroy Road,
Woollahra, Sydney

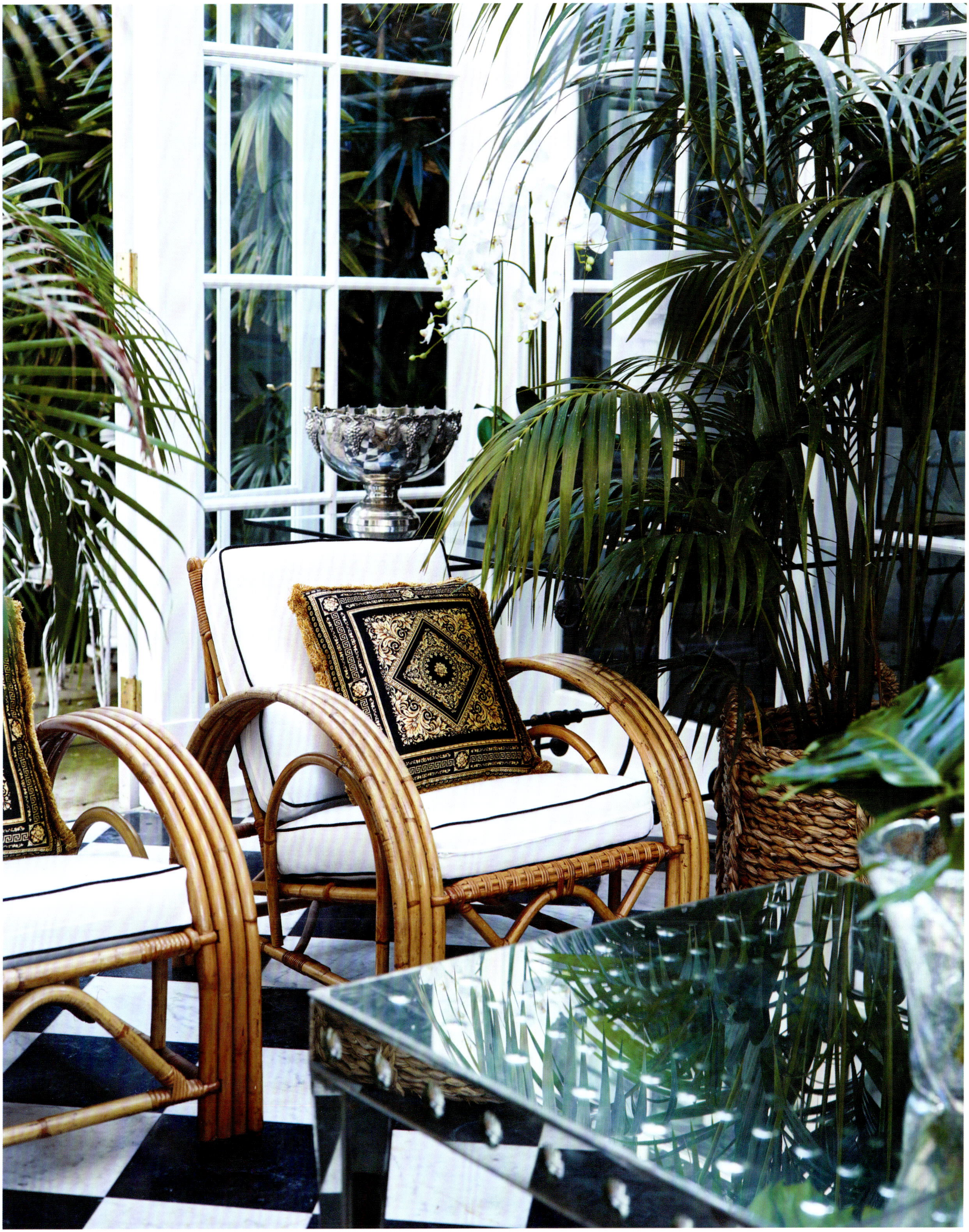

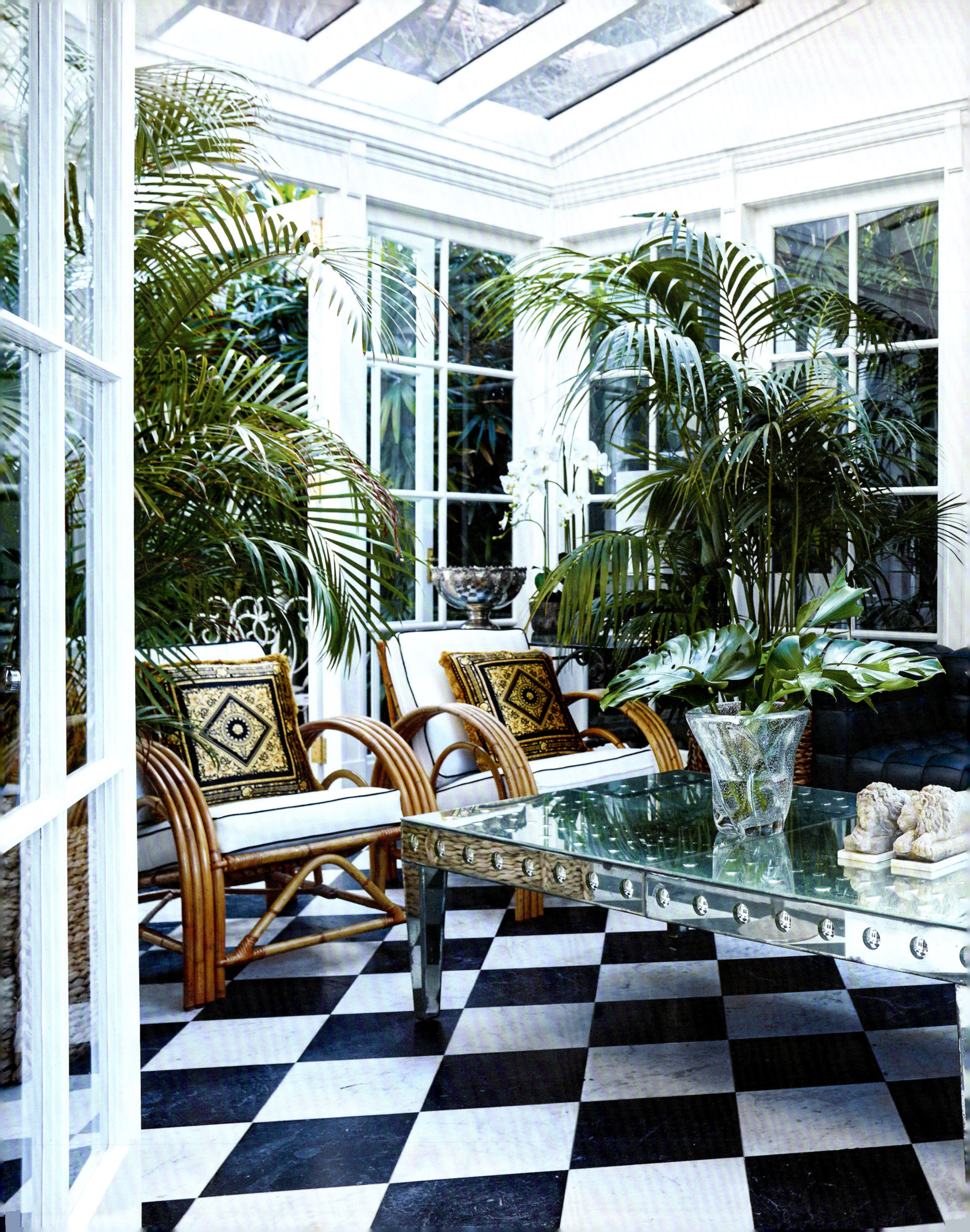

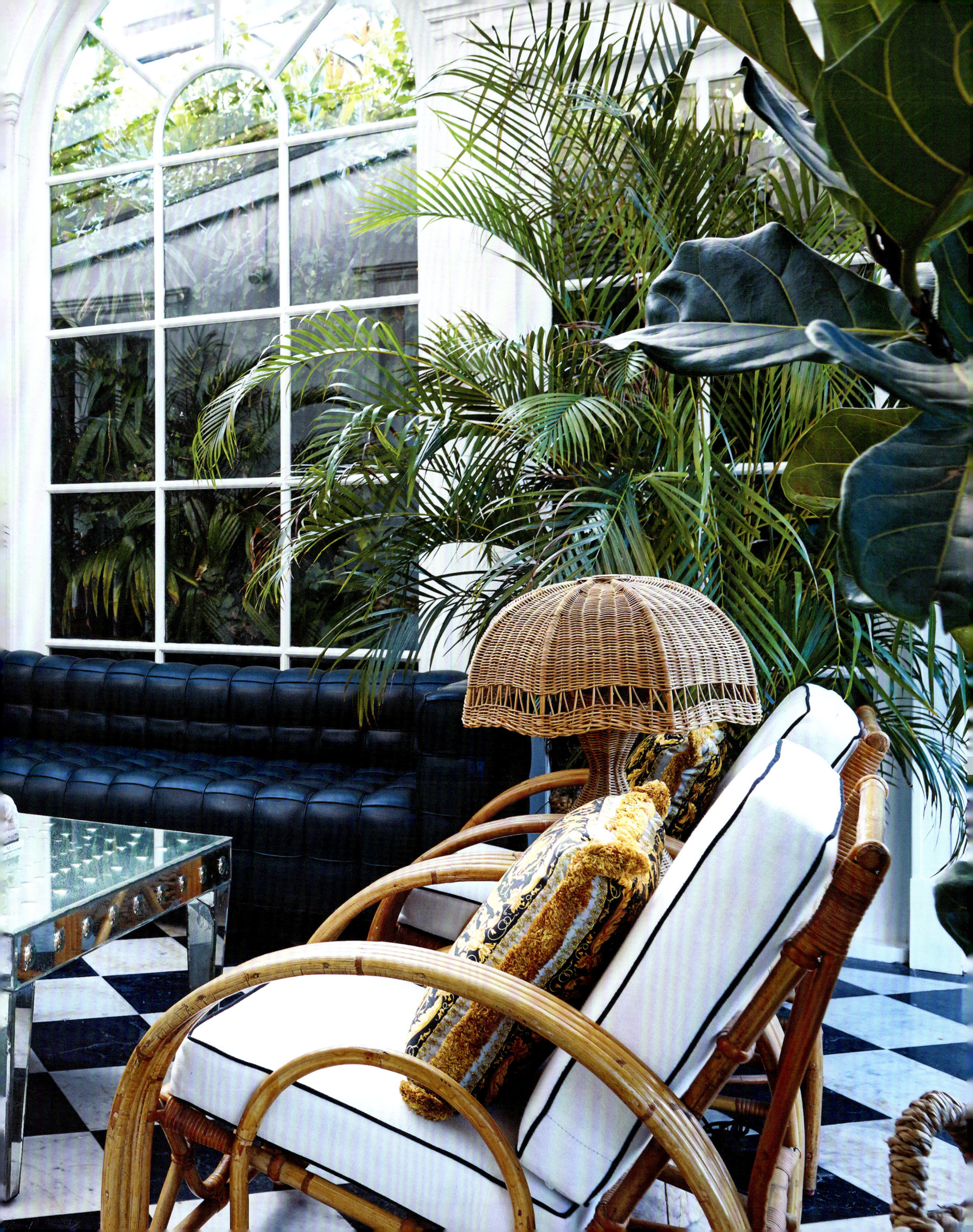

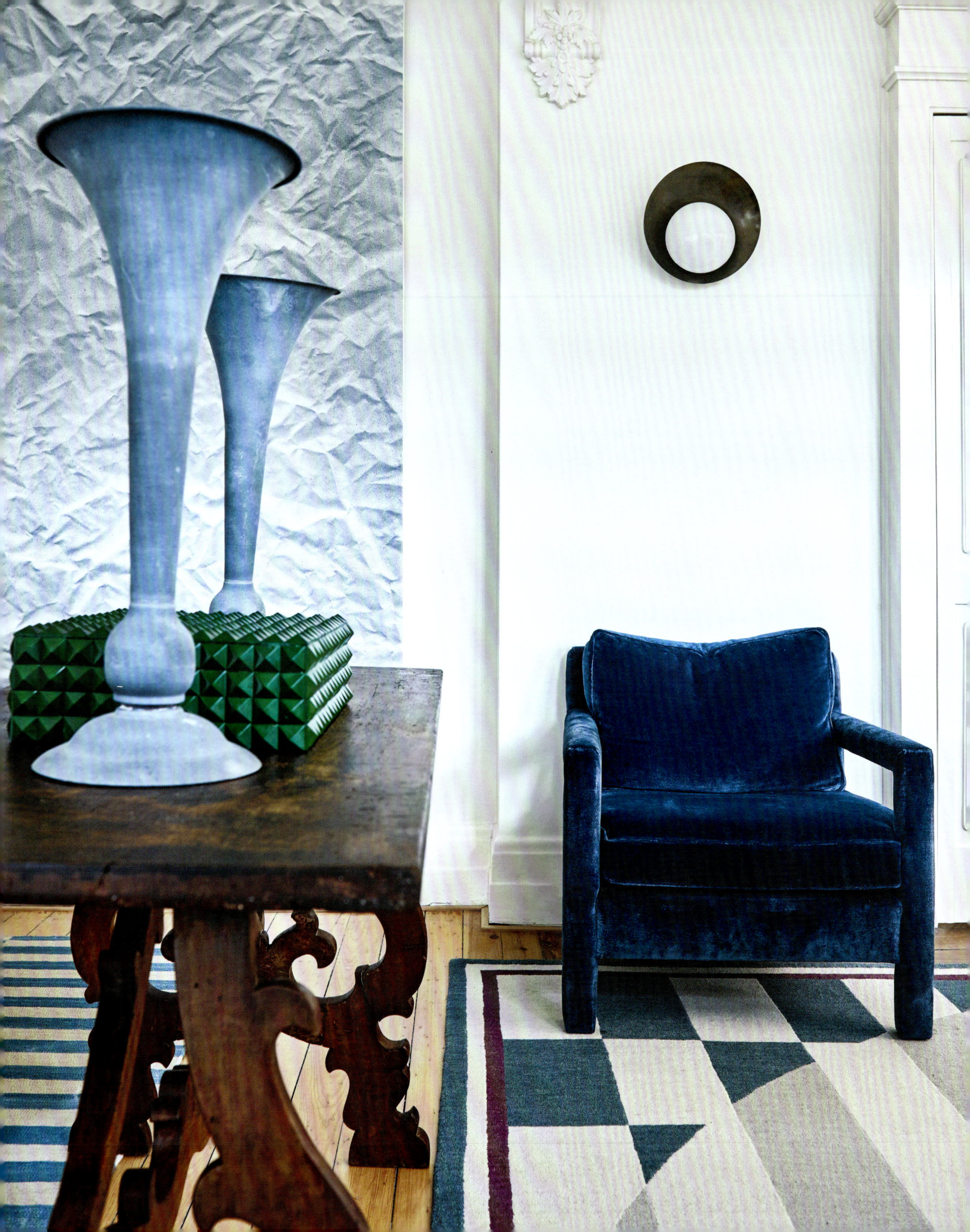

Perhaps I'd been to Singapore recently and was dreaming of Raffles. Perhaps it was just standing in the light-filled conservatory, with its glass walls and ceiling offering endless vistas of the greenery outside. Either way, I knew that for this room I wanted to create the sort of setting you might find in an old-fashioned colonial hotel—all leafy plantings and casual glamour.

It's quite unusual to discover a conservatory in an Australian city-center home—this is the sort of space one tends to associate with grand country houses and murder mystery games. But this beautiful Victorian-era house, set in an old-world part of Sydney's eastern suburbs, has an innate grandeur that springs partly from its surrounding gardens and partly from its original design. The conservatory is central to its layout, linking to formal living and dining rooms, and for the owners, a couple with three children who are keen entertainers, it was clear that this would become a much-loved and much-used space. Of course, the challenge is envisaging all this when the reality is rather different. Standing there on my first visit, the conservatory was a run-down area being used as a storage room, with an old carpet and peeling paint. Elsewhere, elements of the house had received makeovers that were more 1980s than 1880s, such as the pine floorboards, which had been stained a lurid shade of orange. My intention is always to bring out the best of what a house can be. This five-bedroom home had some fabulous bones and original finishes, which I wanted to honor so that the character of the place would sit in harmony with its owners' contemporary lifestyle. The interior design involved nudging recently modernized elements back to a style more in keeping with the traditional structure, such as reinstating old cornices and sanding back the floorboards for a raw finish. For the conservatory floor, I introduced black-and-white marble tiles in a checkerboard pattern to announce this as a special space. Together with cane furniture upholstered in white bouclé fabric, ceiling fans, and rattan planters containing oversized palms, they create that colonial hotel vibe, with the palms maintaining a connection to the greenery outside. I like to think of the garden as another room and I believe indoor and outdoor layers should work as one, an effect that is enhanced here by the natural light that floods this space.

pp. 217–19 - Old-world glamour beckons in the conservatory, which combines the refined finishes of silk Versace cushions and an antique French mirrored coffee table with the natural, textural appeal of cane and rattan, and the abundant greenery.

Opposite - The zinc plinths, which Patrick and I discovered in a New York antiques store, give a strong sculptural quality to the space. They also pick up the blue tones of a custom velvet-upholstered chair, the two rugs and a Sean Wadey artwork behind.

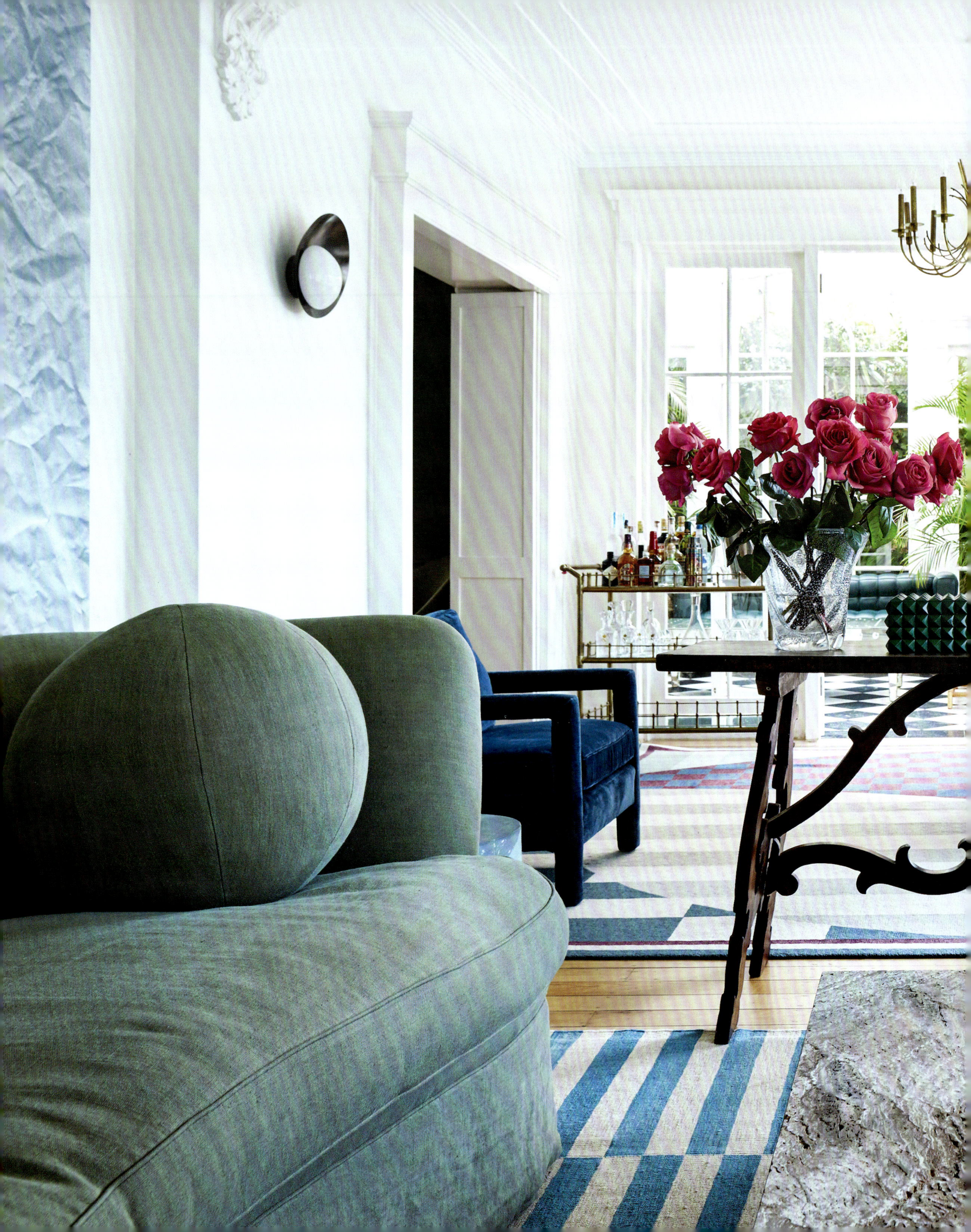

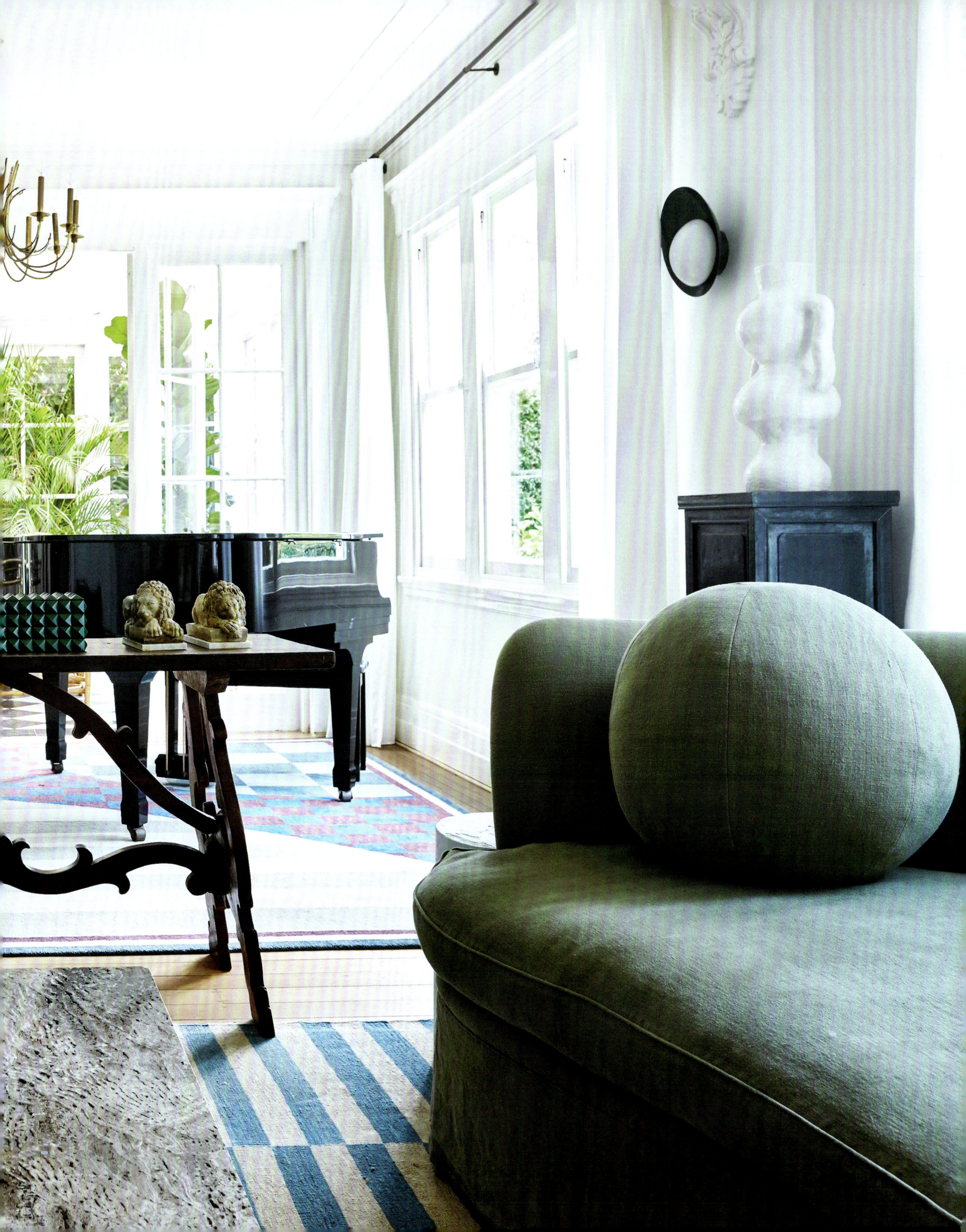

The myriad colors of all that foliage helped to determine the vision for the interior décor, so sofas in the softest sage green linen were a pleasing choice for the living room. Finding the right shade of green paint for the dining room became a little contemplation of nature in itself, which entailed trying several shades on the walls to see how they responded to light at different times of the day. I think there's a wonderful serendipity about the fact that the perfect shade turned out to be one called "Bay Leaf." Those herbaceous hues instill a sense of calmness in the rooms, which is reinforced by the natural textures of certain materials. In the conservatory, cane and rattan bring this earthy element; in the living room, it appears in the wool of a blue and white kilim rug and the travertine of a coffee table. These tactile, rustic components balance the refined, burnished finishes of the antique pieces that reflect the more formal aspects of the house. There is another theme at play here too. One of the owners works in the fashion industry, and I wanted to introduce some fun, glamorous elements to acknowledge her passion. Upstairs, an unused bedroom has been transformed into a lavish walk-in wardrobe, painted a gorgeous sky blue and featuring shelves for handbags and a charming cushioned window seat with extra storage. Elsewhere, the fashionable thread weaves its way through the house via little touches that elevate various spaces, from a Hermès blind in the family bathroom to Versace silk cushions in the conservatory and a Pucci rug by the living room. Even the dining chairs appear dressed for the occasion, with their loose linen covers and pleated skirts in eight different colors. These were actually a happy accident that resulted from there being simply too many beautiful shades to choose only one. From sage and navy through to pink and rust, their tonal range and contemporary shape provide a playful counterbalance to the antique dining table and somber artworks behind.

And so the modern and the traditional, the relaxed and the formal, happily interact throughout the house. One original feature cherished by the owners is a lovely old butler's pantry, which connects the dining room to the elegant gray-toned kitchen via a swinging door. It's a reminder of a time long before open-plan kitchens, when staff would have brought meals out to the gathered diners. Now, of course, it's the diners themselves doing the serving, but there's still that sense of old-world ways that gives this house much of its charm.

On the other side of the house, separated from the living room by an elegant nineteenth-century Spanish side table, is another treasured heirloom — a grand piano, which sits atop the Pucci rug and is used by adults and children alike. Among all these rooms, the conservatory acts as breakout space and entertainment hub, whether the house is full of guests or just the family relaxing. Sitting among the greenery, listening to the sound of the piano during parties or practice time, you are lulled by the sense of another era, imbued with all the energy of this one.

Previous spread - A nineteenth-century Spanish side table acts as a beautiful yet unimposing divider between the living room and the piano area.

Opposite and overleaf - Curved custom sofas in sage green linen present an inviting setting, contrasted by the "tougher" element of concrete in the side tables and the legs of a gray travertine-top table.

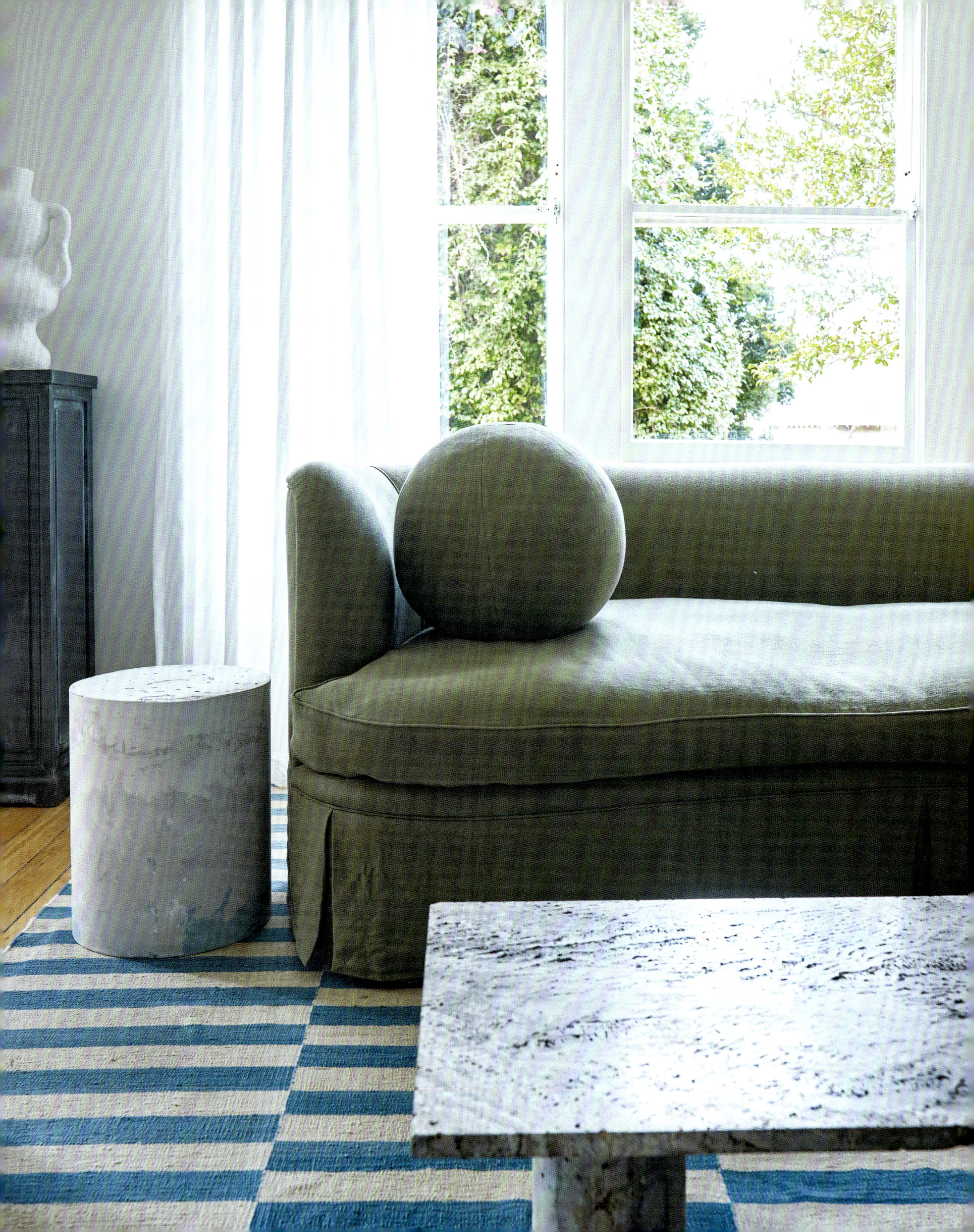

YVES SAINT LAURENT
WOOD
JAMES TURRELL
FANTASTIC MAN
Art Sales Digest
DRESSING THE MAN

BVLGARI
NEWTON
THE FASHION BOOK
LIFE
IT'S ALL TRUE
Cy Twombly

Above and opposite - Ample natural light in the dining room, with its beautiful Murano glass chandelier, allows for the rich play of colors on the walls and chairs.

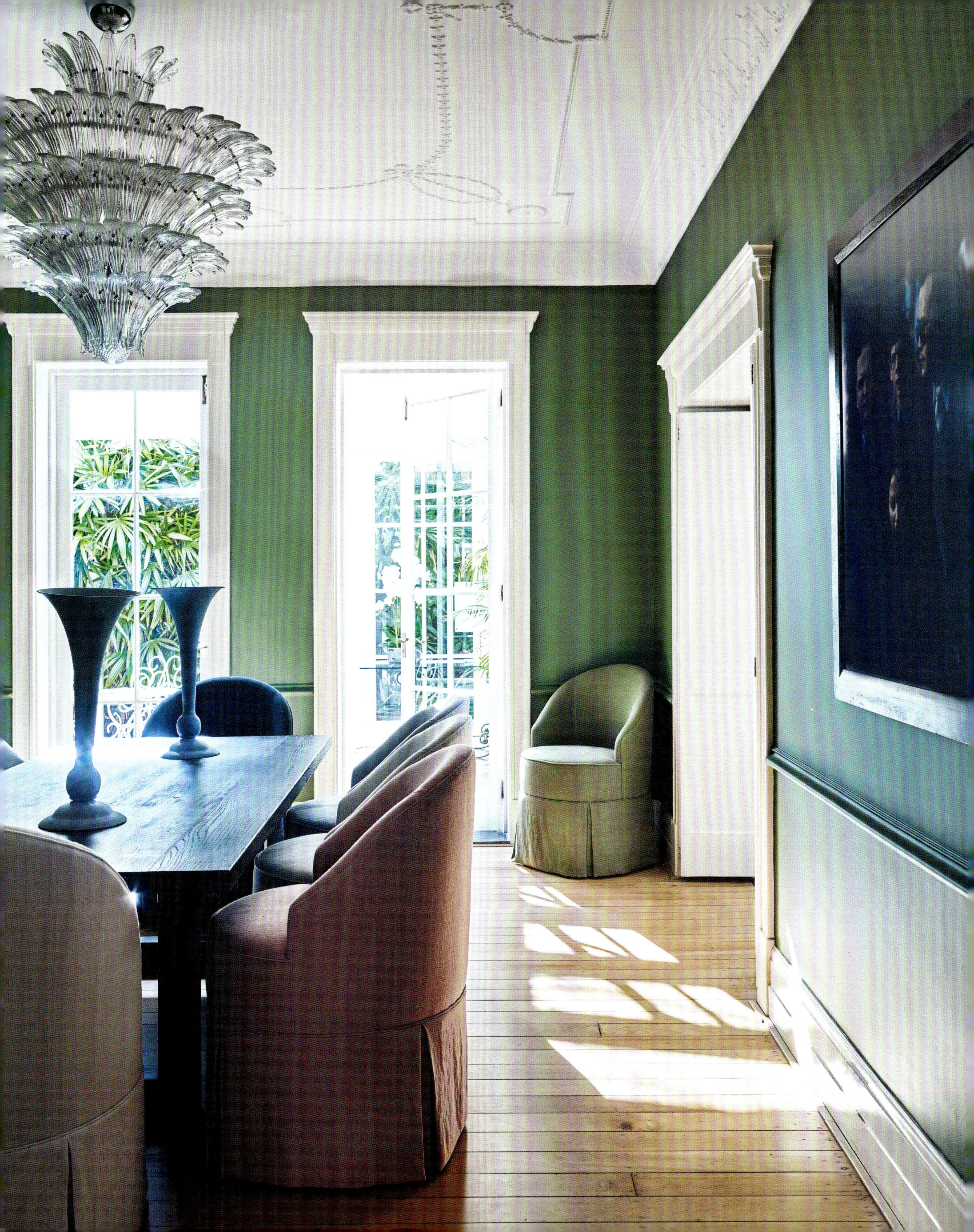

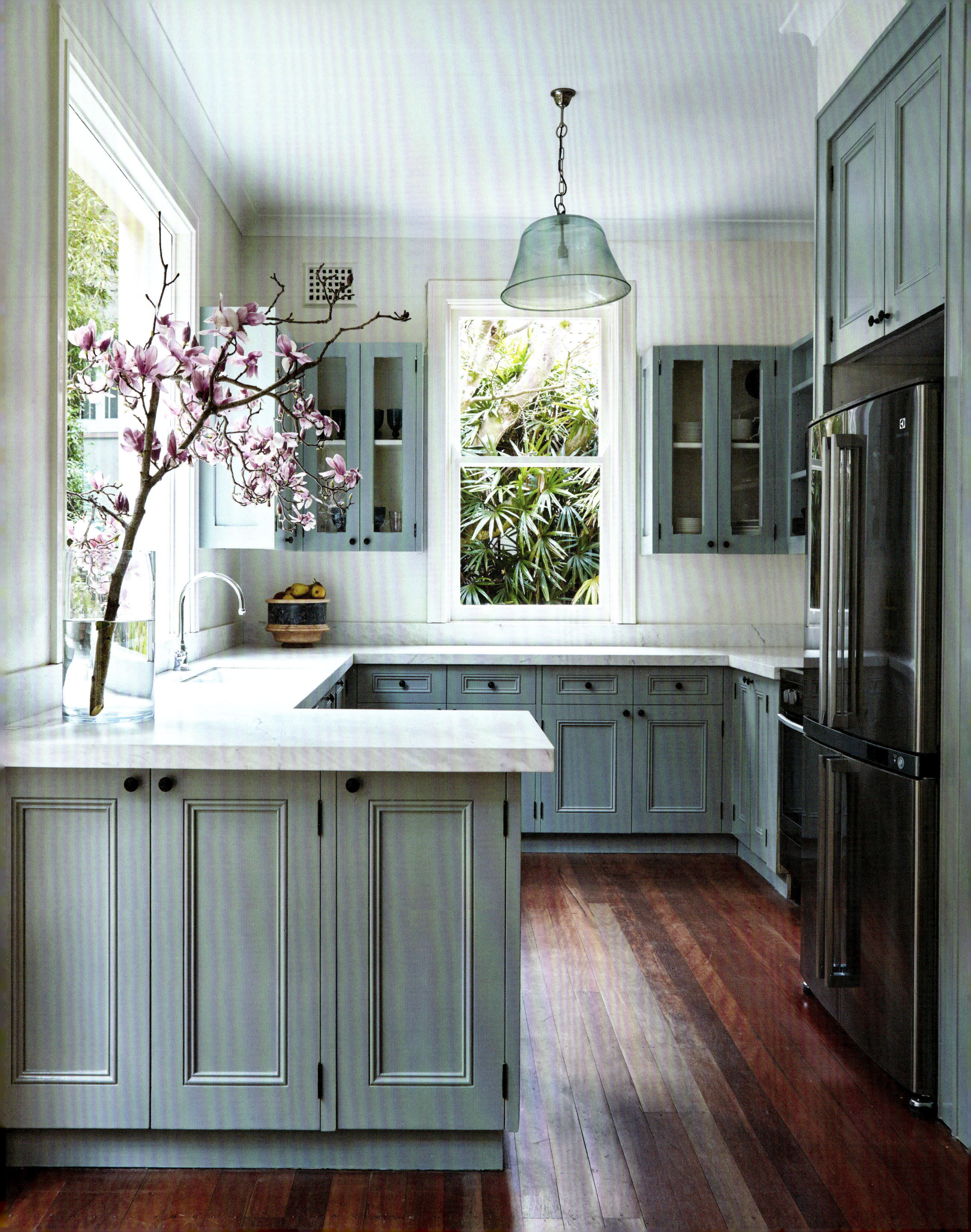

Opposite - Gray painted cabinetry gives a soft look to the old-style kitchen, which connects to the dining room.
Above - More gray features in the lovely sheen of the silk-pile carpet on the stairs, a space that just needed a fresh coat of paint on the walls to revive it.

Following spread (left) - A blind made from Hermès fabric brings a fashionable touch to the family bathroom.
Following spread (right) - More stunning prints in one of the children's bedrooms: Cole & Son Zambezi wallpaper provides a charming backdrop to the warm tones of the headboard in Kelly Wearstler Graffito *fabric*.

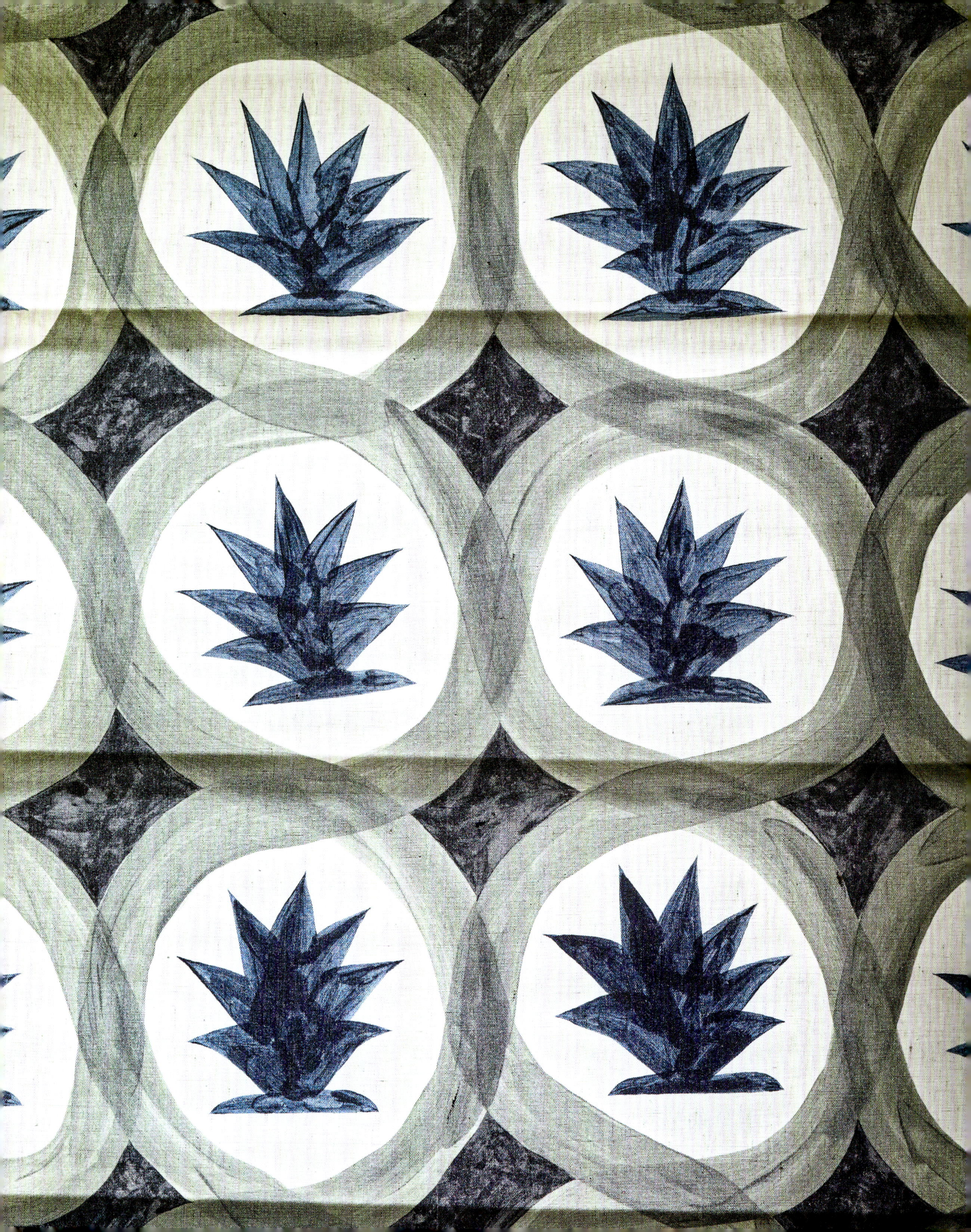

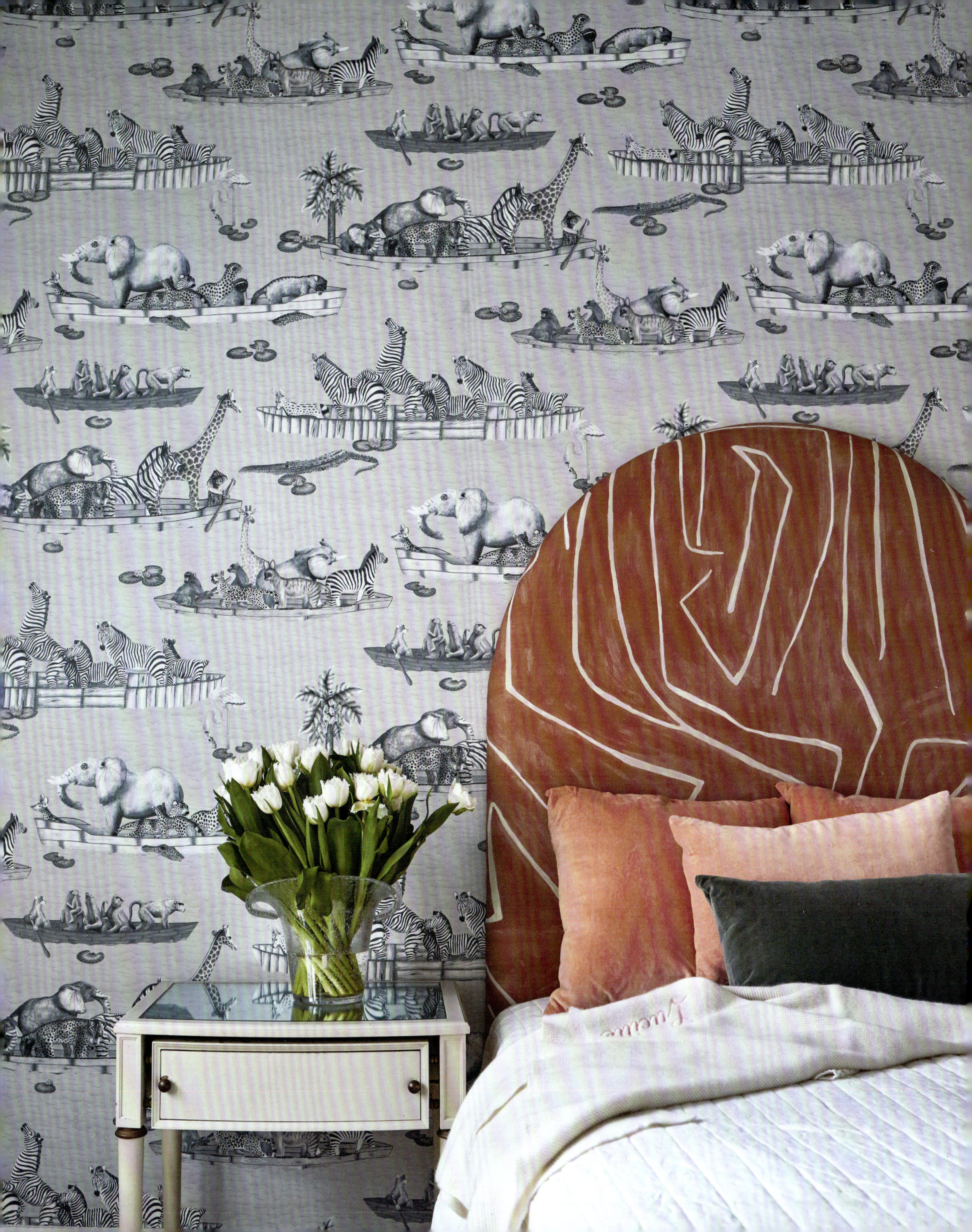

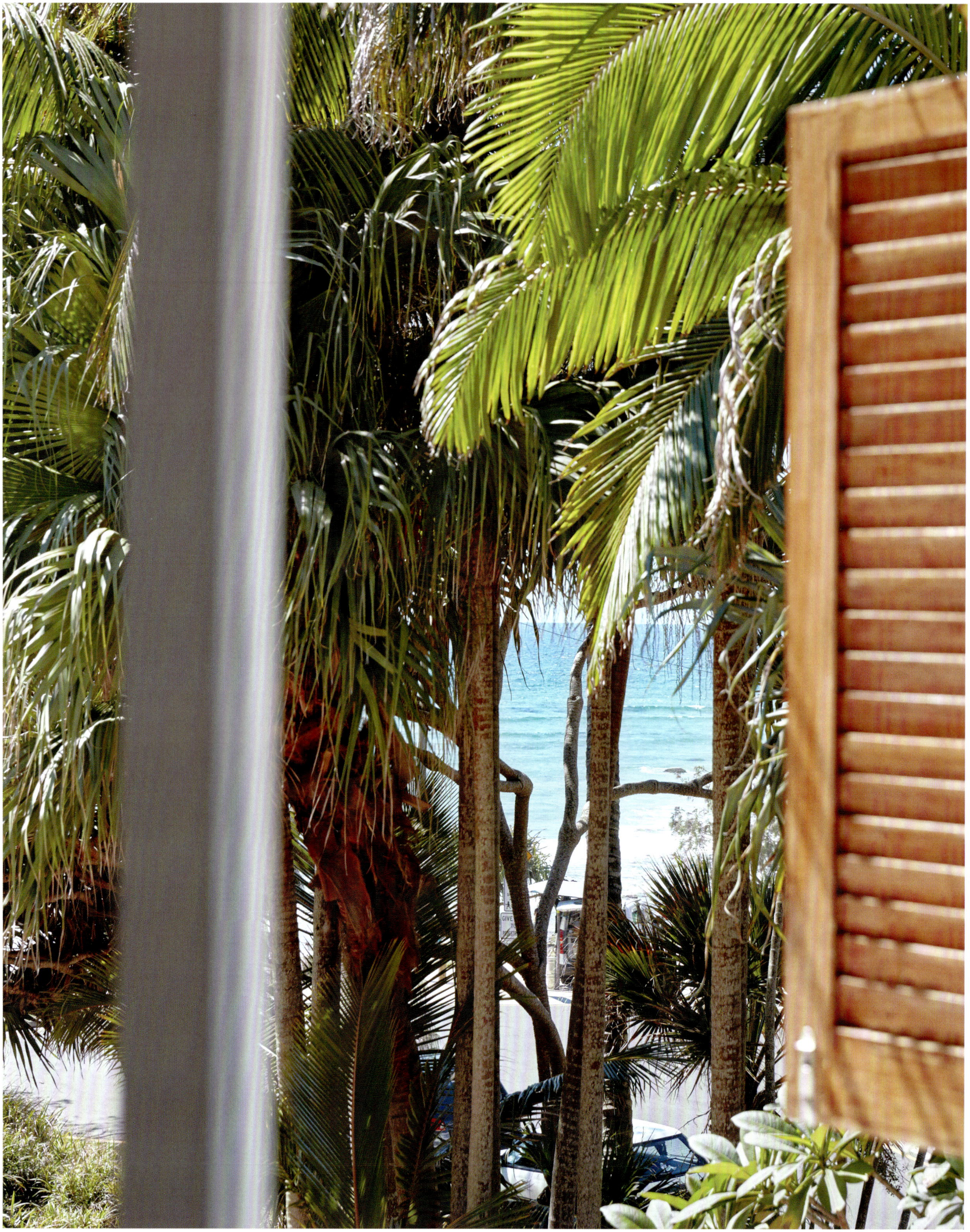

RETREAT

Raes on Wategos,
Marine Parade, Byron Bay

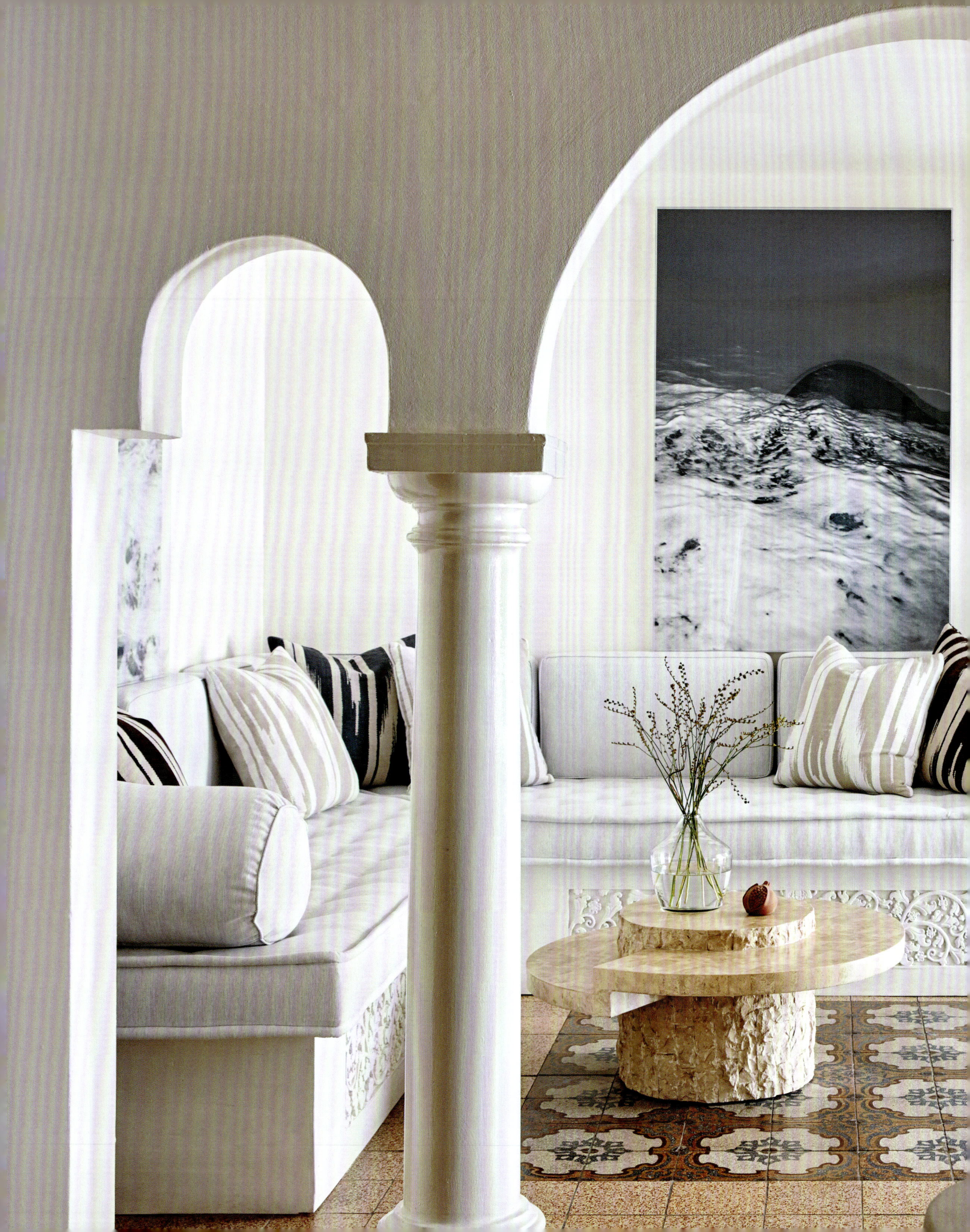

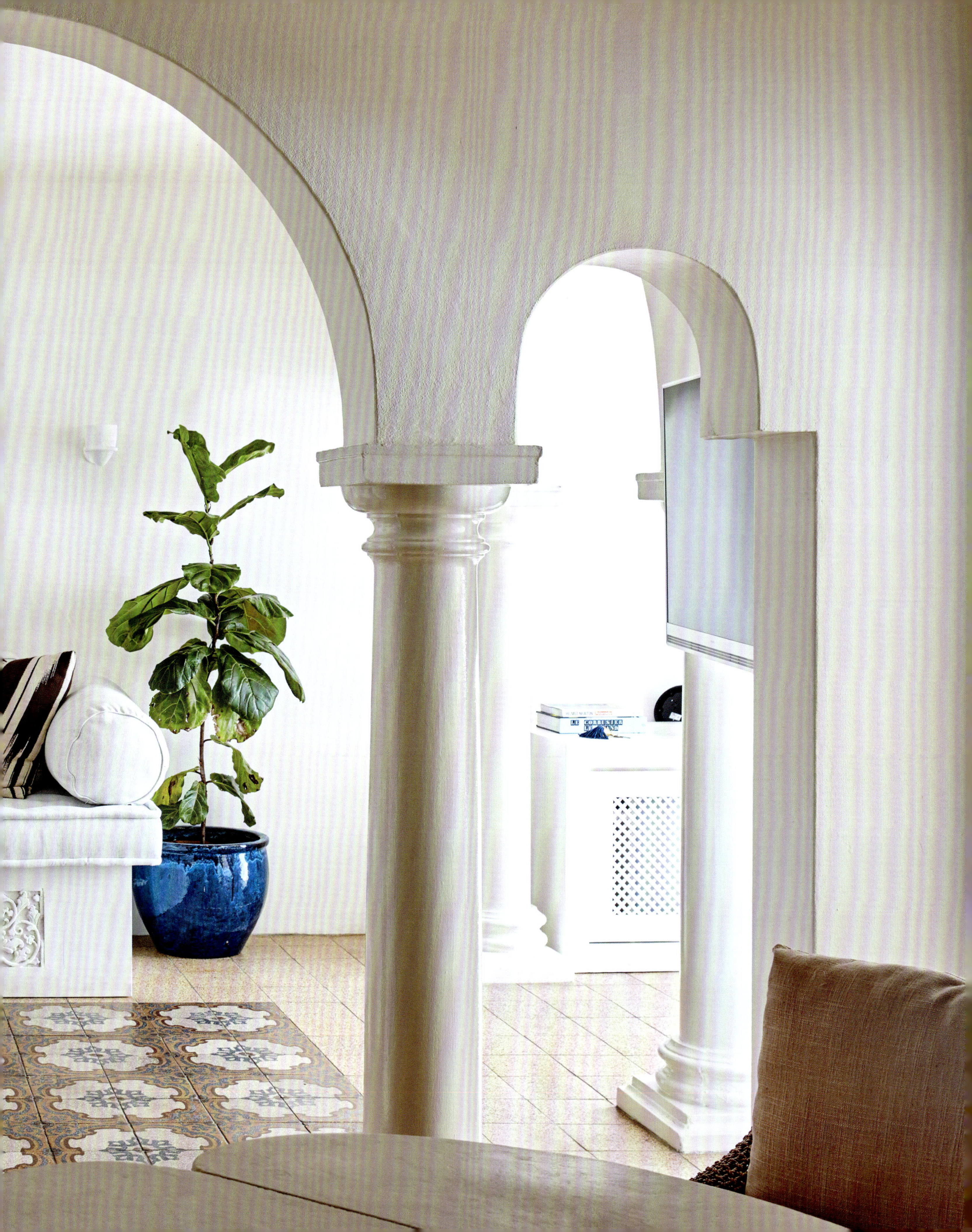

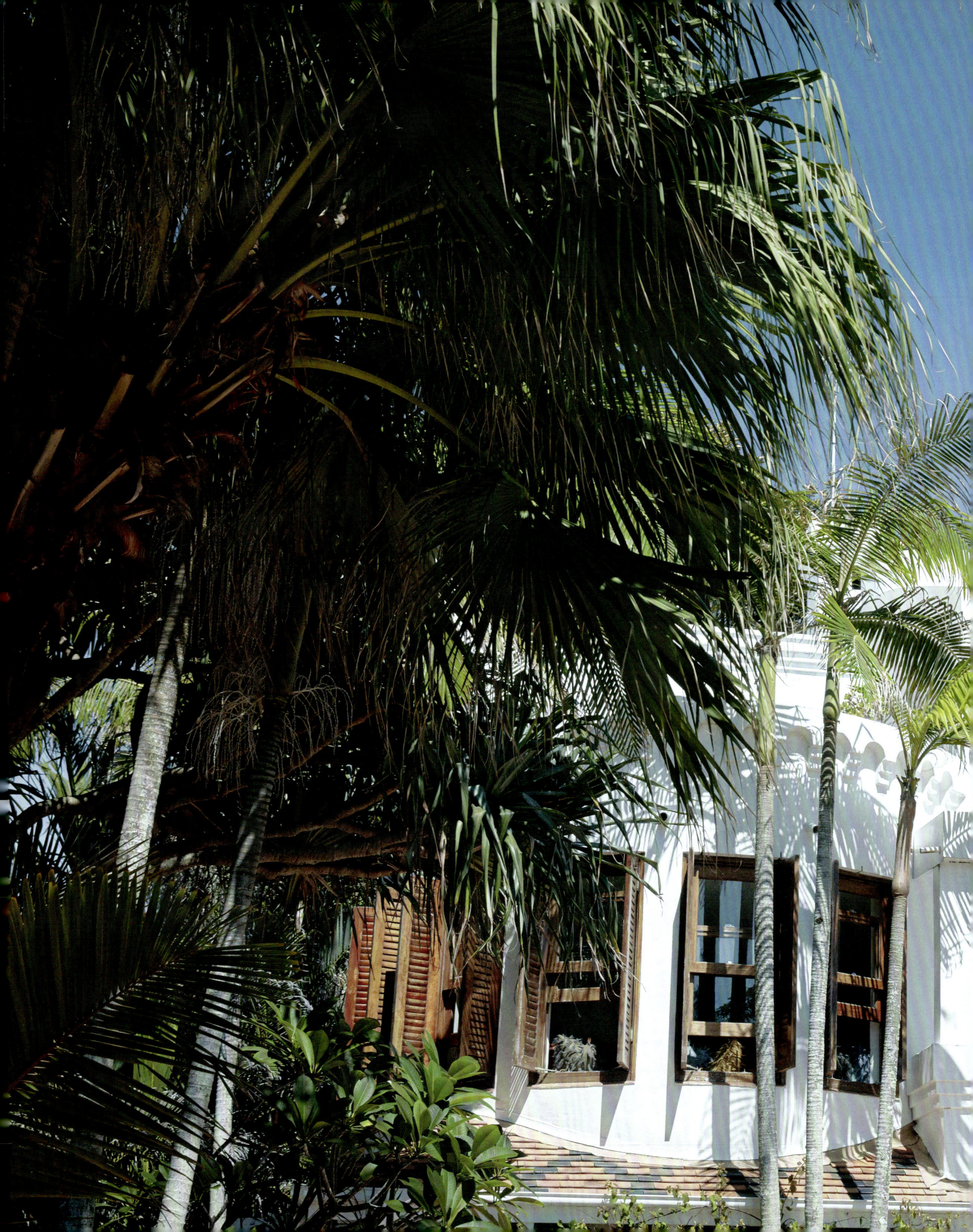

RECEPTION • SPA

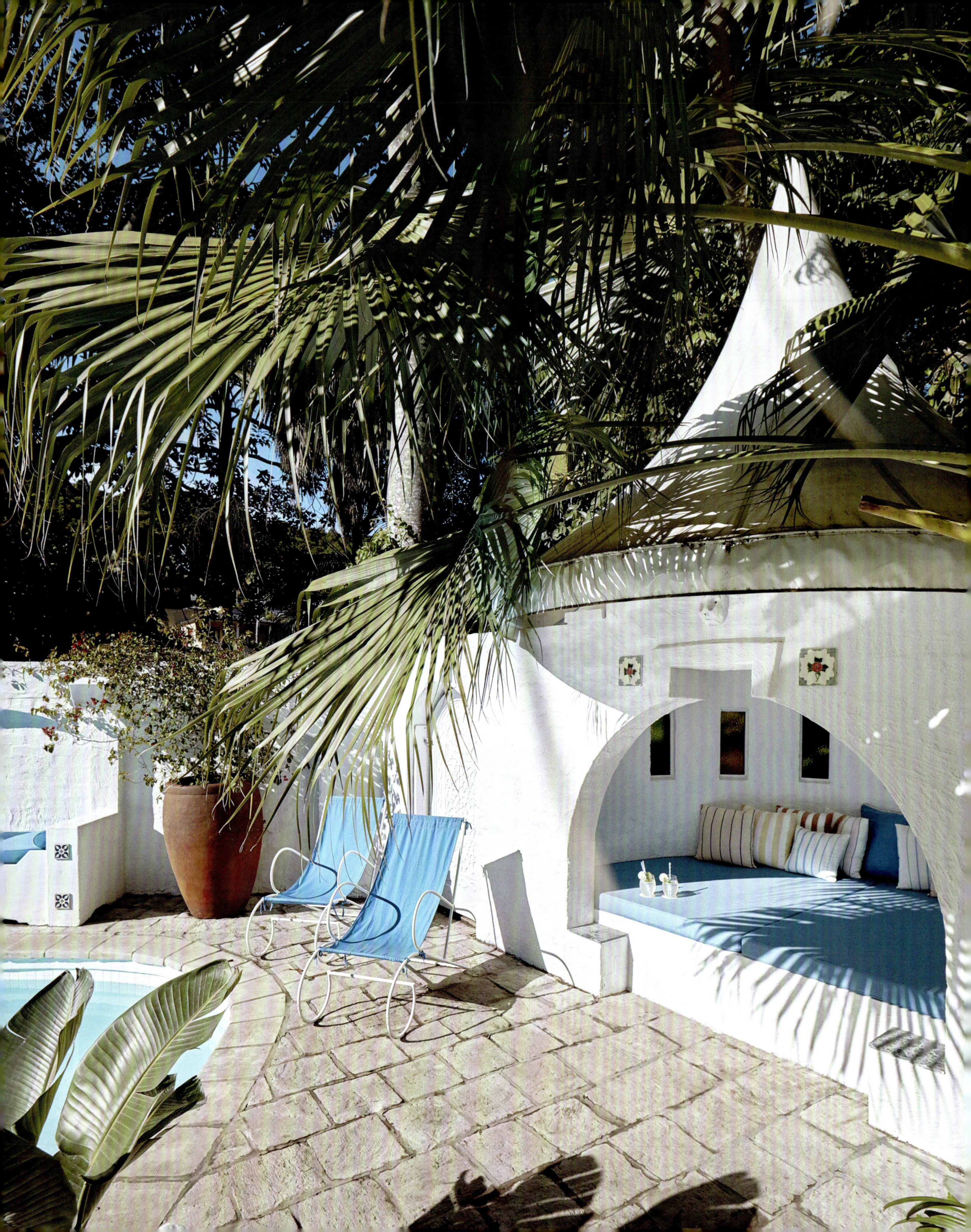

When you travel for work as much as I do, you see inside a great number of hotel rooms. You also become accustomed to identifying which spaces could be better utilized, which layouts could flow more smoothly, and all the little things that could make your stay more enjoyable. To get the chance to consider these elements as part of an interior design job is quite the experience—particularly when your research involves staying at one of Australia's most famous boutique hotels.

Raes on Wategos is an iconic luxury retreat in an equally iconic location—the fashionably bohemian New South Wales coastal town of Byron Bay, which has lately become such a magnet for celebrities. Wategos Beach, which the hotel faces, is an idyllic and tranquil spot that works its transformative magic on visitors. There is something sublimely Zen-like about the beach and the hotel, and even one night here can do wonders for the soul. I was fortunate to spend seven nights, one in each of the hotel's different suites, which was a great way to get a feel for the individual spaces. Built in the 1960s as a rather eccentric residence that later included a restaurant on its grounds, Raes began life as a hotel three decades later, and five years ago its new owners engaged me for an extensive redesign. The building, full of quirky, unloved spaces and unexpected nooks, was furnished in a mix of cultures and styles, where Moroccan tiles fought with dark Balinese furniture and dated purple suede upholstery. The architectural elements, however, were beautiful, with arches, columns, and molded wall details that wouldn't look out of place in a Marrakech riad. A lot of my work involved stripping back unnecessary and distracting furnishings to reveal those elements, and then enhancing or replicating them to create a light-filled, breezy retreat that is all about relaxed luxury.

The Moroccan floor tiles were a gorgeous feature of the hotel, so I restored these where possible and introduced similar new tiles, laying them in configurations to match the originals so there is no jarring distinction between old and new. The tiles vary between the rooms in terms of detail, palette, and finish, giving each space its own personality. In one suite, patterned cement tiles extend across the entire floor, while in another they make up a stunning display in the center of a seating area, surrounded by peach terrazzo tiles. Marble tiles appear in different arrangements, from a large geometric motif to a grand checkerboard design in gray and dusty pink that is almost like a giant Berber print.

pp. 236–37 - A little bit riad, a little bit resort—the Moroccan floor tiles, architectural arches, and corner banquette blend comfort and style.
Previous spread - The building's unconventional lines are especially evident on its exterior. The warm tones of the timber shutters contrast beautifully with the white walls.

Opposite - The signature Raes blue features in the grotto-style daybed and loungers by the pool.

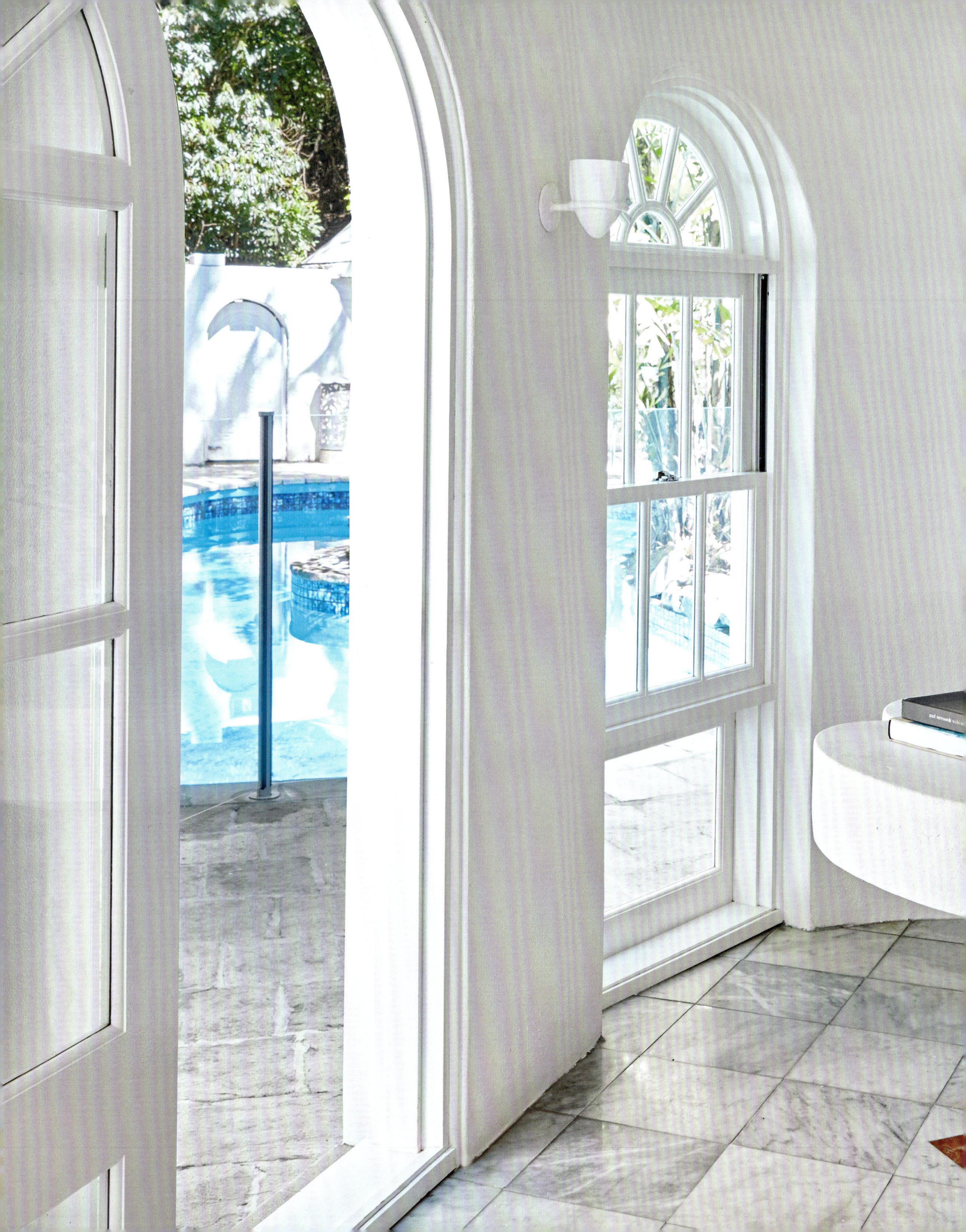

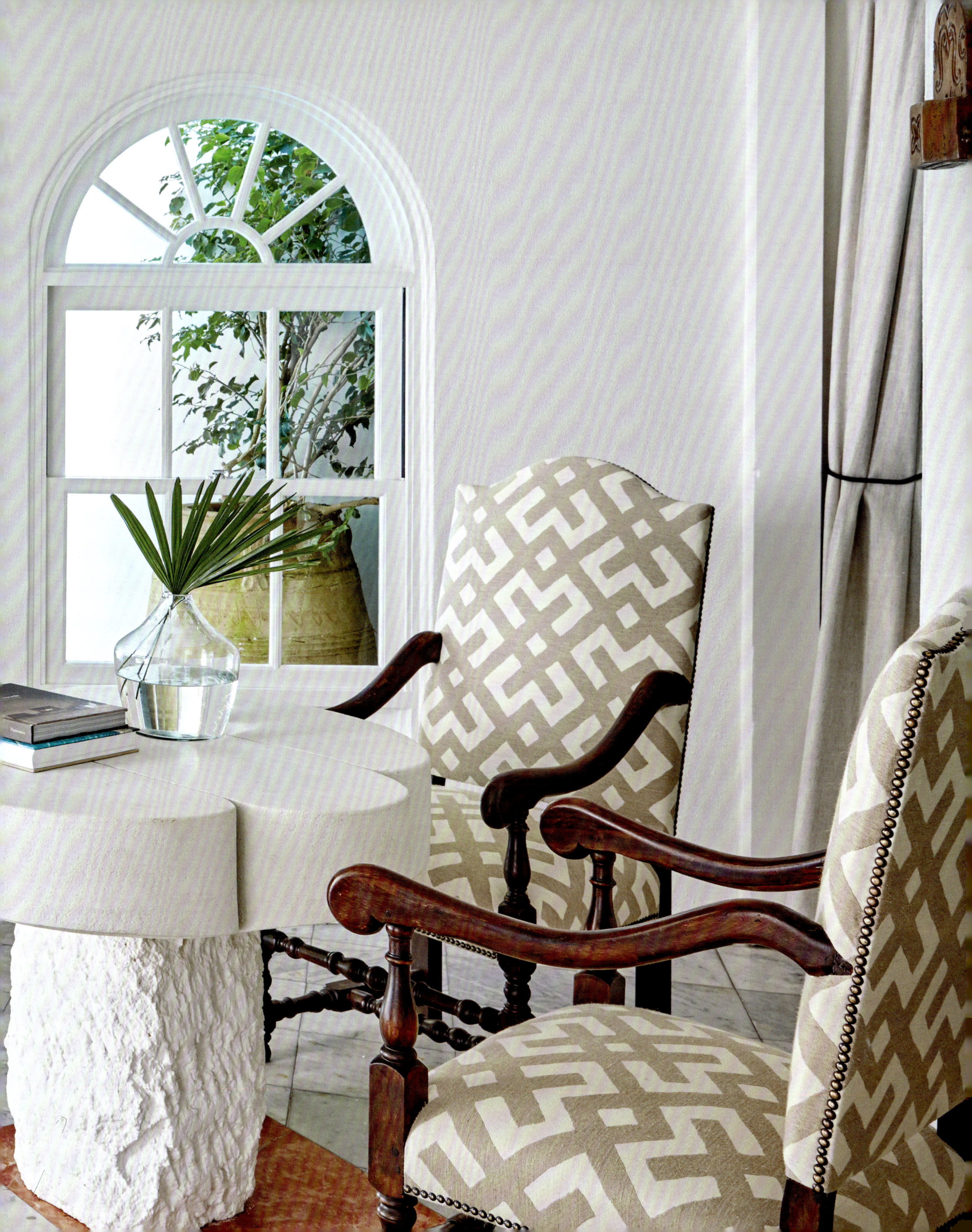

The individuality these tiles bring to each room is a large part of the hotel's charm, enriched by other components of the interior design. I focused on creating enticing little groupings of furniture to suit the layout of each room and make it unique, like a private residence. Every piece has been chosen and every setting arranged to feel as if, like the tiles, it has always been there, timeless in its appeal. I wanted guests to immerse themselves in the experience of their particular room and, on leaving, to anticipate what experiences another visit—and another room—might have in store. Custom seating arrangements and daybeds were key to giving each unused or oddly shaped space a purpose. One suite features a large corner banquette in white linen that wraps around a mid-twentieth-century travertine table, with pops of color courtesy of boldly patterned cushions, a striking photograph of waves, and a blue glazed pot. A smaller built-in banquette in another suite features a simple white French-buttoned seat and stacks of pale blue cushions, with a small French farmhouse-style stool bringing a rustic touch. Elsewhere, in a suite overlooking the pool, a pair of African stools present a raw, organic materiality beside an all-white daybed, which I introduced to revive a neglected corner of the room. Simply decorated with a couple of cushions, it tucks invitingly into a curved nook, which echoes the arches of the surrounding doors and windows. Another pair of chairs in the suite—antique Louis XV-style pieces from France—showcase their classic lines beside a striking contemporary table of carved Australian limestone by stone mason and sculptor Steven John Clark of Melbourne studio denHolm. Clark's creations, a fusion of furniture and art, appear throughout the rooms, also teamed with Malawi cane armchairs for a study in curves and texture.

Being a hotel, there are elements common to the rooms, but I still wanted the design to feel intimate and distinctive. The televisions (an unavoidable feature) are framed in a white plaster box that softens their impact, while white furnishings continue in custom plaster light fixtures, poured concrete desks with lattice-front doors, and loose, pull-back linen curtains. The beds, in white linen with a stone-colored linen valance, feature headboards in a custom-designed shape that is a hotel signature. The effect is low-key and calming yet infinitely elegant, with upholstery chosen for durability, while antiques, cushions, and artworks bring refinement.

White, gray, dusty pink, and the greens of the natural surroundings form the palette for the rooms and common areas, enhanced by the beauty of stone, cane, and timber. One more hue essential to this holiday haven is the inimitable Raes shade of blue, which draws inspiration from the ocean beyond and comes into its own by the pool. Here, it appears on mid-twentieth-century-style loungers and on the cushioned seat of a grotto-style daybed. I created this nook from a strange little cave previously used for storage, adorning it with floral inset tiles and striped cushions by fashion designer Lucy Folk. This may be a shared space but, like the hotel itself, it is so much more: a special retreat in a private piece of paradise.

Previous spread - Beside a carved limestone table, Louis XV-style chairs upholstered in Pierre Frey fabric bring a lovely warmth and classic shape to the contemporary white and gray poolside suite.

Following spread - The same fabric, in a darker tone, appears on a corner daybed, amid Moroccan-style wall treatments.

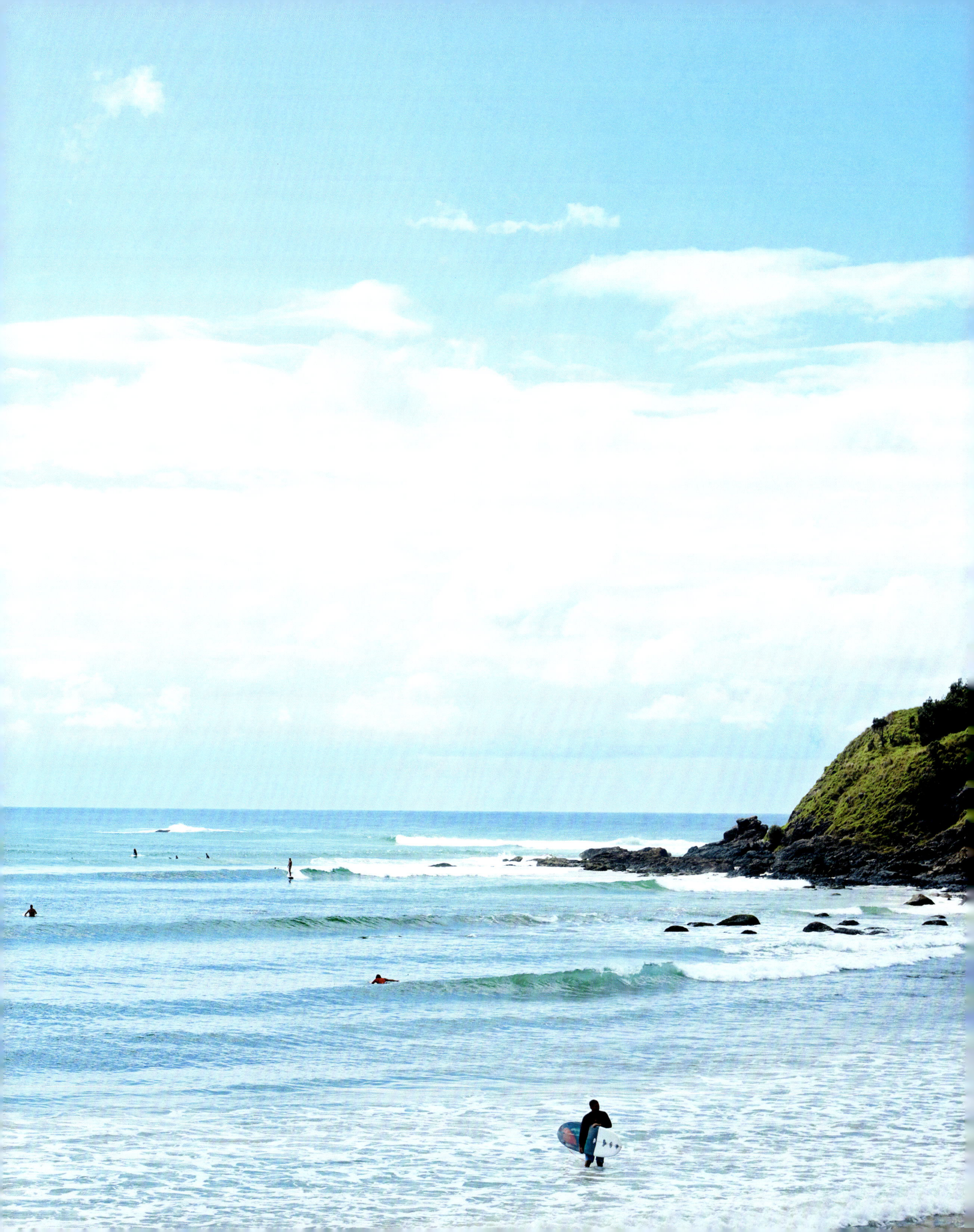

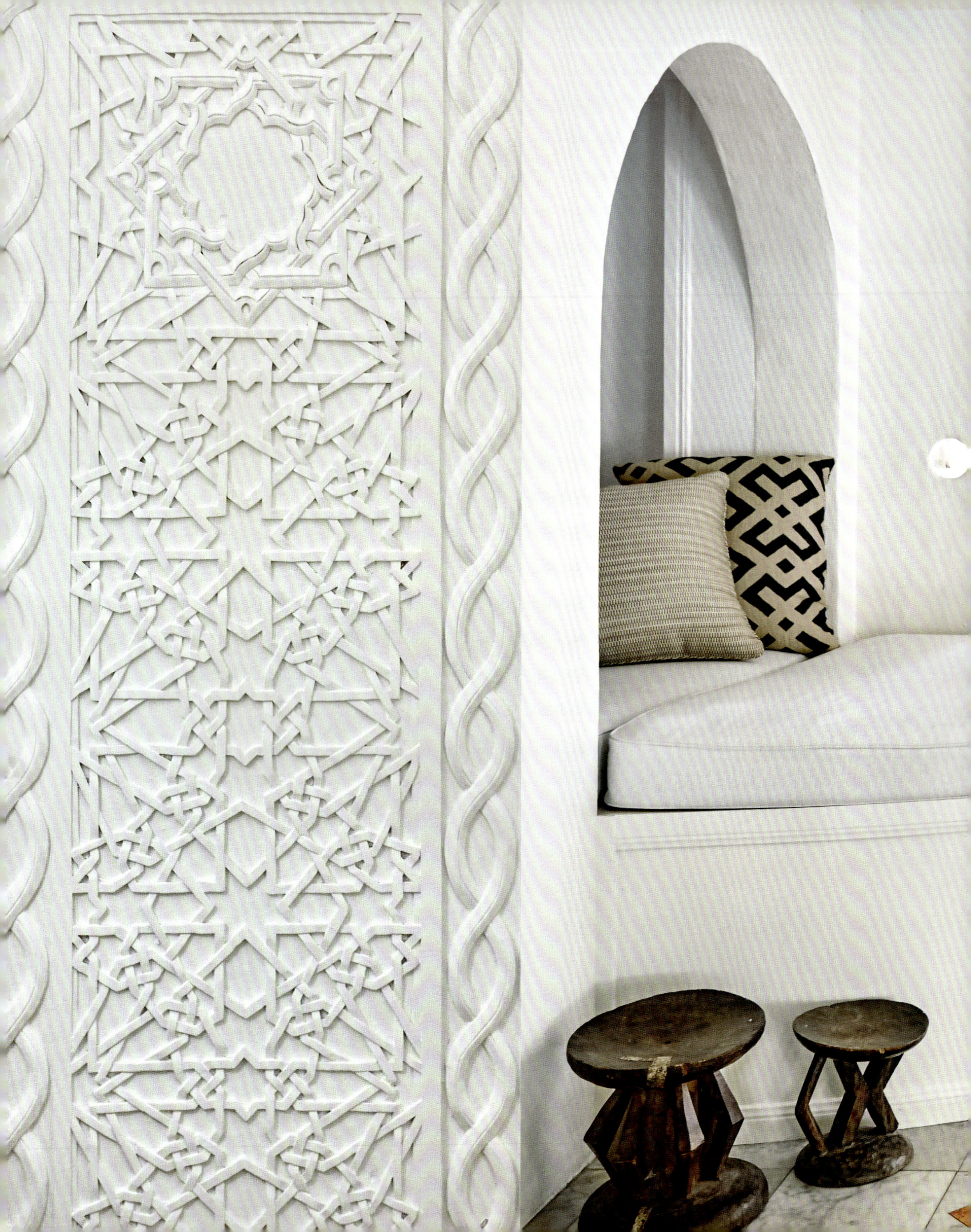

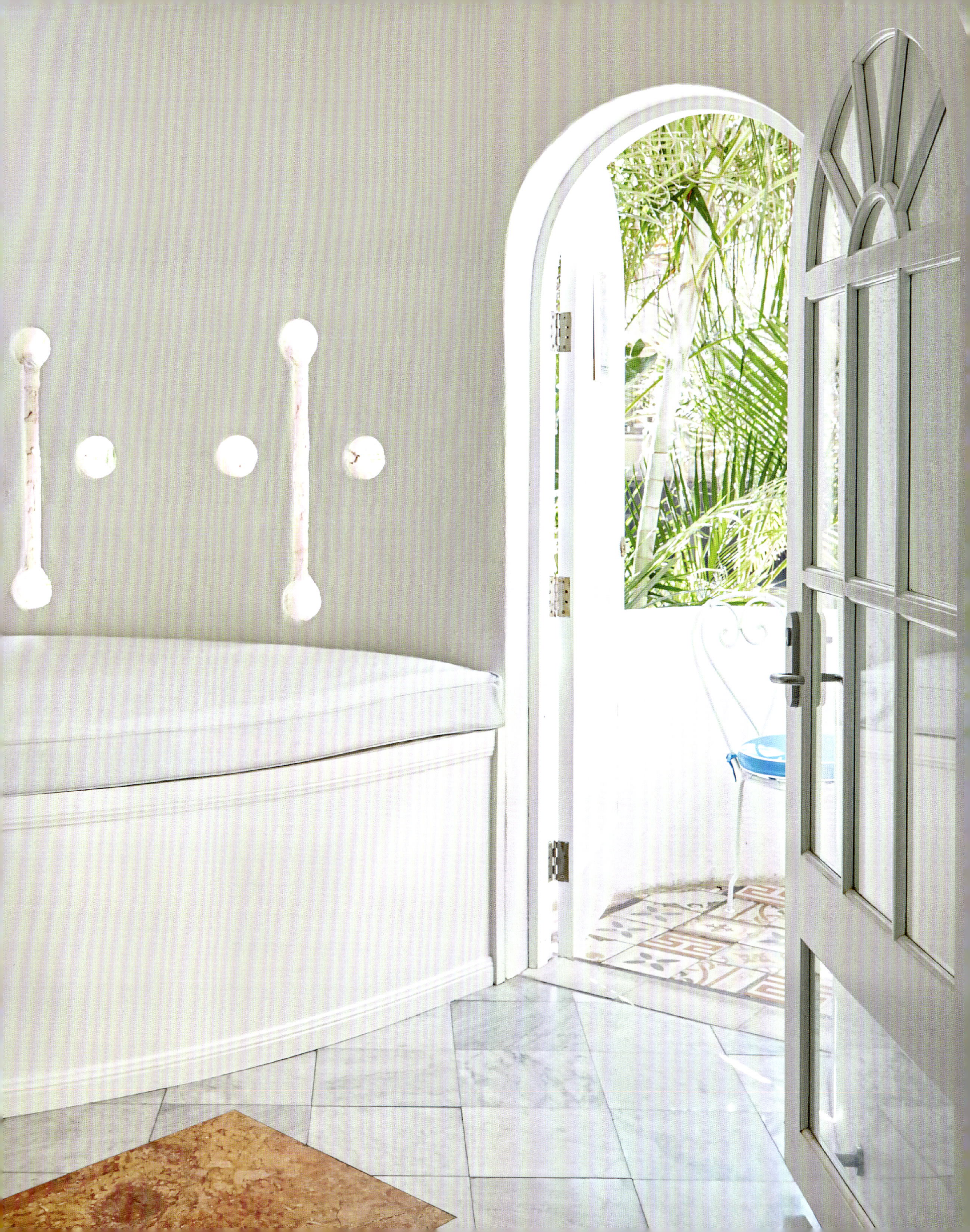

Above - Rattan chairs bring a natural, textural finish that suits the beachside setting.

Opposite - In the rooms, custom linen headboards and curtains make for durable yet stylish furnishings.

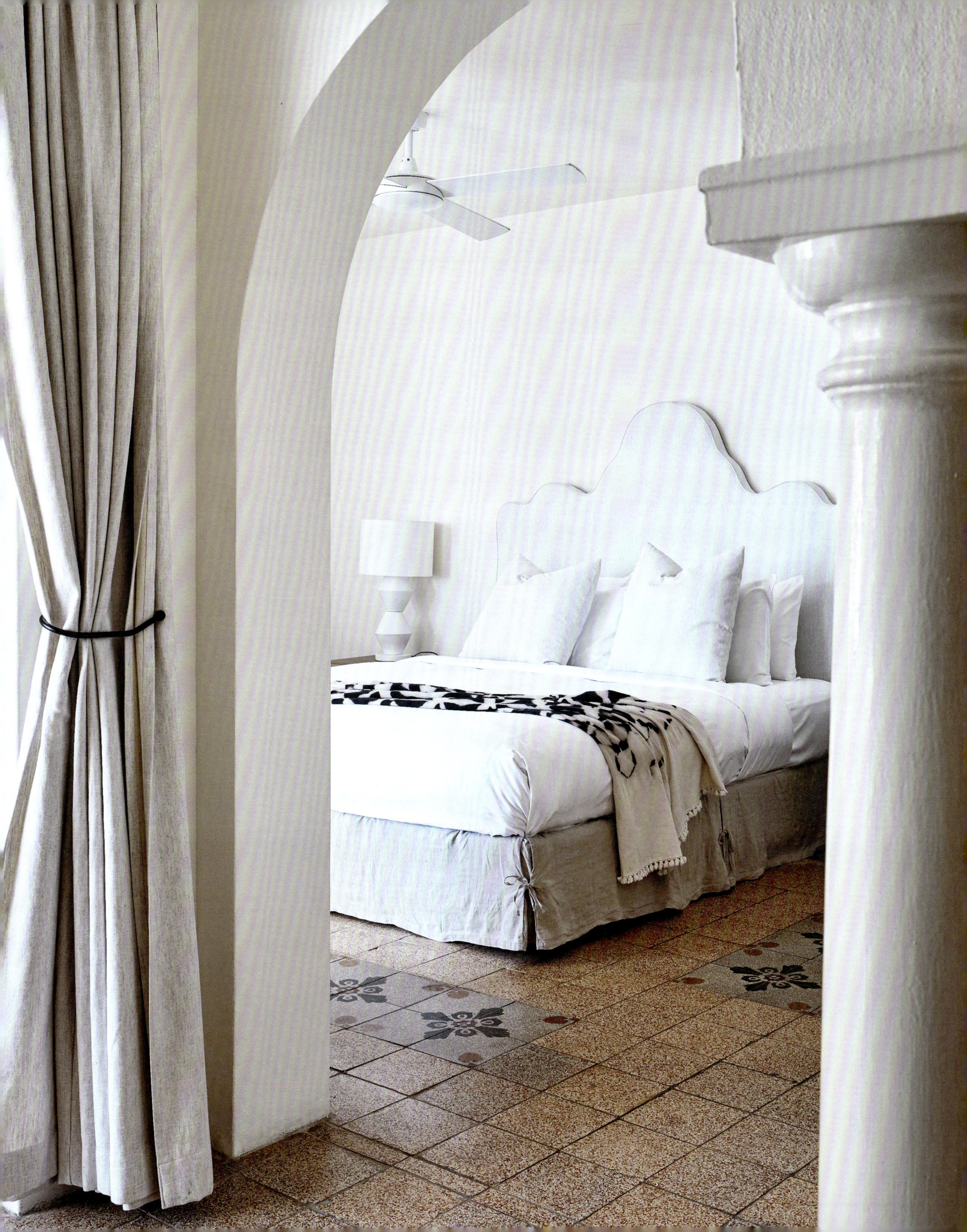

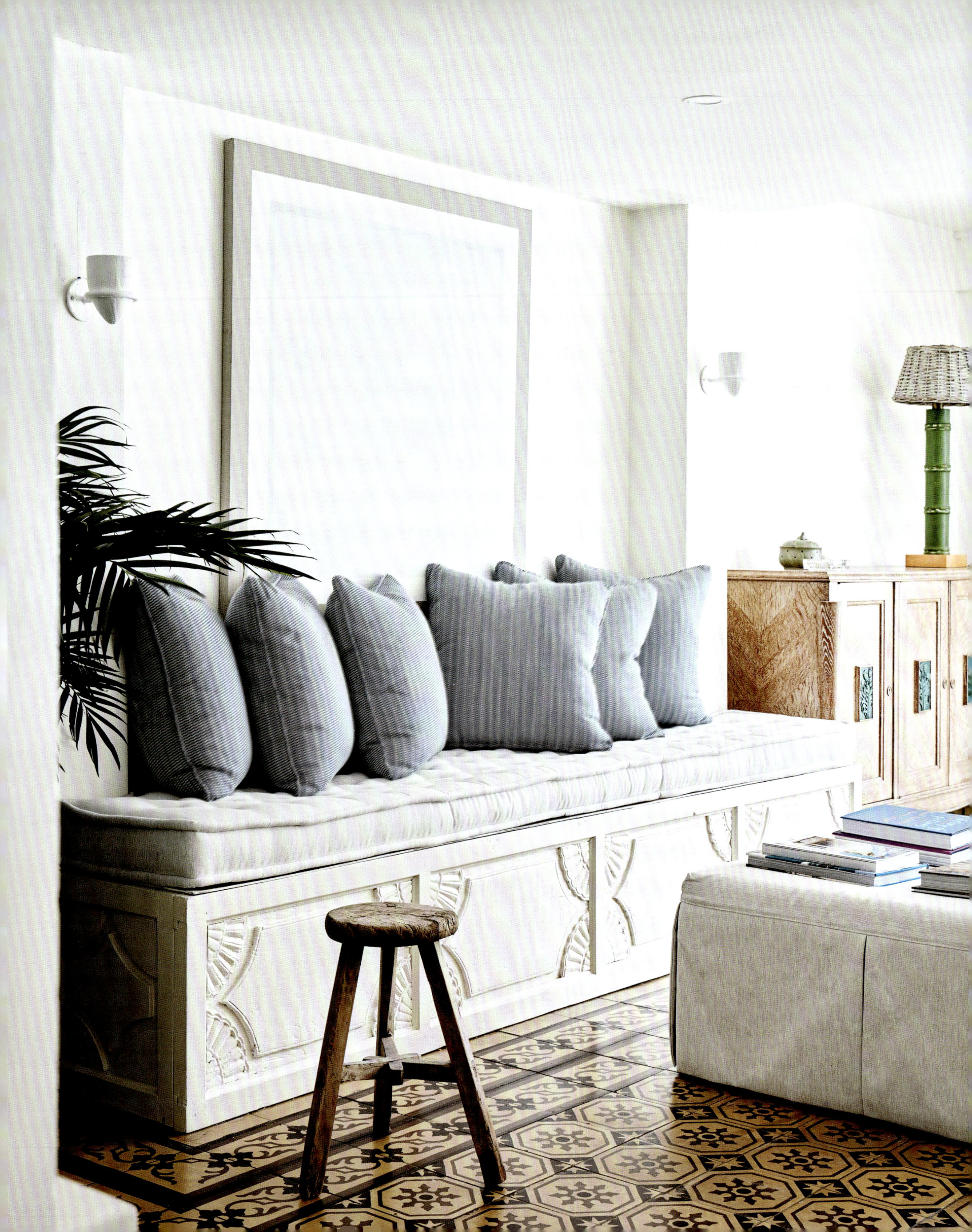

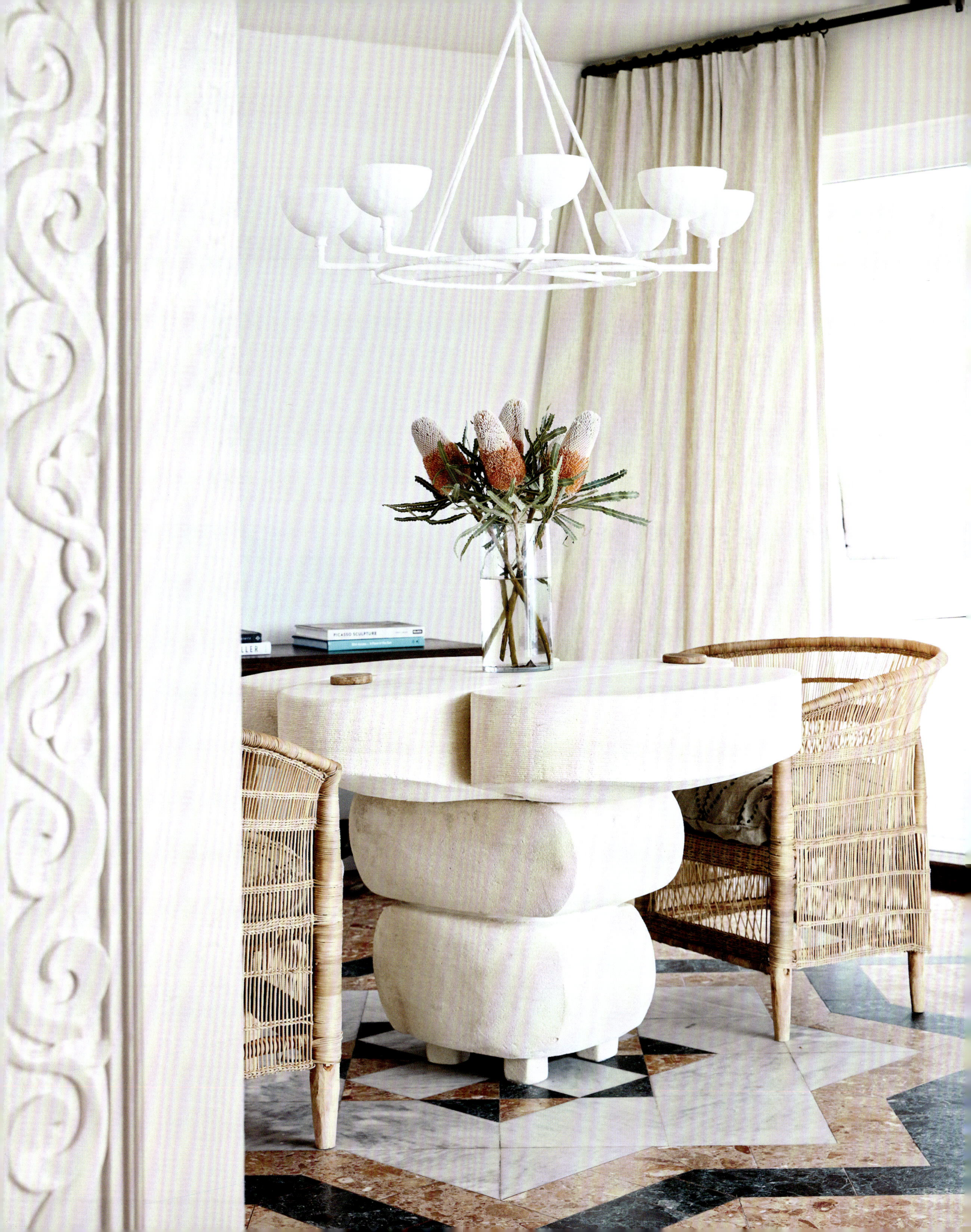
PICASSO SCULPTURE
LLER

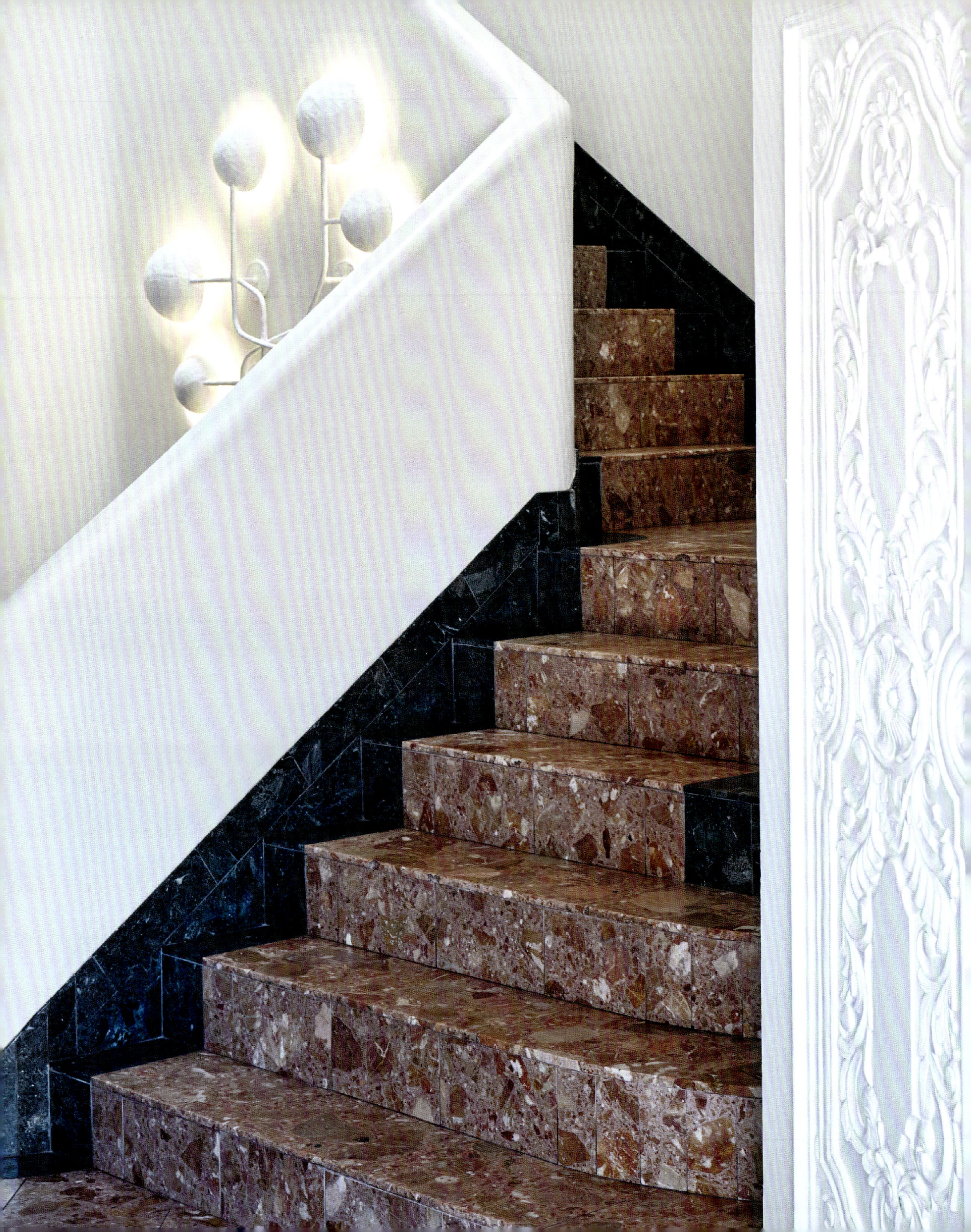

Previous spread - Plaster finishes on a banquette seat, wall relief, and pendant light give detail to the white palette.

Opposite - Elements such as the marble stairs at reception and the arched window (above) emphasize the lines of the building.

Following spread - Gray and dusty pink marble floor tiles create a striking Berber-like pattern, contrasting with the curves of the headboard and keyhole doorways.

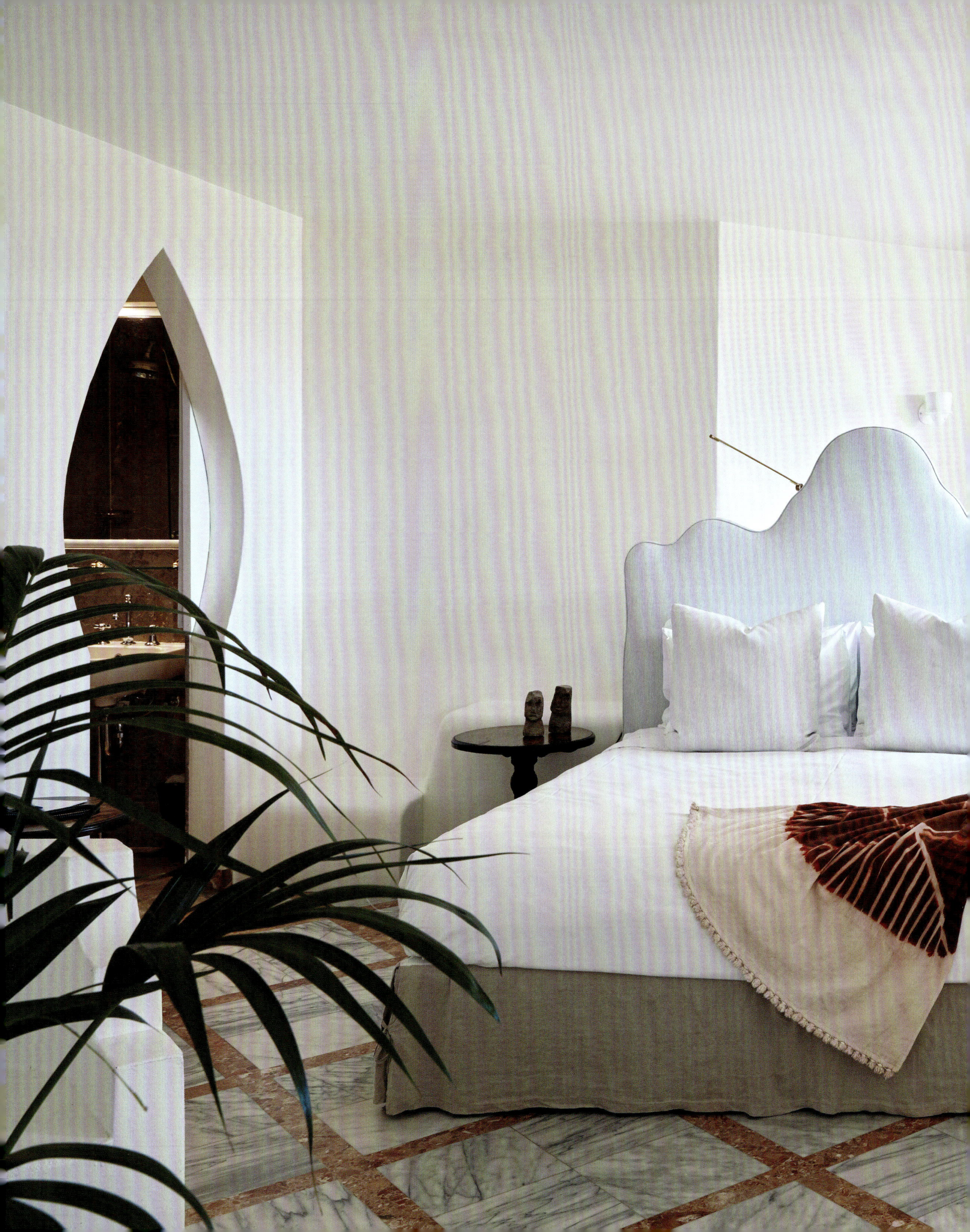

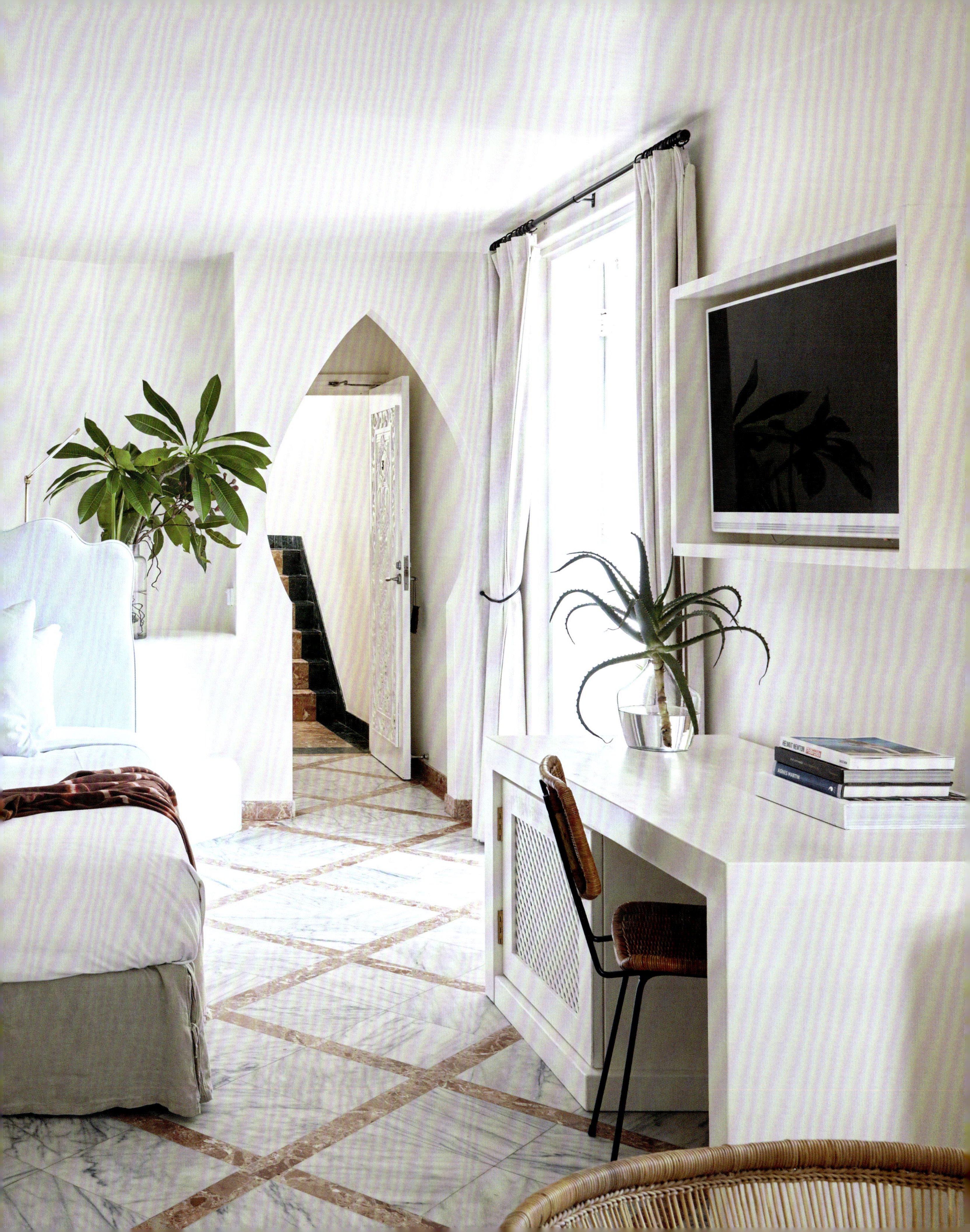

Acknowledgments

This book was a great pleasure to make, and allowed me time to slow down and reflect on how far back my love of interior design began and how natural the journey of a career can be when you truly love what you do. A few thank-yous are in order to seal this book with a kiss. The people below made every page possible, and I hope they enjoy reading this book as much as I enjoyed creating it.

First and foremost, Mum and Dad. They are the cornerstone of my life. They raised my sister, Tess, and me with limitless aspirations: the world was truly our oyster. Thank you, Dad, for dragging me and Tess to the fairs in Europe at 5 a.m. with the lure of a pain au chocolat and finding some treasure to bring home to Australia. You opened up our eyes to the very special universe of antiques, fine art, and interiors from a young age. I don't think either of us were aware of how lucky we were and what we were able to absorb over so many years.

Don McQualter, my first boss, who taught me more than I could ever put in writing over five glorious years under his mentorship. His parting words when I left to start my own business were, "Never limit yourself to what you already know." He epitomizes the noble art of leaving things undone, a little raw, and leaving something for the imagination.

My kids, for making me the luckiest person in the world. And my husband, Patch, for inspiring me every single day. He strives not to best his contemporaries or his predecessors, but to excel himself, and he encourages me to push boundaries.

My editor, Giulia Di Filippo, who has made everything seem easy and effortless.

James St. Johnson, the most talented graphic designer I've ever met, for making beauty unfold in its most pure form.

Special gratitude to Fiona Daniels for patiently putting my words onto paper and bringing out the best in them, and for her sage advice and invaluable input all along.

My sister, Tess, for her endless love and support.

My builders, contractors, and suppliers for making magic happen and for always having an open mind.

My photographers, Sean, Anson, Felix, James, Tess, and Sharyn—what you capture in the lens continues to inspire me.

Alex Eagle, whom I first met on Instagram and later in person on a hot summer's day at the Venice Biennale, and with whom I share a rare aesthetic connection. She introduced me to Rizzoli, and the rest is history.

Lucy Folk, who I've known from the day I was born and who inspires me with her creativity and her unique way of pushing me that little bit further in my design process. May our lives and paths continue to overlap around the world.

My team, past and present, for helping me deliver our work. You keep the wheels turning and I will always be grateful for this. Special thanks to Grace Fernan, who helped secure the materials that make this book so special.

Rizzoli, a heartfelt thank-you for welcoming me to your family.

And finally, my clients, who entrust me with their homes. The greater the trust between client and designer, the more successful the results. Put simply, you are the book.

All my love,

Tam xx

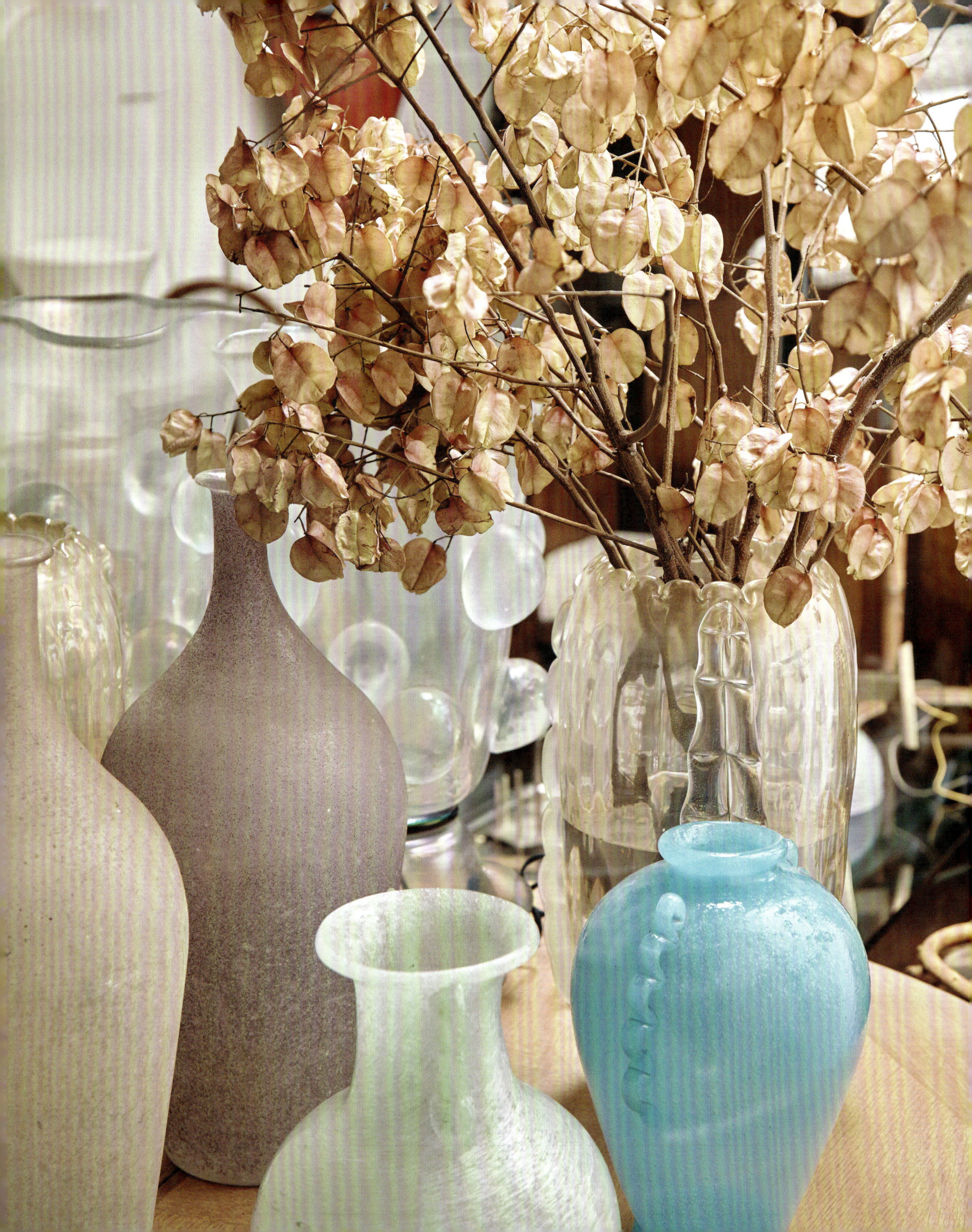

Photography

SANDCASTLE
HIDEAWAY
ATELIER
BUNGALOW
VILLA
TREEHOUSE
SANCTUARY
PIED-À-TERRE
CAPSULE
TOWNHOUSE
VAULT
GREENHOUSE
RETREAT

Anson Smart

Anson Smart

Sean Fennessy

Alana Landsberry

Anson Smart, Tess Kelly

Sean Fennessy

Sean Fennessy

Brigette Clark, Julien Fernandez

Glen Allsop

Sharyn Cairns

Gabriel Saunders

Anson Smart

Sean Fennessy

Tamsin Johnson: Spaces for Living

First published in the United States of America in 2021 by
Rizzoli International Publications, Inc.
300 Park Avenue South
New York, NY 10010

www.rizzoliusa.com

Publication © 2021 Rizzoli International Publications, Inc.
Introduction, project descriptions, and captions © 2021 Fiona Daniels and Tamsin Johnson
Text © 2021 Edward Clark
Quote © 2021 Alex Eagle
Quote © 2021 Lucy Folk

Publisher: *Charles Miers*
Editor: *Giulia Di Filippo*
Copyeditor: *Victoria Brown*
Production Manager: *Kaija Markoe*

Designed by James St. Johnson

All rights reserved. No part of this publication may be reproduced, stored in a retrieval system, or transmitted in any form or by any means, electronic, mechanical, photocopying, recording, or otherwise, without prior consent of the publishers.

Printed in China

2022 2023 2024 / 10 9 8 7 6 5 4 3 2
ISBN: 978-0-8478-7072-1
Library of Congress Control Number: 2021931393

Front cover: *Thomas Street, Windsor, Melbourne. Photography* © Sean Fennessy
Endpapers: *Tamsin Johnson's mood boards. Photography* © Claudia Smith
Introduction: *William Street, Paddington, Sydney. Photography* © Felix Forest

Visit us online at:

Facebook.com/RizzoliNewYork	*Instagram.com/RizzoliBooks*	*Youtube.com/user/RizzoliNY*
Twitter @Rizzoli_Books	*Pinterest.com/RizzoliBooks*	*Issuu.com/Rizzoli*

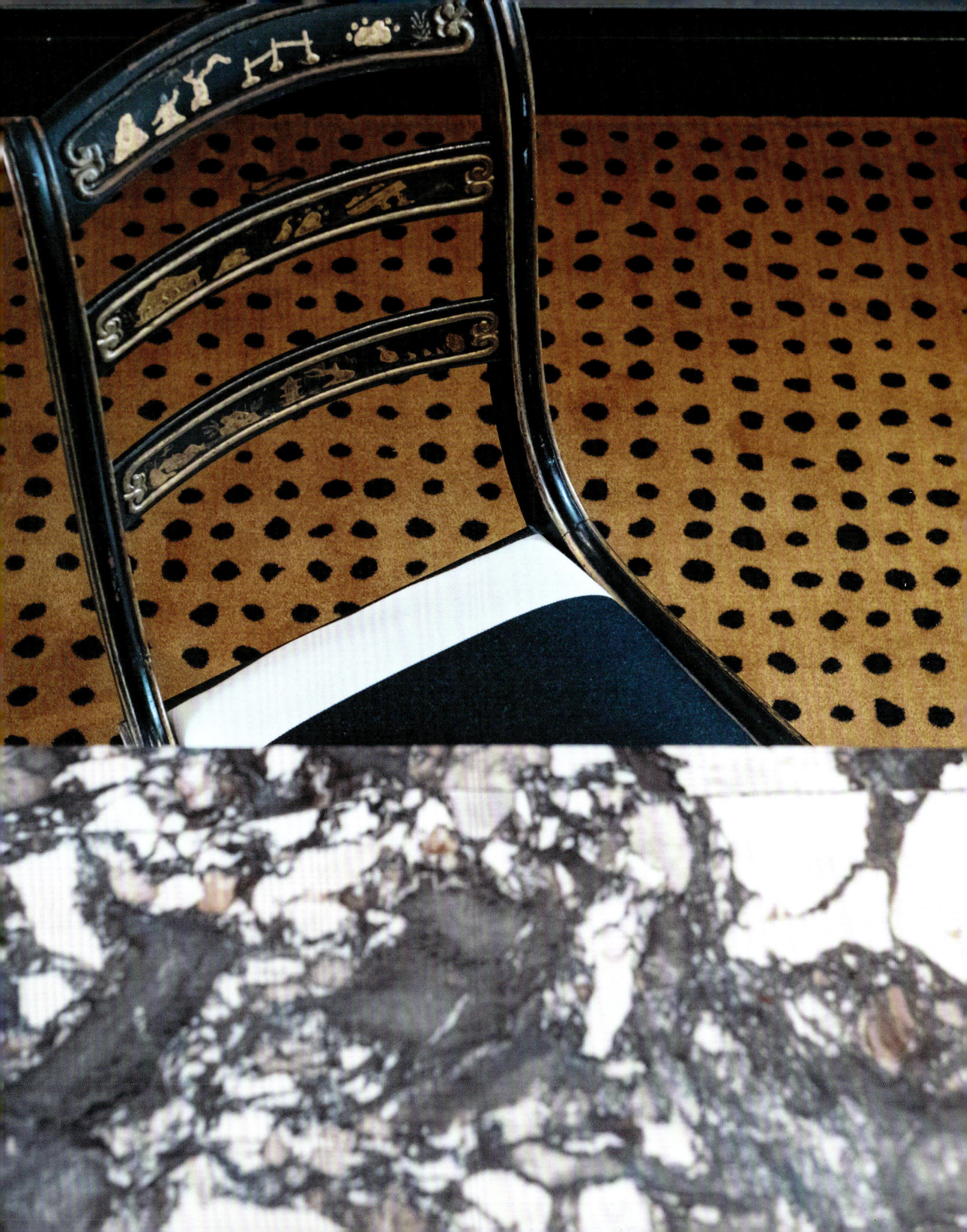

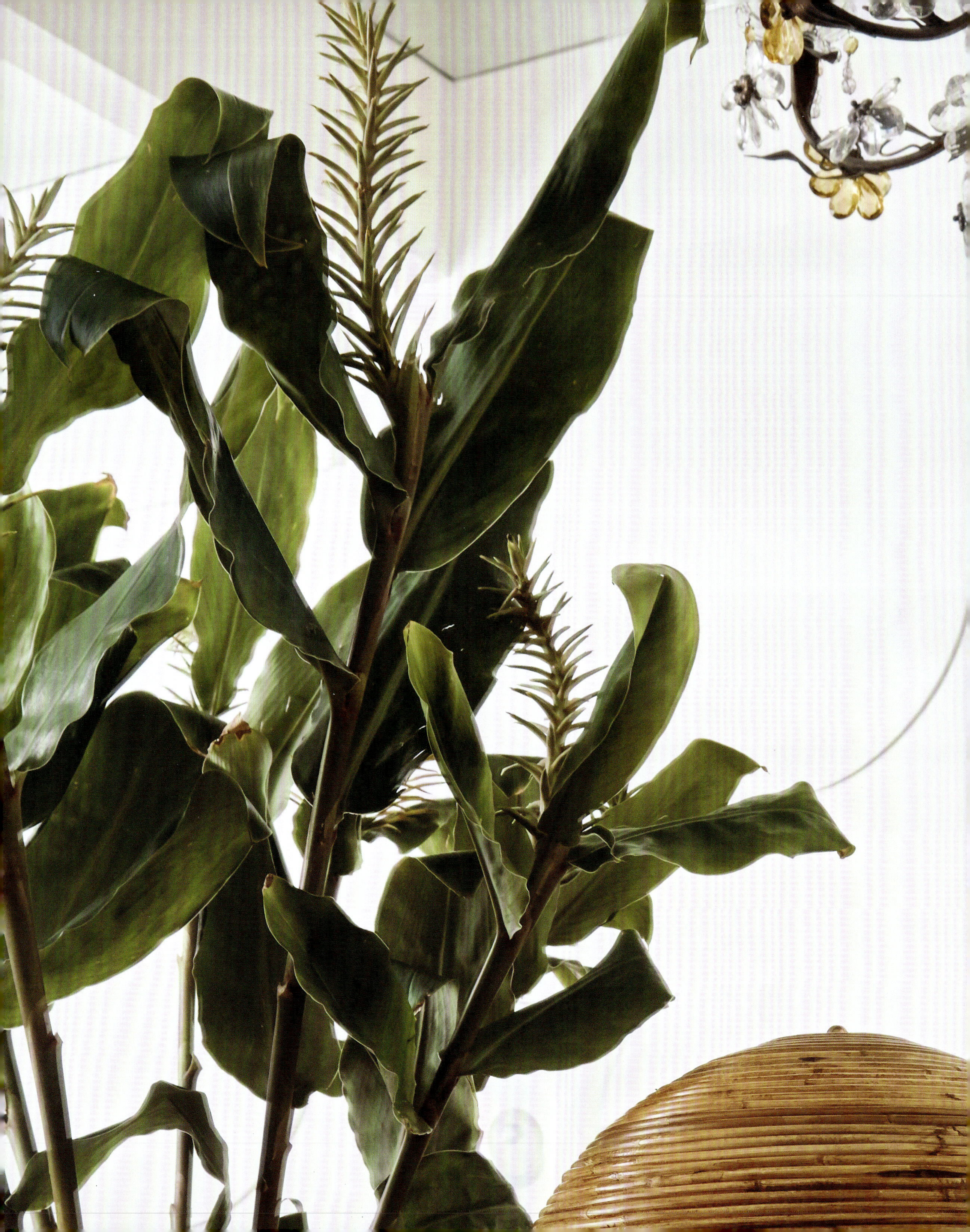

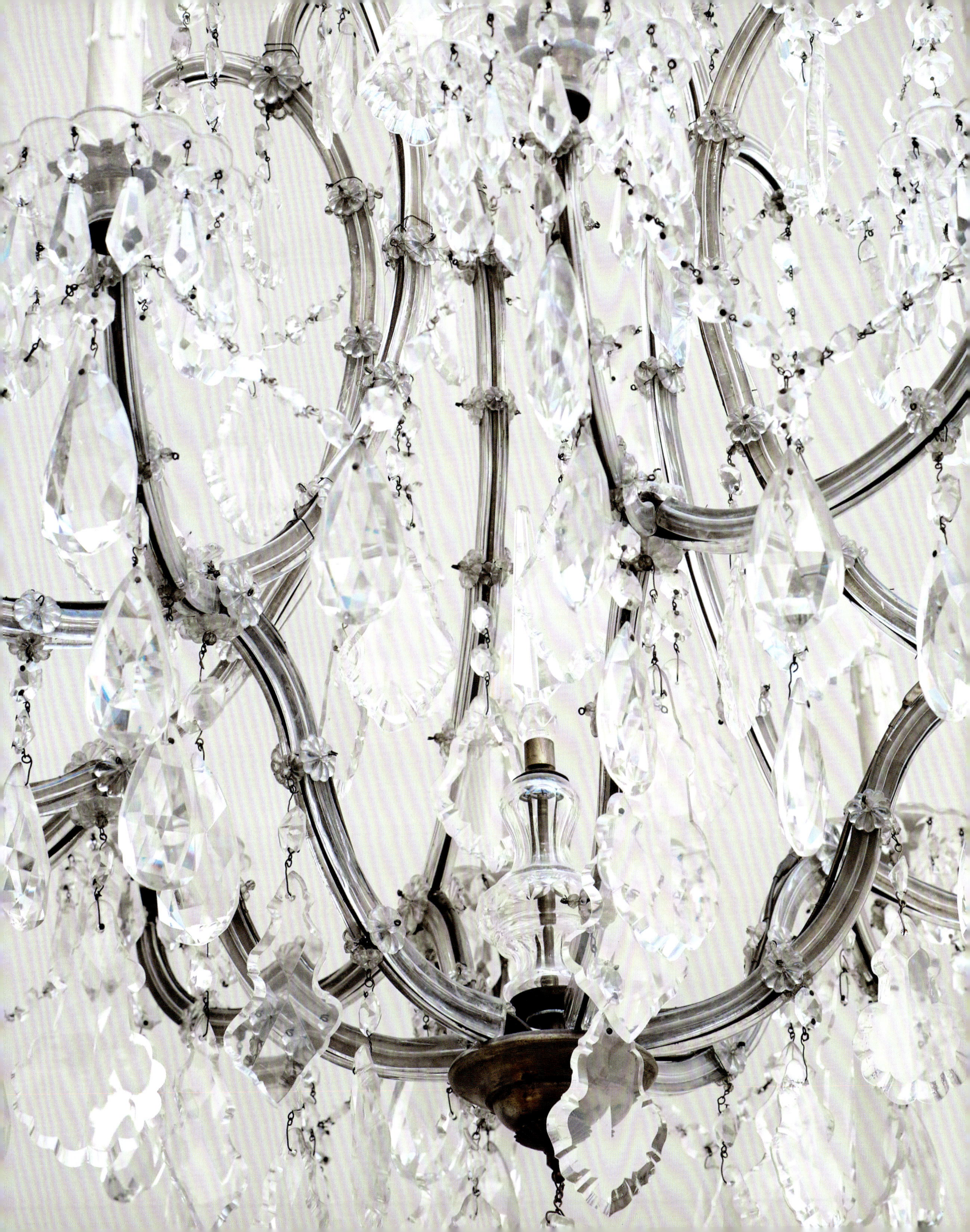

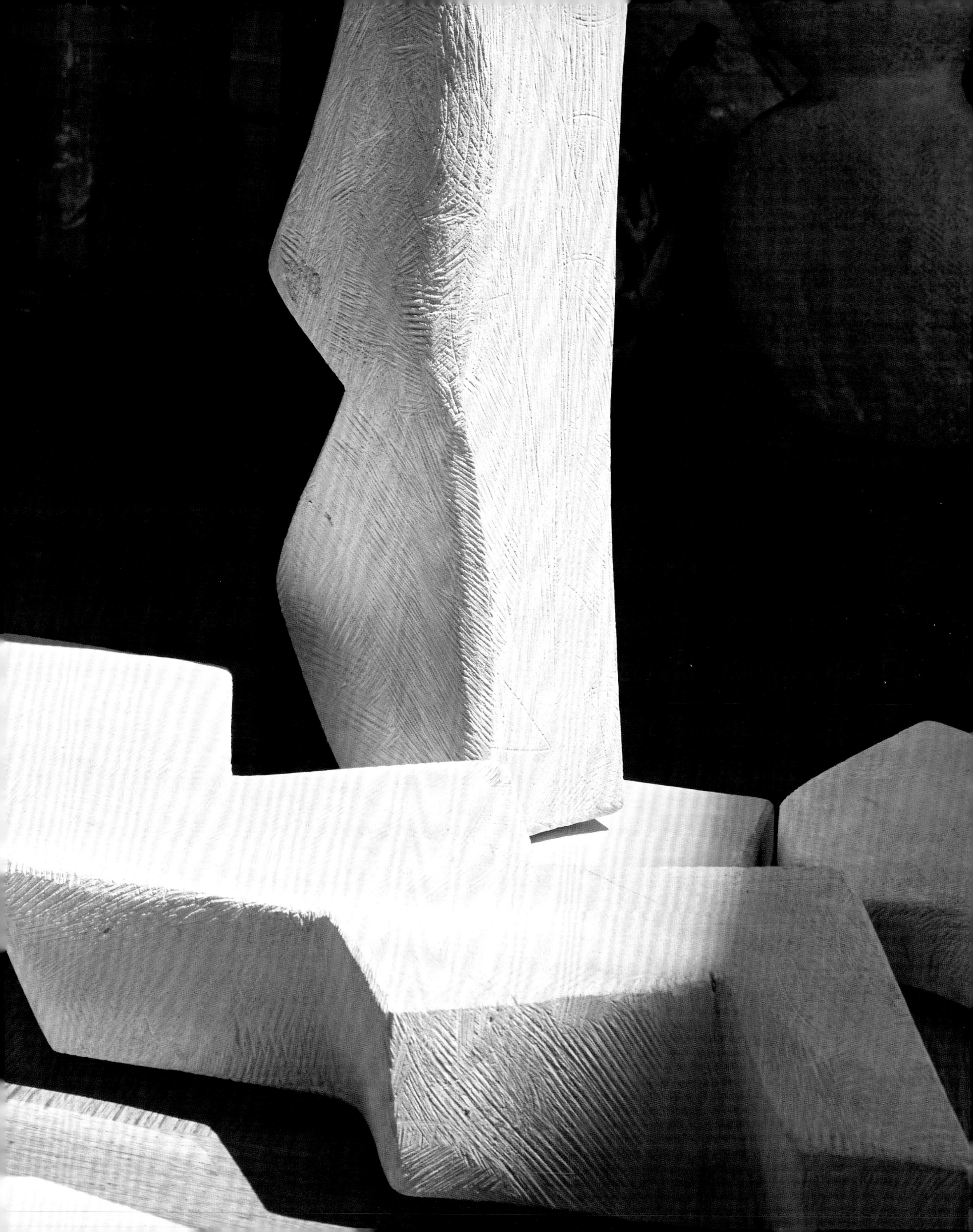

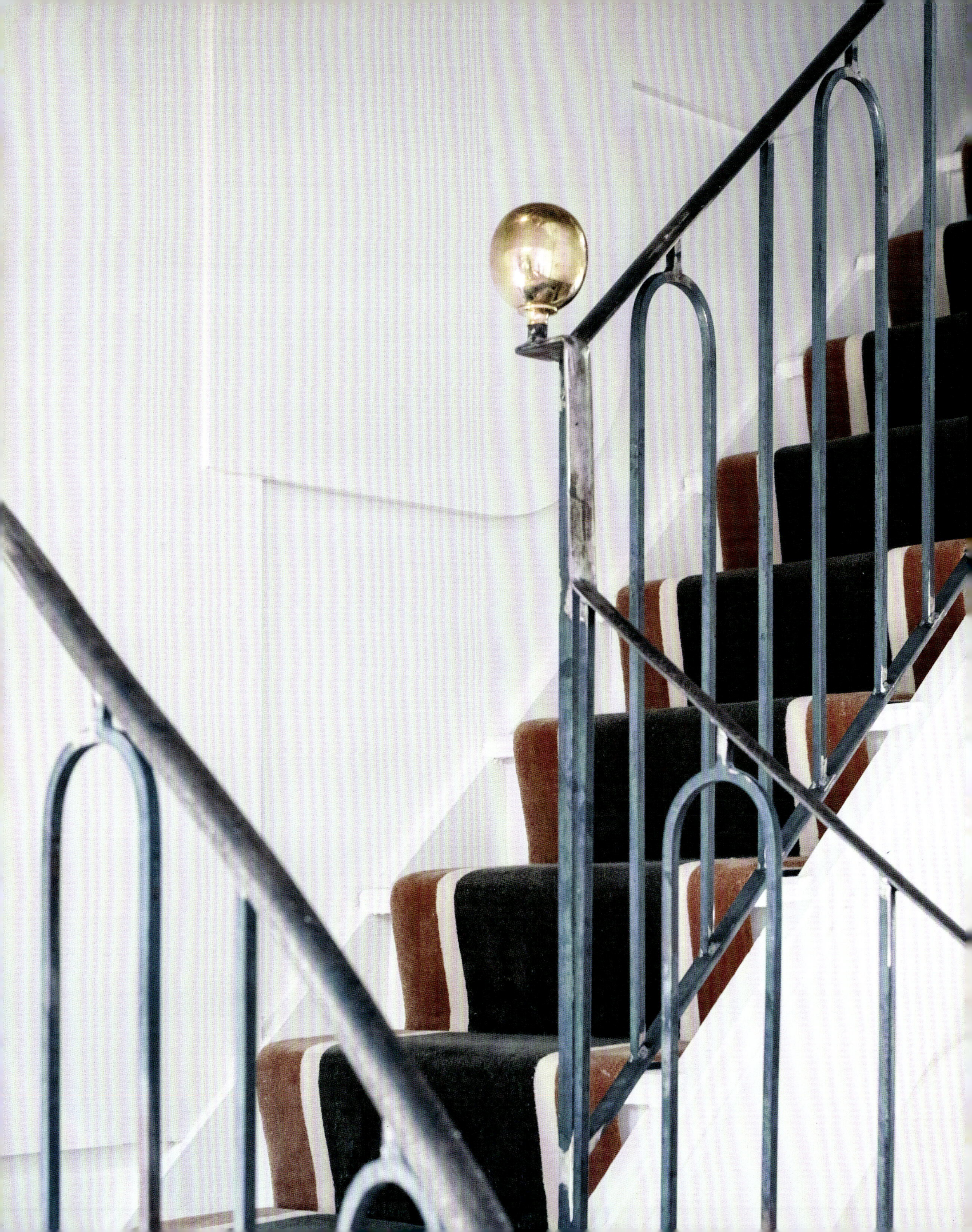

I am Dandy
GENTLEMAN'S GUIDE
HOMO ELEGANS
THE HERMES YEARS
THE FASHION BOOK
THE LONDON FASHION BOOK
BRITISH TEXTILES
INTIMATE CHANEL
THE KILLER DETAIL
THE TWENTIES
FASHION NOW
Riva
UFO
THE BIG BOOK OF THE HAMPTONS
GIORGIO ARMANI
THE BOOK of PLANTS
RALPH LAUREN
PARIS MAGNUM
ESCAPE
HAVANA
ENTRYWAYS OF MILAN
INGRESSI DI MILANO
giorgio armani
VOGUE FASHION
VALENTINO
THE ROLLING STONES

ROCHIER